Risk Culture

Risk Culture

A Practical Guide to Building and Strengthening the Fabric of Risk Management

Erik Banks

palgrave
macmillan

First published 2012 by
PALGRAVE MACMILLAN

Palgrave Macmillan in the UK is an imprint of Macmillan Publishers Limited, registered in England, company number 785998, of Houndmills, Basingstoke, Hampshire RG21 6XS.

Palgrave Macmillan in the US is a division of St Martin's Press LLC, 175 Fifth Avenue, New York, NY 10010.

Palgrave Macmillan is the global academic imprint of the above companies and has companies and representatives throughout the world.

Palgrave® and Macmillan® are registered trademarks in the United States, the United Kingdom, Europe and other countries

ISBN: 978–1–137–26371–1

This book is printed on paper suitable for recycling and made from fully managed and sustained forest sources. Logging, pulping and manufacturing processes are expected to conform to the environmental regulations of the country of origin.

A catalogue record for this book is available from the British Library.

A catalog record for this book is available from the Library of Congress.

Contents

Figures

Tables

1
Successful Risk Management

Risk, or the uncertainty regarding a future event or outcome, characterizes much of what banks, industrial corporations and governmental agencies must deal with on a daily basis. Indeed, risk is a driving force in creating markets, products and, ultimately, revenues and profits. Absent risk, the business world would be characterized by complete certainty and, arguably, little opportunity for innovation or profit. The risk-free world is safe, predictable and rather boring.

Of course, risk also has a dark side: just as it allows for upside opportunity, it creates the possibility of downside losses. Failure to recognize and manage risk can lead ultimately to real problems. Left unchecked, risk can prove particularly destructive, leading in the most extreme circumstances to financial losses and distress.

The very fact that risk exists and has the potential to create these positive and negative outcomes necessarily means that it has to be actively, *and properly*, managed. And, while the quantitative models and governance frameworks for managing risks are by now well established, the behavioral aspects – driven in large measure by the concept of "risk culture" – are still somewhat unclear and under-theorized. We shall, of course, be exploring the theme of risk culture in this book.

In the balance of this introductory chapter we shall put the concept of risk into proper context: we shall briefly explore the different kinds of risks to which corporate (and public) entities may be exposed, and then consider the factors which make up a successful risk management process. We shall then briefly introduce the idea of a risk culture – a topic which we shall develop further throughout the book. We shall conclude with an outline of the chapters which follow.

Types of risks

It is no surprise that risk comes in many different forms, as the operating environment for companies is complex, broad and diverse. Some firms are exposed to risks related to the financial aspects of the economy (e.g., interest rates, currency rates, equity prices), while others are exposed to factors related to variables and processes used in the creation of goods or services (e.g., commodity inputs, legal matters, labor costs, operating variables, physical plant and equipment impairment or destruction, health and safety costs). Some firms are exposed to both dimensions.

While risk comes in many different forms and can be classified in different ways, we shall consider it under two broad groupings: financial risk and non-financial risk, with the caveat that other groupings and levels of detail can also be considered.[1] Before we explore this classification, let us briefly explain the concepts of speculative and pure risks. Speculative risks are those which have the potential to generate a profit or a loss, such as we might encounter in the financial markets. Firms often seek out such risks as a way of creating profits. Pure risks, in contrast, can generate a loss or no loss, but never a profit. Such risks are commonly identified with the insurance market and are often eliminated or transferred. The risk management process created by a firm must typically account for the differences between speculative and pure risks, as their treatment and management is necessarily different. With that in mind, let us turn to financial and non-financial risks.

Financial risk

Financial risks come in many different forms, but for our purposes we can divide them into market risk, liquidity risk and credit risk, each with its own characteristics and granularity.[2] Let us briefly examine each of these.

- *Market risk*: the risk of loss (or gain) based on the movement of a market variable. Within the general class of market risk we can consider specific risk factors that generate an associated exposure. More specifically, interest rates, equity prices, commodity prices, currency rates and credit spreads are influenced by supply and demand forces in a freely traded marketplace, indicating that they can move up or down at any point in time.
  - *Interest rates*: interest rates move up and down on a regular basis, through both market forces and policies or actions established by monetary authorities. As a result of this dynamism, institutions may face higher or lower financing costs and/or lower or higher prices on their fixed-income investments.[3]
  - *Equity prices*: equities (individually and as constituents of baskets, sectors and indexes) can move up and down on a daily basis as a result of market forces as well as earnings expectations and other micro and macro events. Prices can also be affected by index rebalancing, where the removal of constituents from the index triggers selling and their addition triggers

buying. Individuals or institutions holding long or short equity positions in their trading, investment or retirement accounts will be impacted by price movements.

- *Commodity prices*: commodity prices, which represent the value of a range of goods such as energy products, precious and industrial metals, and agricultural products, are subject to daily price fluctuations for many of the same supply and demand reasons noted above. Speculators, traders, hedgers and producers involved in commodities will therefore experience daily fluctuations in the values of their short or long positions. Note that commodity prices also count as a factor of production for many industrial and transportation companies, and can arguably also be included as a form of operating risk, as described in the next section.
- *Currency rates*: currency rates, representing the exchange value of one currency for another, move as a result of supply and demand activity fueled by hedgers and speculators as well as the macroeconomic policies enacted by various national governments. Institutions that directly or indirectly hold currency positions in their investment accounts, or are exposed to currencies through their production, trading, import or export activities, will experience gains or losses on a daily basis through currency movements.
- *Credit spreads*: credit spreads, representing the tradable component of credit instruments such as bonds, money market instruments and traded loans, can move on a daily basis through market forces and the short-term outlook of a borrower's creditworthiness. As credit quality improves, the institution's spread tightens against a risk-free benchmark; that is, its all-in borrowing cost, including the base risk-free rate as well as the idiosyncratic risky credit spread component, declines. The reverse occurs as creditworthiness deteriorates. Investors who hold such credit-sensitive instruments may therefore experience daily fluctuations in the value of their holdings.

Market risks can also be defined in terms of their risk parameters. In particular, risks can arise from directional, volatility, correlation, dividend, basis, curve and repricing movements. These parameters can be applied to one or more of the classes defined immediately above.

- *Directional (or delta, gamma)*: the risk of loss (or gain) resulting from small (delta) or large (gamma) movements in the direction of any one of the market risk factors detailed above.
- *Volatility*: the risk of loss (or gain) resulting from the change in movements in market risk factors.
- *Correlation*: the risk of loss (or gain) arising from changes in the relationship between two or more assets with specific market risk characteristics.

  - *Dividend*: the risk of loss (or gain) arising from changes in estimated future corporate dividend payouts.
  - *Basis*: the risk of loss (or gain) arising from changes in the relationship between an asset and an underlying derivative hedge.
  - *Curve*: the risk of loss (or gain) arising from changes in the shape of a market risk curve (e.g., interest rate or volatility).
  - *Repricing*: the risk of loss (or gain) arising when an asset or liability is renewed at a less (more) favorable rate (e.g., for losses, a lower rate for an asset reinvestment or a higher rate for a liability or funding transaction; vice versa for gains).

  Higher-order risks can also be considered, but we shall ignore these as they are not immediately relevant to our discussion. They are, of course, critical to a proper risk identification process.

- *Liquidity risk*: the risk of loss (or gain) based on the ability to access funding or to liquidate or pledge assets on a short-term basis in order to generate cash sufficient to meet expected or unexpected obligations. We can divide liquidity risk into various components: asset liquidity risk, funding liquidity risk, joint liquidity risk, liquidity contingency risk and liquidity mismatch risk.
  - *Asset liquidity risk*: the risk that assets held on the balance sheet will not be realizable with enough time or value to generate proceeds needed to meet obligations. A typical balance sheet contains assets with a range of realizability, from the instantaneous (e.g., cash) to months or years (e.g., fixed assets). The actual composition depends heavily on the nature of the company and how it deploys its capital in order to create revenues: financial institutions tend to feature fairly liquid balance sheets, with assets that can be converted into cash very quickly through sales or pledges, while industrial companies are far more likely to feature a large proportion of fixed assets (e.g., plant, property, equipment) that can generally be converted into cash only through a security charge or encumbrance; actually disposing of fixed assets in order to raise cash is not generally a viable solution as it could take a long time to realize fair value, which is of little use when an emergency payment must be made. In practice, corporate entities tend to keep an inventory of cash and marketable securities or investments on hand in order to cope with unexpected payments. An insufficient amount of such assets may lead to losses when attempting to secure liquidity.
  - *Funding liquidity risk*: the risk that a company will not have access to sufficient amounts or types of financing to meet obligations coming due. This aspect of liquidity risk relates to the liability side of the balance sheet. In practice, companies use a variety of liabilities to fund their operations,

including short-, medium- and long-term capital markets instruments and loans; these may be unsecured or secured on fixed assets, and may feature fixed or floating interest rates. Such funding can be accessed to pay for regular operations or to make unexpected payments. However, there is always a risk that certain forms of funding may be withdrawn or made available only with conditions, particularly during times of financial stress. If a company is unable to use different funding options to meet its obligations, it may find itself paying more for a particular form of financing or turning to the asset side of the balance sheet in order to generate the required cash.

- *Joint liquidity risk*: the union of asset and funding risk can lead to a form of joint liquidity risk which represents an extreme cash spiral. In essence, a firm that is unable to access its liability facilities to generate cash may then be forced to turn to its assets, either selling or pledging them to create cash. Any such action is likely to have a negative effect on the firm's creditworthiness, which may cause lenders on any remaining liability facilities to either cancel or alter their lines. Capital markets investors providing liquidity via commercial paper or medium-term notes may also choose not to roll over their investments. This places the company in any even more precarious position, and may require another series of asset disposals or encumbrances, and so forth, until the company is unable to raise any further monies; this is likely to culminate in some type of distressed sale or bankruptcy.
- *Liquidity contingency risk*: a catch-all category that considers the financial pressures that may be imposed when sudden, unexpected events require a greater amount of cash than previously estimated (even greater than estimated under "stress" scenarios). Such unexpected events may strip through asset and liability funding sources more severely than anticipated, leading to financial distress.
- *Liquidity mismatch risk*: liquidity mismatches occur when the pattern of cash outflows is not properly matched by cash inflows or other cash access. In most cases this is a rather benign problem that can be solved by drawing down from other funding sources, but in more extreme cases it can create larger losses.

- *Credit risk*: the risk of loss related to the inability or unwillingness of a counterparty to honor its contractual obligations, which may take the form of loans, leases, bonds or derivative contracts. Like market risk, credit risk comes in a variety of forms, including default risk, pre-settlement risk, settlement risk, contingent risk and sovereign risk. There is also, as noted above, a market-driven form of credit risk, so-called credit spread risk, which represents a key intersection between credit risk and market risk.

- *Default risk*: the risk of loss should a company, as an obligor to one or more creditors, cease to make payments under financing or other contractual obligations. In most cases the cessation, which becomes a defined event of default, occurs when a company is unable to make appropriate payments as a result of financial deterioration.
- *Pre-settlement risk*: the risk of loss attributable to any financial contract that is defined by a dynamic or changing exposure amount. This most often relates to financial derivative contracts (e.g., forward, swaps, options) that are characterized by a notional amount but whose actual risk exposure is a fraction of the notional (and reflects the mark-to-market value and some potential future exposure). Should a default occur, the amount owed to creditors will relate to the mark-to-market value and replacement cost.
- *Settlement risk*: the risk of loss due to the brief period between a company delivering cash or assets and receiving in-kind assets or cash, at which time default occurs. Settlement risk is typically associated with foreign exchange and international securities transactions, which do not necessarily settle on a same-day basis as a result of time zone or timing differences.
- *Contingent risk*: the risk of loss arising from some future exposure that may be generated in the course of dealing with a company. While pure default risk, noted above, is the result of a drawn loan or issued bond, a contingent risk relates to the possibility that an undrawn bank line will be tapped at some future time, adding to exposure and the prospect of losses in the event of default.
- *Sovereign risk*: the risk of loss arising from the unilateral actions of a sovereign nation or governmental entity. This type of risk can come in various forms, including a debt repayment moratorium and debt restructuring or repudiation. These events can cause the de facto equivalent of a credit loss. It is worth noting that certain "non-default" sovereign actions can also be imposed to the detriment of corporate or financial parties dealing in the country (e.g., capital controls or asset expropriation). These are not strictly credit events, but they can generate losses for the affected parties.

Non-financial risk

Non-financial risks relate to a broad range of operating risks that a company is likely to face in the normal course of its business – and, as the name suggests, exclude all financial exposures. The precise non-financial risks a firm may encounter depend on the industry in which it operates and the specific construct of its business; as a result, there is a systemic element and an idiosyncratic element to such non-financial exposures. While the list of possible risks in this area is quite long, we can define the key areas as business risk, strategic risk, legal risk, operational risk, and property and casualty risk.

- *Business risk (sometimes referred to as operating risk)*: the risk attributable to a weak operating environment, where demand for goods and services is insufficient to generate the revenues needed to create a satisfactory return for stakeholders. Business risk is often perceived during an economic downturn or when a specific market segment is suffering from some form of dislocation. For instance, during a recessionary period, consumer demand for a broad range of goods and services tends to decline, putting pressure on the operations of firms providing such goods and services. This pressure can be considered systemic, affecting all companies in the sector to some degree. In a "micro" sense, a firm may also suffer from lack of business if its own products or services have fallen out of favor or are no longer seen as competitive or compelling, or if business production has been interrupted, and so forth. When business activities decline and revenues fall in tandem, companies operating with a high cost base may find themselves unable to generate a net profit (and may, in some cases, post net losses). Cash flow and liquidity may also be affected, and in the most serious situations this may lead to financial distress.
- *Strategic risk*: the risk that strategic business decisions fail to yield the desired results, or that they lead to loss of competitive advantage or squandering of financial or other resources. If an institution is to prosper over the medium and long term it must have a strategic plan that allows it to evaluate and act on expansion, product development, mergers and acquisitions, multi-year investment, and so on. If any decisions related to these areas fail (or are in some way mishandled), the institution may lose capital, market share, business opportunities, reputation and even investor confidence.
- *Legal risk*: the risk of loss should some aspect of the legal process within a company's operations fail to function as intended. This risk can take several forms, including flawed contracts which fail to protect the company's interests in commercial matters, declarations of *ultra vires* on existing contracts (a party acting outside legal authorization) and lawsuits related to a product or service deficiency. Legal risks may force an institution to take active legal steps to protect its commercial rights (which may be resolved favorably or unfavorably, suggesting some degree of gain or loss) or to take defensive

legal action in order to protect itself against legal claims (suggesting more of a pure risk, where the outcome may be either the payment of damages or the dismissal of the legal action).

- *Operational risk*: the risk of loss attributable to any error or defect in the company's standard operating process, procedures or infrastructure. Common forms of operational risk include losses attributable to the compromise or collapse of core IT infrastructure (which can result in business interruption), accounting or financial fraud, erroneous payments, departure of key personnel, and loss of patents or intellectual property.
- *Property and casualty (hazard) risk*: the risk of loss due to damage to or destruction of productive property which leads to business interruption and, potentially, additional expenditures on property replacement (depending on insurance coverage). This category also includes the risk of loss arising from employees' health and disability issues and their relative inability to contribute to the work process.

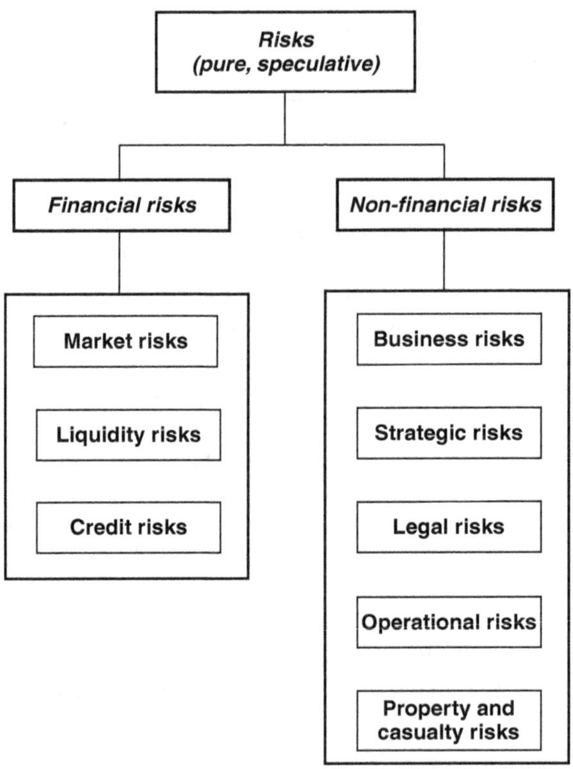

Figure 1.1 Overview of risk classes

Clearly, non-financial corporate entities also face risk of loss on the costs of any inputs that are used in the manufacturing of goods intended for sale: as input costs rise, the cost of goods sold increases, and if a company cannot pass on the cost increase to its customers (or has not protected against these increases through a hedging program), it will suffer reduced profits (or an outright loss). In the main, however, such risks can be incorporated into the market risk category above, primarily with regard to the directional risk associated with a commodity used as the main raw material in a productive process (e.g., steel in automobile manufacturing and fuel in the airline and transportation industries). Costs associated with salary increases and other selling, general and administrative expenses are a further source of potential margin compression if not managed prudently.

Figure 1.1 summarizes key types of risks.

Successful risk management

Since institutions can face a broad range of potentially damaging risks, it seems obvious that the truly successful ones will be those that can properly manage their risk exposures. Proper management leads to maximization of value (for corporate entities so charged by their shareholders), minimization of costs (for governmental entities attempting to serve constituents, taxpayers or other stakeholders) or both.

This endeavor is commonly described using the broad term "risk management" – which involves the active management of all risk exposures that impact an organization. Risk management is nothing particularly new: risks have existed throughout history, and those affected have attempted to deal with their effects. That said, awareness and formalization of the topic have increased significantly in recent decades as the operating environment has grown more complex, volatile and global, and as methods and mechanisms to deal with risks have become more sophisticated.

The fundamental risk management process

While risk management practices vary across industries and firms, they typically constitute a multi-stage process that includes governance, identification, quantification, management and monitoring, as depicted in Figure 1.2. Once established, the risk process should ideally be enduring and inculcated in a firm's daily operations. Nevertheless, elements of the process must be reviewed constantly, as a firm's risk exposures may change over time. Let us explore each element of the typical process in more detail.

Risk governance

Any sensible risk management process must begin with an overarching risk governance framework. Risk governance can be defined as the set of

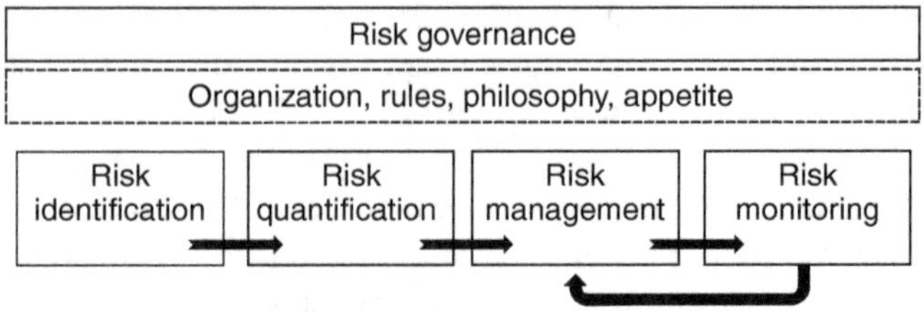

Figure 1.2 The fundamental risk management process

organizational structures and rules that govern risk activities, authorities and behaviors, and that define clearly the firm's risk philosophy and risk appetite.

In the first instance, a firm must establish a proper organizational structure: one that allows it to consider and manage its risk exposures, regardless of type or quantity. There is no single model which fits every industry, or every firm within an industry; much depends on the nature of the company, its business, its strategies and its stakeholders. Many companies prefer to establish a dedicated risk management unit that operates independently of the risk-taking businesses. While the structure, prominence and authority of the risk function can vary, it is not unusual for such a unit, headed by a chief risk officer (CRO, or equivalent), to report directly to the firm's CEO, COO or CFO.

Of course, management of risk is not the sole responsibility of the independent risk managers. It is increasingly common for companies to consider the formation of risk management along multiple lines of defense. We may, for instance, think of these lines of defense as follows:

- *Board of directors*: responsible for directing the concept of risk management and strategic risk issues, setting governance rules, approving the risk philosophy, approving the risk appetite, setting the tone of risk management.
- *Executive managers*: responsible for defining the risk philosophy and merging business and risk strategies, developing the risk appetite, being aware of key exposures, setting the tone of risk management.
- *Business managers*: responsible for managing day-to-day risks within the parameters they have been granted, creating a proper risk awareness in the business environment.
- *Risk managers*: responsible for promoting the firm's risk culture, setting and enforcing risk policies and limits, stressing the portfolio, consulting with business managers on risk-related activities.
- *Auditors*: responsible for auditing the control process and ensuring the proper degree of assurance management.

Clearly, many parties have a role in the process. The importance of such broad participation cannot be stressed enough: in a complex firm operating in a complex environment, the task of effectively managing risk is bigger than a single individual (e.g., CRO) or division (e.g., risk management group). It must be a shared role, but one where the responsibilities and accountabilities are very clearly defined. Figure 1.3 summarizes these lines of defense.

Beyond the establishment of these formal lines of defense, it is important for those in the leadership ranks to reflect the fact that risk management is ultimately everyone's concern. While the firm may have a formal risk management structure, reality and pragmatism suggest that every employee in a company should be considered a risk manager. To be sure, duties and authorities must be defined, but the idea that everyone can play some type of formal or informal role is useful and appealing – and a central tenet of successful risk culture, as we shall discover.

Risk rules, the second aspect of governance, are the guidelines put in place by an institution's board and executive management (and, depending on industry, regulatory officials) so that risky activities can be properly steered. These rules may relate to risk-taking authorities delegated to different parties within an institution, the risk-taking rights accorded to different subsidiaries or group companies, the policies governing risky business, the penalties for violating the risk process, the forms of stakeholder reporting and transparency, the escalation process that must be followed to take more risk, and so forth. In general, rules of this sort must be formal and codified, although some informal rules may also exist; in either event, there must be an expectation that rules are to be obeyed at all times, which means that proper enforcement is paramount.

Another key element of risk governance centers on a risk philosophy, which we can define as a declarative statement of the firm's view of, and approach to, risk-taking. In other words, the risk philosophy seeks to spell out the kinds of risks that the firm is willing to take or that it chooses to transfer or otherwise avoid or eliminate, and how risky activities are expected to contribute to earnings. While this is something of an aspirational exercise, it should become a

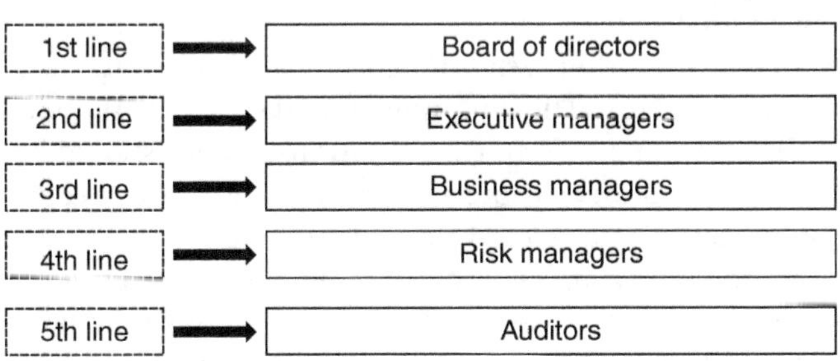

Figure 1.3 Risk management lines of defense

practical part of the risk process. Let us consider two simple examples of a risk philosophy. A financial institution may determine that it will actively assume risk in all European and Asian markets, but will not engage in the US markets. Furthermore, it may decide to take only a limited amount of market risk from pure proprietary activities, preserving its risk capital for core credit-lending risk business. Finally, it may demand that all risk-related business achieve a certain target hurdle rate on a risk-adjusted basis in order to justify use of capital and provide shareholders with a fair return. These aspects of its philosophy must then flow through to its business strategy, risk appetite and policies. An industrial company may define its philosophy in quite a different manner, in line with its focus on core operations. Thus, it may choose to eliminate all financial risks arising from its production, import and export activities, preserving only the attendant business risk that is part of normal operations. Simultaneously, it may be willing to accept a small amount of exposure in terms of property and casualty risks, taking a first loss position (i.e., deductible) with regard to property damage and business interruption, and thereafter requiring transfer of excess risks to an insurance company. Again, these choices have to be reflected in the entire process. Both of these examples are simplified, but they should help reinforce the point that by explicitly defining the perimeter of risky activities, the management and directors of a firm clarify their nature for all internal and external stakeholders. Naturally, the risk philosophy must be revisited periodically as operations, markets or circumstances change.

The third critical dimension of risk governance relates to the quantification of the risk a firm should take. Once organization and rules have been established and a philosophy defined, management and directors must determine how much capital to allocate in support of risky activities. This will, of course, depend on the specific business of the firm: it is no surprise that financial institutions, which are in business to take risk, will allocate a much larger portion of their resources in support of risky activities; that is, they have a large risk appetite. In contrast, non-financial institutions will view risk as either secondary or tangential to core operations, and thus allocate a much smaller (even *de minimis*) amount of resources in support of such activities; their risk appetite is often extremely small.

There are, of course, various ways of defining a risk appetite, which differ by industry and by company. The common starting point is the level of capital available to support the business. Clearly, an institution should never take an amount of risk which, under various scenarios, would outstrip capital and leave it with negative net worth. Accordingly, the sum of all risks (credit, market, liquidity, operational, hazard, etc.) should be less than the amount of available capital (including a safety buffer). Other considerations may be used to help define risk appetite, including maximum leverage levels (a de facto extension of the last point), minimum liquidity levels and credit rating target.

Given the importance of both risk philosophy and risk appetite in the context of risk culture, we shall revisit these concepts in greater detail later in the book. For now, however, we should regard all aspects of risk governance as absolutely essential to the smooth functioning of a risk management process.

Risk identification

With governance issues in hand, the next step in the risk process is to identify risks. In other words, a company must be aware that some uncertainty exists before it can be quantified, managed and monitored. Some risks are self-evident and can be readily identified. For instance, the classes of financial and non-financial risks summarized earlier in the chapter provide an indication of all of the factors which could affect the financial performance of an institution. Some risks are less obvious and are trickier to spot. For example, in the financial world risk variables such as correlation and volatility of volatility may not necessarily be easy to identify (or quantify), but they can certainly affect results. In addition, some risks change over time, particularly as certain contractual or triggering events occur. In fact, the changing nature of the risk that might not be adequately captured is particularly insidious, as it can disappear from the radar screen and might end up being the source of surprise losses. This suggests that risk identification has to be viewed as dynamic, rather than static. Note that a rigorous program of identification typically involves several of the lines of defense described earlier.

Risk quantification

Once a risk has been identified, we advance to the next stage of the risk management framework, which centers on quantification. In some cases the quantification exercise is simple and straightforward, and involves only the most elementary mathematics. For instance, a bank can quantify how much it will lose on a foreign exchange position by multiplying the size of the position by the actual or anticipated move in the exchange rate; this will provide an indication of gain or loss. Alternatively, a company can compute the sensitivity of its earnings to different levels of revenues, and thus create a picture of its business risk given a strong or weak level of demand. Such analyses and projections are very common.

In some cases the quantification exercise is rather more complex and involved; indeed, certain models for valuing portfolio market risk (e.g., value-at-risk), credit risk (e.g., credit defaults, correlations, recoveries, exposures) or derivatives (e.g., complex options) are mathematically quite sophisticated. Unfortunately, the more involved the quantification process, the greater the room for error, as assumptions used to create a risk estimate may or may not hold true (particularly during times of stress). Any risk identified can, and should, be quantified in some way, so as to help with decision-making – but the shortcomings of the quantitative process need to be understood and ultimately factored into any decisions taken.

Quantification is, of course, a substantial subtopic of its own, and many academic and practical works propose different ways of analytically assigning numbers to risky events. In considering the risk management framework, it is important to remember that quantification is very difficult and that it is rarely perfect (although it is sometimes posited to be), so results derived from this stage of the process have to be examined with a judicious, even skeptical, eye.

Risk management

Management of risk is the fourth step in the risk framework, and brings us to the heart of initial and ongoing decision-making. Having identified and then quantified risks, a firm needs to determine how best to manage the potential impact by considering a series of issues, such as why a risk should be accepted, the level of return that is expected from the risk (or the downside that is being protected), how the risk might affect the current profile, the end result that is foreseen, and how the risk should be mitigated or eliminated (and at what cost), if that becomes necessary. All of these are essential points in arriving at a proper risk decision. Note that decisions are typically taken on an incremental basis but need to be considered in the context of an entire portfolio.

Of course, in a sophisticated institution the decision to take discrete risks cannot be made in a vacuum, without reference to some overarching strategy – which takes us back to the idea of a risk philosophy. The management of risk must be intimately linked with the firm's risk philosophy and must adhere to the tenets set forth therein. Not surprisingly, the actual management of risk has to be viewed as highly dynamic, as circumstances can change from one day to the next; simply accepting, or protecting against, a risk and not revisiting this decision periodically is not a rational behavior. It is worth noting that while all aspects of the risk framework are essential, decision-making surfaces as *primus inter pares*. This is the action that sets in motion the entire chain of events that can lead to good or bad results. Risk management decisions are elemental in a company's progress.

Risk monitoring

The last stage of the risk process involves monitoring, which relates to creating transparency around what has been decided in the management stage. Monitoring arms risk takers with fresh information so that an adjustment in the decision can be made, if needed. In fact, a firm can have no sense of trend or progress with regard to risks if it cannot monitor them in some fashion. Monitoring thus acts as a feedback mechanism and, if functioning properly, should lead to a reaffirmation or readjustment of risk management decisions. It also acts as a control mechanism, allowing risk managers to compare risks taken with the appetite or the operational risk limits, helping ensure compliance.

Monitoring takes many different forms, some ad hoc and some formalized, the latter type tending to occur when an institution is operating in a highly regulated environment where external regulatory rules impose minimum standards of reporting and monitoring. In general, directors and executives require succinct, useful risk information that allows a comparison of exposures against risk appetite and that can be used for strategic decisions. Business and risk managers (and other control parties) need a greater level of detail so that they can both monitor against risk limits and make more precise tactical calls on how to proceed with a series of exposures. Naturally, some external stakeholders will also receive summary risk information, allowing them to assess trends and issues. Regulators and rating agencies may receive additional detailed, and confidential, information. Regardless of detail or audience, it should be emphasized that the monitoring task can often be quite formidable, particularly for a large and complex institution with multiple risk-related activities taking place in numerous subsidiaries or legal entities. Indeed, the process of creating useful, timely risk monitoring systems should not be underestimated and depends heavily on technology and data infrastructure.

Other factors influencing risk management success

With some understanding of governance, identification, quantification, management and monitoring let us now consider additional factors that can help a firm create a truly successful platform.

- A firm must have a clearly defined business strategy that reflects all dimensions of risk and explicitly ties revenue generation to risk exposures. While this is an essential part of the risk process, it is not always understood or followed. It is not uncommon, for instance, for some risk-taking firms simply to increase their future revenue budgets without regard for the risk implications; in other words, they fail to link the revenue strategy with the risk appetite. This becomes an even more critical issue when a firm is simultaneously seeking to increase revenues and reduce risks – a practical non-starter. Synchronicity between the two is essential.
- A firm's management must have an understanding of risks. In other words, those responsible for guiding the firm must be in a position to gauge the size of current and future risks and their impact on the company's revenue profile. Again, while this might be stating the obvious, the behavior is not necessarily practiced in all institutions. To be sure, periods of turmoil or crisis seem to raise awareness about the firm's risk profile among top management

and board members, but this effect can sometimes be short-lived. The effective institution will embed this behavior permanently.

- A firm's management must have an in-depth understanding of profit and loss (P&L) generation. Simply put, this means executives must understand how money is made and lost. For firms that are actively involved in risk-taking (e.g., financial institutions), this P&L explain process must cover all sources of risk – credit, market, liquidity, operational. For those firms that face risks as a by-product of core operations, the exercise is still vital: it is critical, for instance, to know how much is made or lost as a result of business risks, input cost changes, property and casualty damage, operational errors, lawsuits, business interruption, and so on. Without a detailed ability to track and analyze P&L, an institution cannot make rational risk-related decisions.
- A firm must be proactive and flexible, able to anticipate, and react to, changes in the macro environment and their effect on P&L, risk and the balance sheet. The operating environment of the 21st century is particularly dynamic and interlinked. This means that dislocations and opportunities can occur with greater speed, and have greater impact, than in any previous era. A firm that is in command of its risks and understands how they impact revenues and other aspects of the business strategy is a firm that can make proactive adjustments to protect against, or take advantage of, new market scenarios.
- A firm must be willing to say "no" to business that appears misbalanced from a risk/return perspective – regardless of what competitors may be doing. It is obviously tempting for firms to try to win as much business as possible in an effort to maximize market share, broaden client activities and increase dominance. However, if business is not priced correctly from a risk perspective (i.e., if the firm takes the loss leader approach), then the firm will soon find itself with a misbalanced book of business – one where risk-related losses outstrip revenues. Accordingly, the ability to reject business that does not make sense from a risk/return perspective is an essential ingredient in wise risk management.
- A firm must have some minimum level of infrastructure that properly reveals its risk profile. We indicated earlier that risk monitoring is an essential component of the risk management process. Monitoring dozens, hundreds and even thousands of risk factors or positions on a continuous basis is a complex undertaking that requires at least some investment in technological infrastructure. Accordingly, this is a key requirement for any firm that hopes to implement a proper risk process.
- A firm must have a minimum level of technological and operational integrity to support its business operations. Operational risk is a very real and damaging – and generally avoidable – class of exposure that can be managed with an appropriate base of technology and operational processing.

Investment in such infrastructure can be seen as a form of protective premium payment to eliminate (or at least dramatically reduce) instances of operational failure, and should feature prominently in any risk framework.

- A firm should foster a sense of teamwork and cooperation among all those with a direct or tangential relation to risk. While this again seems obvious, at least some institutions preserve an "us versus them" mentality – a silo approach that pits revenue generators against those with a control function (including the financial control, legal, compliance, audit and risk management departments). Such divides can be destructive and work counter to the effective management of risks. Accordingly, mechanisms which foster cooperation must feature prominently, and a shared vision and partnership among top management must be apparent for all others to see.
- A firm must have the ability to communicate clearly at all levels. This again goes back to basic organizational management issues, and yet it remains a problem for some firms. The idea is simple, yet powerful: when professionals from different areas and at different levels are communicating effectively (and not hoarding or guarding information), the likelihood of avoiding or minimizing problems, including those of a risk-related nature, improves. Equally, the chance of making informed risk decisions increases.
- A firm must have an internal culture that is attuned to risk – regardless of function or discipline – and that allows it to migrate from a risk control to a risk management mindset. This is clearly the central idea behind risk

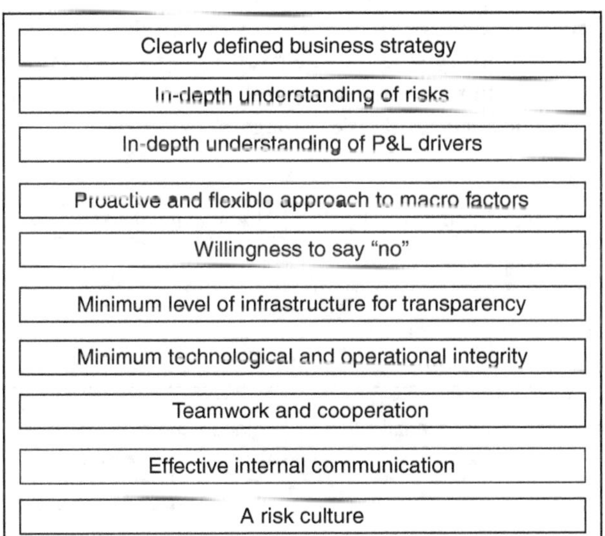

Figure 1.4 Factors influencing risk management success

culture and the themes that we explore at length in the book. In fact, we shall begin this exploration in the section immediately following.

Figure 1.4 summarizes additional factors which can contribute to risk management success.

The idea of risk culture

Let us now return to Figure 1.2, introduced earlier in the chapter, which depicts a typical risk management process. As we have seen, these essential building blocks must exist in order for the mechanical aspects of the discipline to be carried out properly. And, as we have also indicated, they are necessary, but they are not sufficient, conditions. To be truly effective, the risk management process must become second nature; that is, it must be practiced as and believed to be normal behavior in the normal course of business. Anything less will lead to erratic and inconsistent application.

This is, in effect, the idea of risk culture – a state where risk management processes are so intuitive and so embedded in the fabric of an institution that they exist subconsciously and are practiced as a matter of course. We shall introduce a series of formal definitions of risk culture in the next chapter, but for now we may say that an effective risk culture surrounds all aspects of the risk process and ensures that risk activities are firmly tied to business strategy; the link between the two is strong, cohesive and consistent, leaving no room for misalignment.

Following from our discussion in the last two sections, we can expand the risk management process to include the essential element of culture, along with its linkages to both business strategy and the supplemental factors noted immediately above. These elements, summarized in Figure 1.5, make up what we may define as the successful risk management process.

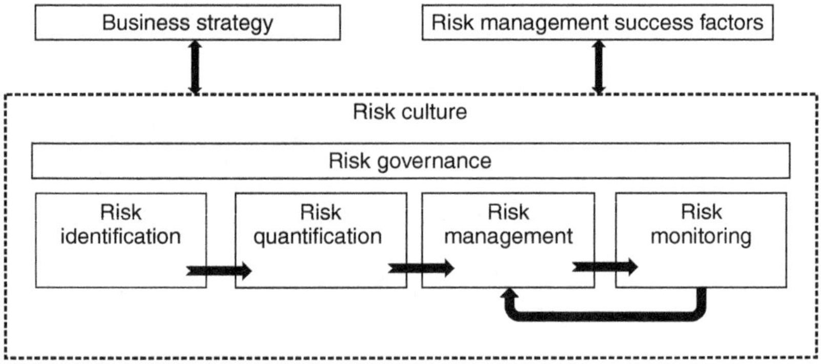

Figure 1.5 The successful risk management process

Outline of this book

With these brief introductory concepts in hand, let us now consider the structure of the book. In the next chapter we shall take a first look at risk culture, considering a variety of definitions and examining why risk culture features as an increasingly prominent topic in financial and business circles. In Chapter 3 we shall analyze how risk culture is perceived by a range of external stakeholders – including shareholders, regulators, creditors, rating agencies, clients and other interested parties; we shall also consider how such stakeholders view the essential items of risk culture, and whether they can truly influence the process. In Chapter 4 we shall consider, in a theoretical sense, some of the deficiencies and problems that affect institutions in their pursuit of risk management excellence; many of these shortcomings are related, not surprisingly, to a weak or non-existent risk culture. In Chapter 5 we shall expand on this topic by presenting case studies of real firms that have suffered as a result of risk culture problems. With some background on flaws in hand, we shall devote two chapters, 6 and 7, to a consideration of various actions that can be taken to help build or strengthen a firm's risk culture – recognizing and emphasizing that the journey can be a long and complex one. In Chapter 8 we shall consider how an institution might be able to gauge its own success in building up a risk culture. In other words, we shall investigate metrics and signals that suggest progress is being made in reaching some of the key goals which are indicative of a strong risk culture. To contrast these gauges of success we shall also analyze some of the behaviors or actions that might suggest sufficient progress has not yet been made. Finally, in Chapter 9 we shall summarize the topic with some concluding thoughts on the complexity and importance of building a risk culture, the consequences of getting it right or wrong and what the future holds for this topic.

The ultimate theme or goal of this book is, of course, to reveal more about the qualitative side of risk management, and specifically those issues which center on the development and strengthening of a risk culture. Much work has been published over the years on many of the quantitative approaches to risk management – all of which is incredibly important, and feeds into the overall topic of diligent management of risk. And while the numerical and methodological dimensions of risk management are a necessary element, they represent only half of the picture; the qualitative, experiential dimension of risk management – what we might consider the fabric of the discipline – is equally important. Here we find relatively less discussion and written work, perhaps because the subject is less precise and more subjective. In fact, there are no tidy formulas or simulations or processes that can define and drive a risk culture. Nevertheless, we intend to provide some essential building blocks in this book, in the hope that these will help further the discussion.

As a final note it is important to indicate that risk culture is something which should concern institutions from all sectors of the business and economic world. While much attention is rightly focused on risk management and risk culture as they apply to financial institutions – including banks, insurance and reinsurance companies, hedge funds and other investment conduits – everything we discuss and consider in this book applies equally to corporate and governmental institutions that are exposed to risk, either as a direct result of daily operations or as a by-product of such activities. Indeed, there is little difference between the bank that takes credit and operational risk, the industrial company that is exposed to business, commodity and reinvestment risk, and the governmental pension fund that carries investment and market risk. If these institutions, all representing different components of the economic chain, are negligent in building a proper risk culture to help manage risk, they will all suffer the same types of consequences. Accordingly, risk management and risk culture apply equally to the bank, the pharmaceutical company, the airline company, the public utility, the government space agency, and so on. With these preliminary thoughts in mind, let us now begin a more detailed discussion of risk culture.

2
A First Look at Risk Culture

To begin our journey we shall lay out in this chapter a series of definitions of risk culture presented by different sources, and then propose a working definition of our own. We shall then consider some of the general characteristics of risk culture, and introduce a simple diagnostic test that can reveal areas in which a firm may be strong or weak. We shall then consider the practical manifestation of a strong risk culture; in other words, we shall describe some of the qualities that exist in firms which have a successful risk culture. Note that we shall revisit these points later in the book when we consider deficient risk cultures and the steps that can be taken to build and strengthen a culture. Finally, we shall consider some overarching "simple rules" of risk relating to risk culture; these can be viewed as commonsense considerations when implementing a risk culture.

Some definitions of risk culture

We are now set to consider some formal definitions of risk culture. We should note, first, that risk culture is only one of the strands that create and define a company's overall culture and personality. Indeed, corporate culture – which we can define as the values, philosophy and traditions shared and practiced by a company's employees – is a much broader topic that touches on organizational issues and social issues. Morgan considers organizational culture to be "the set of beliefs, values, and norms, together with symbols like dramatized events and personalities, that represents the unique character of an organization, and provides the context for action in it and by it."[1] Schein has defined organizational culture as "a pattern of shared basic assumptions that the group learned as it solved its problems that has worked well enough to be considered valid and is passed on to new members as the correct way to perceive, think, and feel in relation to those problems."[2] While these are important and useful definitions, an in-depth discussion of organizational or corporate culture is beyond the scope of this book. Nevertheless, it is helpful to keep these broader definitions in mind when thinking about risk culture as an important subset. So, pursuing a narrower focus on risk culture, let us examine a handful of definitions to build a foundation.

Our first definition comes from consulting firm McKinsey, which has stated that a risk culture comprises "the norms of behavior for individuals and groups within an organization that determine the collective ability to identify and understand, openly discuss and act on the organization's current and future risks."[3] The emphasis of this definition is on behavioral norms and communication as applied to a firm's risks. A second definition comes from consulting firm KPMG, which sees risk culture as "the system of values and behaviors present throughout an organization that shape risk decisions. Risk culture influences the decisions of management and employees, even if they are not consciously weighing risks and benefits."[4] This definition is a little broader: while it still emphasizes the behavioral aspects of risk culture, it extends the concept by addressing or incorporating the behaviors of those who may not even be dealing with risks as part of a conscious, daily set of activities. KPMG has further indicated that "everyone should consider him or herself a risk manager with a shared understanding of the organizational risk appetite, underpinned by a clear governance structure for managing risk, incorporating 'three lines of defense': the first line being the business unit; the second the independent risk management function itself; the third internal audit."[5]

Towers Watson, the insurance risk consulting firm, concludes that "risk culture, a component of organizational culture, embodies an interactive system of values and normative behaviors."[6] Again, the focus is on values and behaviors. Consulting firm PricewaterhouseCoopers (PwC) considers risk culture to be "the tone setting and ethical environment in place at all levels. These touch upon lines of reporting, internal and external risk management communications and policies that reinforce risk management."[7] The emphasis here is on both behaviors and governance mechanisms. Further, notes PwC, the right culture is one "in which the right people do the right thing at the right time regardless of circumstances. No matter how sophisticated the systems or controls, the underlying culture must be committed to ethical decision-making."[8]

Rating agency Standard and Poor's notes that a risk culture "begins with fostering open dialogue where every employee in the organization has some level of ownership of the organization's risks, can readily identify the broader impacts of local decisions, and is rewarded for identifying outsize risks to senior levels. In such cultures, strategic decision-making routinely includes a review of relevant risks and alternative strategies rather than a simple return-on-investment analysis."[9] S&P's view therefore includes communication, empowerment and expertise.

Another important definition comes from the Institute of International Finance (IIF), an influential financial industry trade group, which stated in its report after the financial crisis of 2009 that risk culture "can be defined as the norms and traditions of behavior of individuals and of groups within an organization that determine the way in which they identify, understand, discuss, and act on the risks the organization confronts and the risks it takes."[10] The IIF further recommends that "all employees be aware of what risks they are taking, make the right decisions and raise objections when necessary."[11] Again, the focus is on behavioral norms and how these interact with the different stages of the risk management process we discussed in the previous chapter.

The Committee of European Banking Supervisors, in releasing its post-crisis document on risk management modifications in the financial system, defines a risk culture as a state where "Every member of the organization must be constantly aware of his responsibilities relating to the identification and reporting of risks and other roles within the organization and the associated responsibilities to these roles."[12] This approach focuses primarily on individual responsibilities and authorities regarding risk matters. A further definition comes from the Risk Management Association's Enterprise Risk Council, which regards risk culture as "a set of shared values and beliefs that governs attitudes toward risk-taking, care, and integrity, and which determines how openly risks and losses are reported and discussed."[13] As before, the guiding principles are behavioral. Oxford Risk Research puts forth a very succinct definition of risk culture as "the social and organizational determinants of individual risky decisions."[14] This version is rather broad and open to some degree of interpretation.

Naturally, all of these definitions are valid and insightful, and all point to similar elements or themes – namely, the role of behavior in the consideration of risk – reinforcing a point we covered in the first chapter. For the purposes of our discussion we shall introduce a variation of the definitions above, where we consider risk culture to be *an internal sensibility, reflected in the daily thoughts and actions of all of an institution's employees, that reflects knowledge of, and respect for, risk*. Through this definition we emphasize both risk awareness (knowledge of, and respect for, risk) and an automatic, arguably almost subconscious, dealing with risk matters (embedded in daily thoughts and actions). The point to emphasize is that if all employees of an institution – whether or not they are specifically dedicated to risk-taking or risk management or some other form of control – are "risk aware," they help infuse vigilance within the organization. That is, in an ideal world, every employee or member of an organization would, in the first instance, be a risk manager. When a firm's employees take this approach, we can be relatively certain that the idea of a risk culture is well understood, accepted and practiced.

General characteristics of a risk culture

Now that we have a working definition, let us consider some of the general characteristics that are associated with a risk culture. This will illustrate the unique, and sometimes subjective, nature of the topic.

- *Risk culture can be a nebulous concept*: this is the biggest challenge for many organizations, particularly those that are accustomed to following processes and procedures in the consideration and management of risk. After all, there is something elegant and efficient about turning to models, quantitative processes and cost/benefit analyses to handle risk management decisions. Embracing the amorphous ideas of risk behavior and risk awareness, which can be difficult to measure and judge and which are subjective and people dependent, can be a challenge for some organizations. The trick is to make the nebulous as tangible as possible – which is certainly something we are striving for in this text. If the practice of risk culture remains in the theoretical or conceptual realm, it will not – and should not – be taken seriously. It needs to be grounded in order to be successful, which ultimately means that the behaviors and structural enhancements put in place to boost risk awareness must lead to actionable steps and decisions.
- *Risk culture is qualitative, not quantitative*: this is an extension of the first point, and represents one reason why some institutions, at least, are uncomfortable or frustrated with the idea of risk culture. While many other core aspects of risk management can be quantified and tracked in an orderly manner, risk culture does not lend itself to any such process. We know from our definitions that the primary focus of risk culture is on behavior (and, to some degree, governance or organization). Behaviors can be difficult, sometimes impossible, to quantify (although they can perhaps be categorized), so any measure related to the performance and success of a risk culture is bound to be qualitative rather than quantitative, subjective rather than objective.
- *Risk culture is changeable and evolutionary*: this seems obvious but is so important it deserves some explanation. Since many of the prescriptions of a risk culture are behavioral in nature, and since behavior is influenced directly and indirectly by people, environment and circumstances, it stands to reason that a risk culture will be – or should be – malleable. Unlike the rather defined (and somewhat rigid) typical four-step risk management process, the surrounding risk culture should ideally be able to adapt to changing factors. It is also an evolutionary concept: if properly nurtured, it builds on itself

over time. So, while the idea and practice of risk culture may seem somewhat alien or even forced in the earliest days of implementation, they will evolve into something quite natural over the years – assuming they are respected.

- *Acceptance and implementation of risk culture will vary by firm*: some firms view the concept of risk culture as important and think that spending the time to get it right is worthwhile. Others certainly do not. They may choose not to pursue the initiative, unless they are somehow forced to do so by regulators, rating agencies, shareholders or other stakeholders – although even that forcing has limits, as we shall discover. Even in firms that agree that risk culture is the right thing to do, acceptance and implementation are bound to vary: for some they come easily; for others they do not. The depth and rapidity of acceptance will be a function of many of the practices we consider later in this book. At this point, however, it is worth noting that perhaps the single most important contributing factor to the successful fostering of a risk culture and its subsequent implementation comes from an institution's leadership: if executive managers and board directors believe in this task and set the right tone by making it a corporate priority, it becomes easier. If this tone from the top is missing, the task will be far more difficult. A corollary is that successful implementation needs many "parents" or sponsors; in other words, the more people that drive this practice, the more widespread it will become. Obviously, if leadership does not believe in fostering a risk culture (or believes only to the extent of carrying out a pro forma exercise rather than inculcating a state of behavior) then failure is almost guaranteed. Equally, if leadership cannot get others to drive the process through the ranks, it will not spread very far.
- *Risk culture is a journey with no end*: at the risk of introducing a cliché, it must be said that there is no true endgame or finish line with risk culture – certainly not as compared with a risk process in general, where appetite, models, reporting, capital allocation and so on can be decided, implemented and completed. For reasons mentioned earlier in this section – personal, institutional and environmental dynamism – risk culture is an evolutionary process, one without end. To be sure, certain markers or milestones will be passed along the way which will provide a sense of progress, success or shortcomings. But there will be no final point at which a firm and its leaders report to stakeholders that the task of implementing a risk culture has been completed. In fact, we can point to examples of firms that let slide previously strong and well-regarded risk cultures: the cultures were not properly nurtured, suggesting that the very behaviors that are so helpful in creating risk awareness disappeared or were squashed.
- *Risk culture will determine success in aligning business strategy and risk strategy*: we noted in Chapter 1 that a key component of the successful risk process is synchronizing the business plan with the risk strategy (philosophy and

appetite). While these can be forcibly linked through budgeting processes every quarter or year, a forced exercise will likely be regarded as artificial, and they may ultimately become delinked. If risk culture is well embedded, in contrast, then the likelihood of successfully and continuously aligning the two strategies is much higher – precisely because the two will move in tandem every single day, as the practices which characterize the risk culture are carried out automatically. Not surprisingly, when the business and risk strategies are not synchronized, a certain amount of confusion, even chaos, will ensue. This can, in the final analysis, lead to conflicts and bad decision-making.

- *Risk culture cannot be a box-checking exercise*: in a world characterized by a heavy dose of regulations, rules and oversight, institutions may feel tempted to add another task to the list of things that they must do. In other words, they may consider risk culture just another task to implement following some formulaic process in which all the required boxes are checked in order to get to the end goal: a new risk culture. The box-checking approach can easily work with some aspects of risk management; for instance, a credit risk portfolio model can be built in a series of individual steps, which can be checked off in sequence. When all the individual steps have been checked off, the model is complete and can be put into use. The same applies to many other process-oriented risk tasks. But this approach cannot work for risk culture. Implementation of risk culture, as we have noted previously, is typically an organic, multi-year process that depends on the behaviors of leaders and employees. To be sure, leaders may demand that their employees work toward the implementation of risk culture by following certain behaviors, but if no one truly believes in these behaviors, or if the exercise is seen as part of yet another "must-do" list, then the result will be artificial and ineffective.
- *Risk culture should be shaped by the needs of the institution, not the demands of stakeholders*: every institution is unique in its character and operations, and carries with it the specific personalities of its leadership and its employees. Accordingly, one institution's risk culture is going to be different from another's. Thus, the most effective approach to implementing or strengthening risk culture is to allow each institution to do what is correct for, and appropriate to, its own situation. While investors, creditors, regulators, industry groups and other stakeholders may want institutions to develop their risk cultures, there are limits to what they can do to influence the process, and ultimately they should not force specific measures on individual institutions. Doing so would almost certainly lead to the creation of forced or artificial cultures, which, as we have just noted, will be ineffective.
- *Risk culture must allow for national cultures*: many companies' activities and workforces span multiple national borders, and enlightened managers take

account of the cross-cultural differences that invariably arise by being sensitive to different ways of conducting business and professional affairs; they realize that one size does not fit all and that flexibility and appreciation for cultural nuances are essential to success. The same is true of a risk culture. The well-planned and well-integrated risk culture in a multinational company will provide for different ways of thinking and acting on risk matters – as long as the essential risk process framework remains sound and consistent. Indeed, with the integration of cross-cultural flexibilities it is quite possible that local operations will feel even more committed to building and practicing the overarching concepts of the risk culture: they will be partners rather than mere overseas subordinates.

- *Risk culture relies on good governance, but it does not come solely from good governance*: risk management is a complex task that relies on proper structure and rules to be effective. In fact, we can view these as prerequisites of the successful risk management paradigm, as noted in Chapter 1. Thus, it might be tempting to believe that a proper governance setup can shape a firm's risk culture. If we create dedicated organizational structures, governance rules and reporting lines, the suggestion goes, a risk culture will ultimately appear. It is true that a proper governance and organizational setup can facilitate the establishment and subsequent nourishment of a culture by helping promote communications, allowing for proper rotations, creating the right decision-making and escalation processes, and so on. However, this has to be viewed as one element in helping the development of a risk culture, rather than as the sole, or even primary, driver. In light of our previous points, if the behavioral aspects are not present, even the wisest governance and organizational elements will do little to promote the correct actions.

The points above represent practical characteristics of a risk culture. Since they are elemental to our discussion we shall return to some of them later in the book, particularly when we are discussing flaws and remedies.

A brief diagnostic review

Determining whether a firm already possesses a risk culture requires observation, introspection and both objective and subjective measurement. Later in this chapter we shall summarize the practical manifestation of a successful risk culture. However, it is useful first to consider a diagnostic test to determine the true state of a firm's culture.

A test of risk culture can be designed according to certain themes that we explore in more detail in the remainder of this book. Other tests could be performed, but this one provides a clear way of classifying and examining strengths and weaknesses.

Consider the following 10 key metrics that can be used to evaluate the status of the risk culture:

1. Leadership tone on risk
2. Governance processes related to risk
3. Transparency on risk strategy, appetite and exposures
4. Resources devoted to risk management
5. Technical risk skills
6. Decision-making processes, timeliness and success
7. Business/risk management relationship
8. Communications frequency and clarity
9. Incentive mechanisms related to risk-taking
10. Risk-related surprises

These diagnostic measures can be gauged subjectively, on a scale from strong to weak, high to low, efficient to inefficient, and so on. In Chapter 8, when we consider metrics for judging success, we shall propose a slightly more objective link between important measures and the themes highlighted below; for now, a general assessment is sufficient to get the process started. While evaluation of these factors individually is important, since each measurement contributes discretely to our overall sense of a firm's risk culture, it is important to bear in mind that this is not a box-checking exercise. In other words, we should not expect that by performing the diagnostic test and evaluating the current state of affairs, discovering weak points, enacting plans and then retaking the test a firm will create a sound risk culture. Reality is unfortunately more complex, as we shall discover in Chapters 6 and 7.

The diagnostic assessment – created as a questionnaire – can be performed by an external party (e.g., an auditor or consultant), or it can be managed internally. The process should include professionals from business lines and from risk management and other control functions, and should also include a representative hierarchy, from directors, executives and managers to more junior analysts, for example. Each person will have an important perspective. The main point is to approach the test with candor in order to develop a plan to identify the good and the bad, and to then maintain, strengthen or build the risk culture. Table 2.1 is a sample diagnostic scorecard. Each element A to J is graded on a scale from weak to strong, the results are collated, and the total score is classified according to the groupings at the foot of the table. The classification can be used in the development of an improvement plan, as we shall see later in the book.

In the first completed example, Table 2.2, we see a firm that has taken steps to build the right kind of risk culture – perhaps over a period of several years. In going through its assessment we can see that it has scored well with regard to leadership, governance, transparency, technical skills and resourcing.

Table 2.1 A sample diagnostic spectrum

Test category		Strong		Fair		Weak	
		5	4	3	2	1	0
A	Leadership tone on risk						
B	Governance processes related to risk						
C	Transparency on risk strategy, appetite and exposures						
D	Resources devoted to risk management						
E	Technical risk skills						
F	Decision-making processes, timeliness and success						
G	Business/risk management relationship						
H	Communications frequency and clarity						
I	Incentive mechanisms related to risk-taking						
J	Risk-related surprises						

Total score:

Strong risk culture: 40–50; proactive, in command of risks, avoids problems.

Fair risk culture: 20–39; reactive, generally avoids problems.

Weak risk culture: 0–19; unaware, susceptible to problems.

Table 2.2 Diagnostic test 1

Test category		Strong		Fair		Weak	
		5	4	3	2	1	0
A	Leadership tone on risk	X					
B	Governance processes related to risk	X					
C	Transparency on risk strategy, appetite and exposures	X					
D	Resources devoted to risk management		X				
E	Technical risk skills		X				
F	Decision-making processes, timeliness and success			X			
G	Business/risk management relationship			X			
H	Communications frequency and clarity			X			
I	Incentive mechanisms related to risk-taking				X		
J	Risk-related surprises			X			

Total score: 37.

Table 2.3 Diagnostic test II

Test category		Strong		Fair		Weak	
		5	4	3	2	1	0
A	Leadership tone on risk			X			
B	Governance processes related to risk				X		
C	Transparency on risk strategy, appetite and exposures				X		
D	Resources devoted to risk management				X		
E	Technical risk skills				X		
F	Decision-making processes, timeliness and success				X		
G	Business/risk management relationship					X	
H	Communications frequency and clarity					X	
I	Incentive mechanisms related to risk-taking				X		
J	Risk-related surprises					X	

Total score: 18.

Although it must do some additional work on improving the efficiency of its risk processes, strengthening the business/risk management relationship and fine-tuning its incentive mechanisms, it has generally created the kind of environment in which risk-related surprises are minimized. By focusing on those areas that are classed as "fair" the firm can implement fixes that will let it move from being reactive to being proactive on risk management issues.

In the second example, shown in Table 2.3, we see a firm that has a rather weak risk culture. It may not have focused or invested properly on the issue in the past, and it is now paying the price. In this example the company is fair to weak in each of the 10 categories, indicating that it will need to implement a broad-based program to resolve the deficiencies. Of course, until it has begun to build and strengthen its risk culture, it will remain susceptible to risk-related problems and surprises.

Practical manifestation of a strong risk culture

If risk culture can be regarded as a set of structural mechanics and behaviors which infuse a sense of risk awareness through all levels of the organization, it is helpful to explore, in general terms, how risk culture manifests itself in the successful organization. This means, in effect, examining some of the characteristics that would result in a firm being assessed in the diagnostic stage as having a strong risk culture. This examination will also allow us to consider, in Chapter 4, the deficiencies and flaws that can affect organizations with a weak risk culture.

- *Respecting risk, and keeping it aligned and balanced*: a company that takes risk, in whatever form, must have a healthy respect for what risk can do – both positively and negatively. When a risk culture is properly embedded, professionals at all levels – directors, executives, managers – have a strong appreciation for how risk can benefit the company and its business model, and how it can damage or hurt operations. Leaders and managers can ensure proper control of all risks, align risky business activities with risk tolerance and create a strong link between risk and return. Companies that ignore the power of risk do so at their own peril. Consider a large multinational automotive company that is exposed to operating risk, interest rate and currency risk, credit risk, legal risk, and property and casualty risk. Since the firm's leaders know that the operating results are substantially affected by this range of risk variables, they take the multi-stage risk process seriously and strive to make sure it is well implemented and supportive of business strategy.
- *Leading by example*: a firm with a properly embedded risk culture will be led by directors, executive managers and other leaders who practice what they preach and set a tone they expect others to follow: they are fully aware of the nature of risk and of a risk culture (along with its drivers and its benefits), and they practice the requisite behaviors as a matter of course. Importantly, employees in the organization can easily see this behavior in action, and this guides them to behave similarly. Extending the example immediately above, we can imagine the directors and the executive leaders of the automotive company being fully committed to the diligent management of risk so that the company's operations remain sound and profitable. The leaders may show this commitment by spending time on the key risk issues affecting the firm, properly considering the philosophy, appetite and key exposures, and chairing the relevant risk committees; they may also require their managers to be fully aware of the firm's main risks and to communicate potential risk issues and problems on the horizon before losses are sustained.
- *Remaining flexible and responsive on risk matters*: a firm with a strong risk culture will tend to display flexibility and quick responses when it comes to risk matters. In other words, it will be well placed to deal with a new or unexpected risk opportunity or crisis, to reshape its risk profile in the face of a changing environment or to anticipate risk dislocations – all in a relatively short time frame. When the risk culture is strong, awareness of the key risk

drivers is second nature, so those in charge will be responsive to changing situations: they will be armed with the information and tools they need to protect against or take advantage of a situation. A firm that has no such awareness will never be as responsive, and may suffer as a result. Consider the example of a global investment bank that is active in both trading and securities underwriting. It has developed a strong awareness of risk and its key risk drivers over many years of successful business practice, and is therefore able to use this knowledge, and its technical risk skills, to determine how it can take advantage of changing market circumstances. For instance, if it knows that difficulties are developing in the emerging market debt area and that its own book could be susceptible, it may move quickly to put on some hedges and to begin discreetly selling down its positions in order to be well protected in advance of any dislocation – and before many other banks and securities firm rush to do the same thing.

- *Making risk awareness actionable*: it is all well and good for a firm to have an awareness of risk that is deeply embedded in the minds of risk takers, risk managers and leaders, but it cannot stop there: a truly strong risk culture ensures that awareness translates directly into action. All risk-aware employees use their knowledge to take specific actions to manage risk properly and to ensure a safe and profitable environment. This helps take the conceptual and theoretical aspects of risk management into the realm of the practical, with real decisions and results that positively affect a firm's operations. Thus, if an industrial company with a strong risk culture has employees with a good appreciation of the firm's risks and risk processes, as well as the operating environment, it will expect these employees to propose actions to take better or more diversified risks, to establish protective hedges, to reduce the risk appetite in advance of changes in the economic climate or to invest more resources in a robust risk management platform. Each of these steps reflects an actionable item coming from an awareness of risk.
- *Acting as a partner, not an obstacle*: in well-run firms the risk management functions are separate and distinct from the business and revenue functions, for obvious reasons of independence, oversight and control. This is a key relationship, and the degree to which these "opposing" functions are partners or adversaries will help determine how successfully the firm manages its risks. In an ideal world the relationship is constructive and serves the best interests of stakeholders. Indeed, it should be relatively obvious that, in the properly functioning firm, where risk management is a respected partner, operating efficiently and being consulted for views when a risky transaction is contemplated, the risk process is stronger and more effective. There can still be natural tensions and differences between the two groups, but both will tend to act in a manner that protects the firm. Under this construct, there is mutual recognition that it sometimes pays to

walk away from business that is too risky or could in some way damage the firm. Alternatively, it sometimes makes sense to take additional, "smart" risk. This ideal scenario does not always exist: in many organizations the relationship between business and control functions is more confrontational; business leaders seek only to maximize revenues and client satisfaction (booking occasional "bad business" as a result), and control leaders seek only to protect shareholders (rejecting occasional "good business" as a result). This type of relationship is not conducive to building or strengthening a risk culture, as tensions and conflicts can overwhelm any sense of doing what is right. Consider the example of a bank that actively takes credit, market and liquidity risk. It has an aggressive team of lending officers and proprietary traders who are accustomed to taking and managing risk. However, these professionals are experienced enough to know that getting additional support, advice and views from the risk management team can help them make the right risk decisions. Accordingly, they forge partnerships with their risk colleagues through constant communication and by seeking their opinions well in advance of transacting any business being considered. The risk team, for its part, takes strides to educate itself thoroughly on the business front, and is well aware of the nature of the business lines and of the risks being run. Risk managers make themselves available for consultation and to support requests for more risks of the right kind. They also give their business colleagues early warning signals on the overall environment and potential areas of macro and micro weakness. As a result of these relationships, the risk team is a full partner with the business team in driving rational risk-related deals.

- *Not trying to slip one by the goalkeeper*: in the strong risk culture, revenue generators prefer to act as the first point of analysis and evaluation – rejecting those deals that do not make sense and forwarding those that do make sense to their risk partners. In the opposite scenario, when business partners have aggressive budgets to meet they may be tempted to book as much business as possible, without regard for the risk implications of their actions. In the extreme they may simply take repeated shots on goal in hopes of landing some in the net. They are abandoning their natural role as the first line of defense. Continuing with the example above, on the basis of the bank's approach to both business and risk, we can assume that its lending officers and traders act as a true line of defense, vetting business before considering whether to pursue it from a risk management perspective. This is the complete opposite of the dysfunctional behavior of pressing risk managers to approve as much business as possible – whether or not it makes sense to do so.
- *Promoting the free flow of information*: strong communication built atop free-flowing information is central to the strong risk culture. This is a two-way street, with business and control professionals sharing critical

information about opportunities, concerns, risks, market environment and so forth, in an effort to build useful intelligence that can lead to stronger decision-making. When this communication occurs as a matter of course, professionals are taking fully informed actions, to the benefit of all stakeholders. When the free flow of information is impeded, decision-making is necessarily flawed, as it will be based on incomplete facts. The silo mentality that characterizes dysfunctional communication is detrimental to building the proper culture. Let us take the example of an integrated energy company which is exposed to a range of risks: energy prices, interest rates, currencies, property and casualty exposure, and general business risks. In order to properly control these risks – and so keep the company's revenue base strong – management has determined that it is essential for business managers to keep risk managers and other control personnel informed about their risk-related business activities. Equally important, it has mandated that its risk managers keep business professionals apprised of changing market conditions, portfolio concerns and stress test results. Through this reflexive communication and the free flow of thoughts, opinions and data, the energy company is striving to ensure appropriate levels of awareness.

- *Displaying strong expertise*: a successful risk culture embodies deep, shared expertise. To be sure, those who run businesses and generate revenues and those who manage the resulting risks have their own areas of expertise, arising from many years of experience and practice, but the enlightened organization is characterized by a good degree of cross-functional knowledge: business professionals who are aware of risk issues, and risk professionals who are conversant with business issues, structures and markets. Joint expertise permits the two otherwise separate groups to speak the same language and, per the point immediately above, encourages the free flow of information. Joint expertise also gives each party greater sensitivity to the other's issues, allowing for more reasoned decisions. Continuing with the example above, we would observe that the business and risk leaders working for the integrated energy company have managed to acquire a broad base of skills in both the energy sector itself and risk management as it relates to the industry. The business leaders running individual units have a good base of risk knowledge, and the risk managers who are meant to oversee the company can speak and act intelligently when it comes to business matters. This type of joint expertise means the two groups are at once able to understand each other's viewpoint and to use the broadest base of expertise to protect the firm and to advance business interests.
- *Promoting empowerment and accountability*: professionals need and want to be empowered to make decisions that affect the fate of their unit, department or function. This applies to revenue generators and to risk managers:

each needs to be given the responsibility to act. It is equally true, of course, that professionals who are imbued with certain authorities must be held accountable: they should take credit when things go right, and accept responsibility when things go wrong. A firm with a strong risk culture has professionals who bear the burden of mistakes and problems without shedding accountability or pointing the finger at another party. This is particularly important when it comes to risk-induced losses. When such losses occur, there may be a temptation to simply blame risk managers for failing to capture or control or stop the risks and attendant losses. Alternatively, risk managers may seek to blame business colleagues for proposing the business in the first instance, without properly vetting it. Either approach must be seen as disingenuous. It is far better when all parties accept responsibility and move to fix the problem in a timely fashion, without acrimony. Let us consider the example of a university endowment fund that is responsible for prudently managing the investable assets of the university, generating returns to be applied to development of the school's infrastructure and curriculum. Under the terms of the endowment, the university's board of regents has devolved responsibility for active management of the fund to the endowment's fund managers, who must deal in asset classes and products in line with a broad risk strategy, but who have significant discretion to direct capital into specific investments. The fund managers are able to act rapidly and flexibly, without having to seek additional approvals from the board of regents, and can use all their professional expertise to try to maximize returns. Of course, the same fund managers will be held accountable should the fund underperform.

- *Not tolerating the treatment of some employees as second-class citizens*: the firm that treats all of its professionals in the same manner is enlightened, and this enlightenment reflects a positive risk culture. Historically, many firms have created two classes of employees: those who generate business and revenues, and those who do not. This divide has the potential to create silos and to lead to feelings of inferiority among those in the non-producing roles, regardless of the importance of their functions. It also has the potential to harm the communication, respect and partnership mentality that are so crucial to the establishment of a risk culture. Firms that view all functions as equal help bridge this divide and create an environment where risk management is respected and regarded as just as important as business generation. This is a logical approach because, in the final analysis, flawed risk management can be as damaging as flawed business practices, while strong risk management can be as beneficial as strong business practices. We can consider the case of a global securities firm that has a large team of producers (e.g., traders, salespeople, research analysts) and a group of risk managers to oversee the business. These two groups of professionals have made efforts to communicate and build relationships over the years, acquiring expertise in each other's areas and working together to build revenues and client business and to protect the firm's financial condition. These relationships, supported by the firm's leadership, mean that everyone is treated equally when it comes to professional respect, opportunities and compensation. There is no specific divided or multi-class system, which would prove destructive to relationships and the overarching culture.

- *Realizing when "no" means "no"*: there are times when the best business for a firm and its clients is to do no business at all. Sometimes this can be decided by the front-line business professionals, who, after evaluating a potential product, deal or proposal, might feel that it is not right for any party. At other times it can fall to the risk management team to reject what might seem to business partners to be a worthwhile endeavor. To be sure, many firms (rightly) have some form of escalation process or right of appeal to the next level in the hierarchy; this is important, as it gives business professionals the chance to be heard if they feel their case is unique, compelling or otherwise deserving of a second look. However, at some point a "no" must be taken as a "no." If the two parties have mutual respect for each other's abilities and have a strong communication link, then the ability to accept the answer "no" will follow naturally. A corollary to this point is that regular escalation to the next level indicates a degree of dysfunction. While an occasional appeal is normal and expected, a continuous stream of appeals indicates some lack of confidence or respect at lower levels of authority. Continuing with the example immediately above, we can imagine that a trader might, for instance, want to position a large block of illiquid securities on a strictly proprietary basis. An analysis of the potential returns and the downside, considering the trade in the context of the firm's existing portfolio and prevailing market conditions, might indicate that the appropriate course of action is to decline the business. The trader, though perhaps disappointed, is willing to accept the "no" without complaint or escalation, because he knows and trusts that his risk management colleagues have provided prudent, well-reasoned arguments as to why the firm should pass on the trade.
- *Seeing all risks, transparently*: if a key element of risk culture is risk awareness, then it should come as no surprise that an institution with a strong culture will examine, discuss and manage its risks holistically and transparently. Much has been written in recent years on enterprise risk management (ERM) as the best way to capture all of a firm's risks and to manage them equitably. In fact, this is a logical approach to risk management, as the sum total of a firm's risks takes account of diversification and correlation and allows for risk-adjusted comparisons and decision-making across business and risk factors. Clearly, a firm with a weak risk culture will be unable or unprepared to

view its risks across types and businesses, suggesting a piecemeal or compartmentalized approach to both transparency and management – which will not benefit the firm's decision-making or value generation. An associated point relates to the clarity of the risk philosophy: a firm with a strong risk culture will be crystal clear about the risks it chooses to take, and why, and will stick to its position, while a firm that lacks a disciplined culture will not necessarily be consistent in its approach to risk-taking, creating confusion with regard to its priorities and imperatives. Let us return to our previous example of the integrated energy company, which runs multiple types of risks in various domestic and offshore centers. In order to keep its entire risk profile in check, the company has instituted an ERM framework that allows executive management, business managers and risk managers to see different slices of risk: financial risks, business risks, hazard risks and so forth, by geography, business segment and portfolio type and in total. This ERM approach lets the firm's leadership focus quickly on total exposures, key exposures and adherence to the overall risk appetite. It also allows all responsible parties to quickly match the actual risks taken with the overarching philosophy – to make sure that all activities remain within the mandated perimeter.

- *Encouraging the power to challenge*: a firm with a strong risk culture gives risk executives the power to constructively challenge the business model, specific business transactions and overarching strategies openly and without fear of retribution. This attitude or approach gives business leaders confidence in their strategies and makes them comfortable with transparency; equally, it reflects the fact that risk management is taken seriously by executive management and directors. If this power is lacking or diminished in some way, it may be indicative of larger problems regarding autonomy, governance and transparency. Let us consider the example of a government-related financing authority that is responsible for facilitating the funding of infrastructure projects. This type of business exposes the authority to a considerable amount of credit risk related to project finance, so deals needs to be analyzed and structured carefully to ensure there are at least two sources of repayment. Let us further assume that the financing authority's business leaders want to expand into transportation funding, focusing on high-speed rail. After considerable study, discussion and debate, the chief risk officer may decide to openly and constructively challenge the proposal by presenting the results of a well-reasoned, detailed analysis. In doing so, the CRO has no fear of retribution or of being harassed or criticized by the business and executive leaders: they understand and appreciate the constructive criticism and the risk concerns, and view the challenge as a fundamental part of the process. Regardless of the ultimate decision taken by the leadership, the CRO and risk team have had an opportunity to openly and freely express their views.

- *Promoting a strong feedback loop*: despite diligence and good intentions, institutions still make mistakes, and some of these mistakes occur in the risk arena. Dealing in risky business necessarily means that a firm cannot always get it right. That said, the firm with a good risk culture will have a strong feedback loop (or "risk memory") that allows it to learn from its mistakes and ensure that it either does not repeat them or reduces significantly the probability that they will occur again. This sort of feedback loop is tied to the communications process, but arguably goes beyond just communications: the feedback needs to lead to adjustments to an institution's risk appetite, strategy and policies. Only then can the negative lessons of history be properly embedded in the corporate culture. Let us continue with the example immediately above. Assume that after much debate and discussion, the financing authority's board and executives decide to proceed with a funding transaction in support of high-speed rail. Let us further assume that two years into the five-year development project, the deal runs aground and the borrower defaults. The financing authority is forced to write off the bad credit on its books. While the loss is unfortunate, the key point is that the firm conducts an analysis, under the leadership of the CRO, of what went wrong and compares the results with both the decision taken and the initial risk analysis to point out lessons learned. When the financing authority is approached about a similar kind of deal in the future, it will have the benefit of a well-documented and well-discussed experience to look back on.
- *Demanding ethical behavior*: most companies have some type of code of conduct or integrity charter or principles of behavior which they use to guide the actions of their employees. The intention is typically to get employees to behave properly and respectfully toward each other, clients and other stakeholders. An ethical approach to business is, of course, essential to a strong corporate culture and is fundamental to a strong risk culture, as it gets individuals to do the right thing, even when things are difficult, complex or unclear. But while all of this is well intentioned, it can serve a useful purpose only if it is truly believed – it the code of conduct is lived, and not taken simply as a form of corporate, politically correct, sloganeering. This ethical behavior must be constant, steady and self-reinforcing, or else it may collapse in the face of problems or difficulties. Imagine the case of an asset management firm that is primarily responsible for managing client funds. As part of the corporate ethos, management has developed a charter that demands absolutely ethical behavior by all employees, at all times. This applies to both internal activities and those that might impact clients directly. In due course the company discovers that one of its most important clients has been mistreated through some erroneous pricing. Management moves quickly to rectify the problem, reimburse the client and take disciplinary action against the account officer. Furthermore, it

uses the example to demonstrate to other employees that it cannot, and will not, tolerate any behavior or action that is not consistent with its charter.

- *Employing rational incentives*: a firm with a strong risk culture has rational incentives and compensation mechanisms that properly motivate and reward and avoid any skewed behaviors. Much has been written about the problems caused by poorly planned incentive schemes that actually encourage bad behavior and excess risk-taking by explicitly rewarding business professionals for pure revenues or the net present value of business which might have been on the books for many years. Enlightened firms avoid these problems, and the resulting behaviors, by aligning incentives with the fundamental risk-adjusted revenue stream over a multi-year period. Let us consider the instance of a bank that specializes in making markets in structured products and complex derivatives. Much of the financial risk that it runs is esoteric, illiquid and long-dated, so the firm has a complex risk profile that needs to be managed intensively, over the long term. In order to ensure its traders are disciplined and aligned in their behaviors, the board has approved an incentive structure that ties compensation over a multi-year period to a matrix of factors, including current-year revenues (not present-valued) and the performance of the risk book over a 5-year and a 10-year period. Under no circumstances do the traders receive an annual payout that reflects the present value of long-term risk. In addition, the directors have converted the payout from an all-cash scheme to a 75% stock scheme with a 5-year vesting period.
- *Keeping a steady hand*: there is a temptation, at least in some firms, to become undisciplined or sloppy when the market environment turns strong: when economic growth, corporate profits and client opportunities are on the upswing, the cautionary stance adopted during a previous downturn may be forgotten. This sets the stage for potentially significant problems when the cycle turns or when a shock hits the system or the company. Firms with a strong risk culture preserve their conservative attitudes and behaviors – as a form of institutional memory – to protect them from changing cycles. Exemplifying this steady hand is central to prudent and proper risk management behavior. While this approach may mean firms sacrifice some additional business opportunities on the margin (which are perhaps attractive only when the markets are strong), it will help ensure negative surprises are minimized and that earnings and revenues are less volatile. The idea of a steady hand also applies to competitive pressure. A firm with a strong risk culture believes in its strategy and its appetite, and is willing to stick with these despite competitive pressures to take more, or different, risk. The steady hand is a sign of maturity and experience; it allows a company to skip on incremental business that its peers may be pursuing aggressively.

Continuing with the example immediately above, we can imagine that after several strong years of revenue growth from well-behaved markets and good client demand, the derivative bank encounters a rough patch: markets get difficult, volatility and illiquidity increase, and clients step to the sidelines. Under these circumstances, management revisits its experiences from past market dislocations and decides to lower its risk appetite, put on some protective hedges, sell some of its more dangerous positions and communicate to both traders and risk managers that the strategy for the next few quarters will be one of conservative positioning and risk pricing – all in order to emerge from the market turmoil in good financial condition.

These practical manifestations of a strong risk culture are summarized in Figure 2.1. We shall revisit them later in the book, when we consider deficiencies and flaws and methods of building and strengthening the culture.

It is worth noting that firms that feature a strong risk culture – firms in which most or all of the characteristics noted above are evident – may have developed this culture many years ago and now be enjoying the fruits of such efforts. Some firms have dedicated themselves over many years to instilling the right attitude and approach to risk, ensuring the proper training, awareness and discipline. Such a program of cultural awareness, built atop the issues we consider later in this book, cannot unfortunately be rushed into play. It is also likely to meet with a certain amount of skepticism, at least in some quarters: another corporate initiative, another set of corporate principles and behaviors. Accordingly, it must ultimately take hold in a gradual, organic fashion, becoming part of the fabric of a firm's operations and character. We might say, in this context, that while the successful firm might have a single formalized risk management function, it will have literally dozens or hundreds of informal ones that operate throughout the business and control functions.

Some simple rules

To reinforce the idea of practical manifestation of a strong risk culture, let us take a look at some of the simple rules that can govern the process. Some years ago I collated a series of rules regarding the implementation of risk management within any institution; the ideas, embodied in *The Simple Rules of Risk*,[15] are built atop basic common sense and cover the complete spectrum of the risk process. A handful of the rules in that book relate specifically to the themes we touch on throughout this book, and can thus be seen as a useful summary reference point; these are included below, along with some additional commentary to tie them into our theme. Curiously, what was true and relevant 10 years ago,

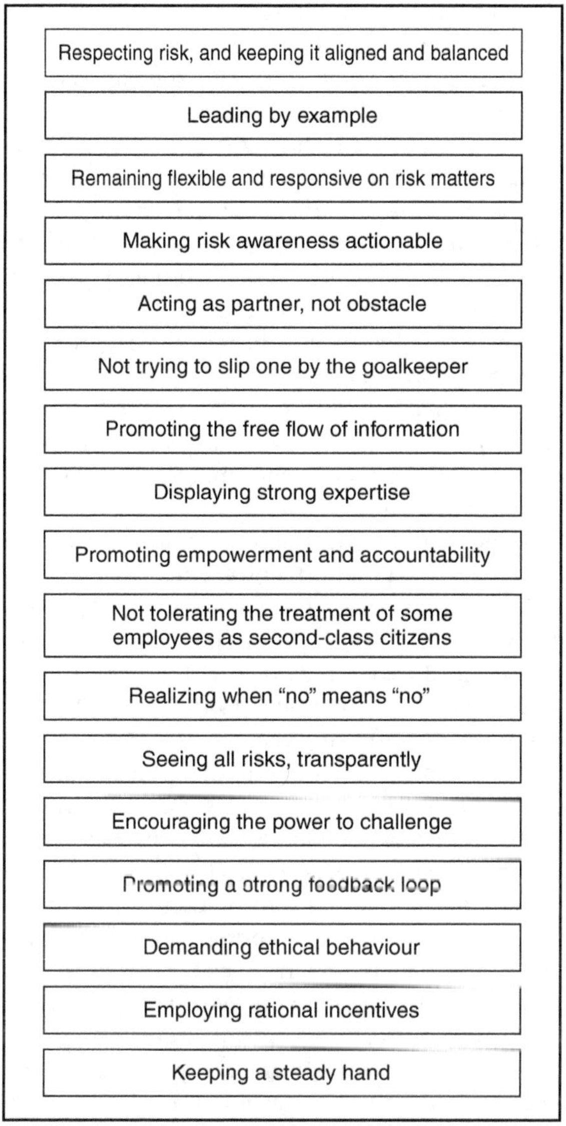

Figure 2.1 Practical manifestations of a strong risk culture

when *The Simple Rules of Risk* was written, remains true and relevant today – perhaps even more so, as the financial stakes have become even greater.

- *Risk-taking should be aligned with other corporate priorities, directives and initiatives:*[16] this rule is associated directly with what we have noted above regarding a firm's business strategy, risk strategy and risk appetite. The linkages must be clear and consistent.

- *Actively assuming risk requires support from key stakeholders and the commitment of necessary financial resources:*[17] this point speaks at once to the concepts of setting a risk appetite and of ensuring sufficient transparency that stakeholders (and shareholders and regulators in particular) are fully informed regarding the risk strategies and exposures a company may take.
- *Risk capacity is not free, and proper compensation must be obtained:*[18] a sound business and risk strategy depends on being properly paid for risks absorbed; the balanced risk-adjusted return concept must be embedded in the business and risk strategy so that the business can be regarded as both enduring to clients and fair to shareholders.
- *Senior management should know the strengths, weaknesses, motivations, expertise and risk behavior of business leaders and risk takers:*[19] this point addresses the risk expertise that must necessarily be embedded within a company's business units and its control functions. A firm should not be taking any meaningful risk if it does not have the right professionals in situ – doing so is a recipe for financial and reputational problems.
- *Once a risk philosophy has been defined, it should be communicated clearly and followed with discipline:*[20] the risk philosophy is the key expression of what a company wants to do with regard to risk; once this has been assessed and formulated it has to be channeled to the key professionals involved in taking, managing and controlling risk, in a clear manner. There should be no ambiguity about what is, or is not, permissible in the risk arena.
- *Clear expression of a firm-wide risk appetite is essential:*[21] in line with the point immediately above, once a company's leadership has defined the financial perimeter of risk-taking activities, it must communicate this perimeter in general terms to relevant external stakeholders (e.g., regulators, rating agencies) and in very specific terms to appropriate internal stakeholders (e.g., business managers, risk managers, financial controllers, auditors).
- *Accountability for risk must run from the top to the bottom of an organization:*[22] this point is, in some sense, another way of crystallizing the idea of a risk culture – a state where everyone in the company feels accountable for risk. To be sure, particular units and professionals have very specific responsibilities for risk. However, more widely, the more employees who buy into the notion that they must protect the firm, the higher the chances that a positive risk culture will thrive.
- *Compensation policies for risk takers must be rational:*[23] incentive structures are designed to incentivize people to do, or not do, certain things. Not surprisingly, if the compensation scheme encourages risk-taking, then that is precisely what employees will do: take more risk. Historically, this has been one key reason for major problems in the financial sector, where large

pay, large risks and large losses have sometimes been highly correlated. Adjusting compensation policies to produce the right behaviors with regard to risk is therefore critical. Note also that rational policies must exist for risk managers.

- *Business managers should be the front line of risk management, accountable in a measurable way for assuming "good" risks:*[24] those who are responsible for generating risks should also be responsible for managing those risks – which necessarily means they ought to be focused on taking "good" or "wise" risks that benefit both the firm and the end client. Business managers who ignore their responsibilities in the direct, firsthand management of risk are extremely dangerous.
- *Risk expertise must be disseminated throughout the organization:*[25] an extension of the point immediately above is that a company that hopes to be truly risk-aware should strive to spread risk expertise throughout the business and control divisions, making as many professionals as possible competent in risk matters. Risk awareness cannot be the sole preserve of the formal risk management unit.
- *General risk education should be mandatory throughout the firm:*[26] bolstering technical expertise on risk matters is a worthy goal, and investing in risk education is a rather simple means of reaching that goal. An organization that is willing to invest in such education (perhaps making it mandatory) will surely receive a handsome return on its investment as more employees become risk-aware. Underinvesting in something as fundamental as risk education is rather short-sighted.
- *Risk specialists should question and probe until they are satisfied with the answers:*[27] one sign of a mature organization with a deep risk culture is that risk managers and other controllers can query and challenge colleagues on risk-related matters until they are truly satisfied with the answers. If the environment is free enough to allow such challenges, then nothing can be hidden and transparency becomes the norm. Clearly, if a company's leaders choose to stifle questions and debate, something wrong may be going on.
- *A constructive relationship between business units and the risk unit can be more productive than an adversarial one:*[28] one recurring feature of companies with strong risk cultures is the partnership approach to management. When business managers and risk managers cooperate to understand the specifics of the business and its risk dynamics, and when they work together to achieve some end, they are likely to be productive and efficient in generating results that are in the best interests of stakeholders. The same effectiveness is unlikely if the relationship is adversarial: conflict, opacity, miscommunication and errors will almost certainly increase, to the detriment of all.
- *Consistency is vital throughout the risk control organization:*[29] arbitraging internal rules in hopes of receiving a different (favorable) decision to proceed with

a piece of risky business is a technique used by some business managers. If a firm's control processes allow for such arbitraging, then it clearly has a problem. Consistency of risk rules and policies is essential to keep all risk takers operating on the same basis.

- *The ability to relate profit and loss to risk is paramount:*[30] a company's leaders must understand how revenues are generated and how risk may create gains or losses. This understanding is so fundamental to corporate operations that it must be regarded as the basis for success. A firm that is so large, disorganized or lacking in infrastructure that it cannot specifically identify how it makes or loses money will eventually encounter deeper financial problems.
- *Risk officers and risk takers should discuss risks on a regular basis:*[31] communication is everything in risk-taking: when those generating and those controlling risks engage in regular dialog about current and prospective risk-related business, they stand a better chance of making the right decisions and anticipating potential opportunities and problems. When this regular communication is missing there is little chance of being synchronized or coordinated on risk-taking matters – which could lead to surprises.
- *When a potential risk problem is discovered, immediate action must be taken:*[32] a firm with a strong risk culture will admit to its problems before they are repeated or become worse. This is a key aspect of transparency and communication and can be a good way of containing a bad situation. A firm whose tendency is to shoot the messenger may eventually discover that risk or business managers are unwilling to highlight any form of bad news, and this silence can serve to compound or prolong an error or loss.

We present this small subset of rules because it helps reinforce some of the concepts that are so important in building and strengthening a risk culture. None of these rules are complex or nuanced; they are basic, commonsense thoughts and behaviors that can, generally speaking, be put into place with a minimum of effort. Again, this does not mean that doing so will guarantee the instant development of a strong risk culture – that can take time, as we shall discover. But observing these rules can help get the process underway.

3
Institutional and Regulatory Considerations

In the previous chapter we defined risk culture and explored some of its characteristics, as well as a number of indicators of firms with a strong risk culture. In this chapter we shall build on the definitional and theoretical concepts by exploring how risk culture plays out in the real world. To begin, we shall consider why firms adopt a risk culture, analyzing the catalysts that can lead them in the direction of change. We shall then explore the results of various risk culture studies and surveys conducted over the past few years. Finally, we shall discuss some of the stakeholders that can influence a company in the area of risk culture. Specifically, we shall describe the changes that can potentially be brought about by shareholders, creditors, clients, rating agencies, industry groups and regulators. Given their importance, and to demonstrate how they can have an impact on culture, we shall focus particularly on certain regulatory and legislative frameworks that have been created in recent years.

Why develop a risk culture?

The first issue to consider is the simple question of why a firm should want to build or strengthen its risk culture. Naturally, the idea of a risk culture sounds good, at least in the abstract. In the previous chapter we saw some positive characteristics that accrue from a strong risk culture, and we can assume that such characteristics are desirable. Thus, the rational firm would want to synchronize its business and risk strategies, have an expert staff that is equally skilled in business and risk matters, create mutual respect between revenue generators and control professionals, develop a functional mechanism to delegate authorities, foster multiple lines of defense for risk matters, promote free flow of information and strong communication bonds, and so forth. All of these factors help a firm "do the right thing" with regard to risk, and we will refer to them as enforcing corporate values related to risk.

But is this the end of the story, or is there some additional motivation? In fact, there is another powerful reason for wanting to instill the proper culture, certainly as far as corporate entities are concerned: value maximization. We are well aware that corporations exist to maximize shareholder value (while also serving other stakeholders, including clients, creditors, regulators and communities). This can be accomplished by maximizing revenues, minimizing costs, expanding into profitable markets and properly controlling direct and indirect risks. It should be obvious that a firm that can manage its risks properly will benefit from a greater upside or a well-protected downside. And while the fundamental four-step risk management process we outlined in Chapter 1 can go a long way toward achieving this goal, it is also clear that the right governance model, coupled with a strong risk culture, will help even further. In short, there is a link between value maximization and a strong risk management process, which includes an effective risk culture.

While some firms may be unilaterally motivated and driven by doing the right thing and by value maximization, not all firms are so enlightened. There may be other forces pushing a less-enlightened firm to recognize the importance of risk culture, and to strive for its successful implementation. Let us consider five of these forces.

- *Regulatory requirements*: in some industries, particularly the financial sector, regulations regarding risk and risk-taking are particularly strict, for obvious reasons: institutions in these industries are in business to take and manage risk, and so they must have robust mechanisms in place to protect themselves and minimize the likelihood of systemic problems. For example, in the banking industry, global financial regulators have set out very clear (and rather strict) requirements regarding risk models, capital treatment and allocation, reporting transparency and so forth. Importantly, regulators increasingly require evidence that both risk and business managers are aware of the risk and capital allocation processes, and that institutions embed such knowledge in their daily actions and activities. The concept and practices of a risk culture could be beneficial in helping achieve these goals. Note that similar types of requirements extend to insurance and reinsurance companies and selectively to other non-bank financial institutions.
- *Loss-making events and disasters*: in some cases recognition of the need for a risk culture is born out of unfortunate circumstances. Firms that experience large loss-making events or financial disasters may feel humbled, and may choose to use the misfortune to examine and then enhance risk processes to ensure those events are not repeated. Ideally, the self-assessment will include a focus on the presence and quality of the firm's risk culture. If the firm believes that the lack of a risk culture (or at least the lack of a sufficiently

strong culture) has been a factor in its losses, it may devote resources and energy to building or strengthening the culture.

- *Competitive advantage*: a firm with a strong risk culture may have a competitive advantage over one with no risk culture, all other things being equal. Such an advantage can arise because the risk culture-oriented firm is able to understand its risk profile more intimately, make fewer risk-related mistakes, optimize its risk resources more effectively, communicate about risk issues more clearly, take risk-related decisions more rapidly and so forth. Risk culture-oriented firms are simply better placed to understand and react to risk issues; it is second nature to them. Firms that lack the same deep risk culture may struggle to understand, react and optimize, leading ultimately to lost opportunities or greater losses. Recognition of this competitive advantage may lead the weaker firm to adopt a risk culture.
- *Shareholder or stakeholder demands*: shareholders or other non-regulatory stakeholders (investors, creditors, clients, rating agencies) may suggest or insist that a firm work to adopt or strengthen a risk culture in order to achieve some or all of the goals discussed immediately above (or those noted in Chapter 2). For example, credit rating agencies may explicitly indicate that enterprise risk management, which includes an element of risk culture, is an important criterion in setting a credit rating. Similarly, institutional investors and creditors may favor investing in or lending to firms that can evidence a strong risk culture, believing that the likelihood of a good or safe return is higher. In fact, the role of stakeholders is so important in this process that we shall cover the topic in greater detail below.
- *Resource optimization*: in the final analysis, it is almost certainly the case that firms with a strong risk culture do a better job of optimizing financial resources than firms that lack a risk culture. The enlightened organization is well placed to understand its risks, its capital absorption requirements and its risk-adjusted revenue opportunities. Since its risk culture is built atop strong communication, joint expertise and mutual respect between risk, control and business functions, its ability to change the risk profile to take advantage of business opportunities may be greater. Firms that lack a risk culture may struggle to understand how their operations generate revenues and attendant risks, and may not be well placed to reallocate capital or otherwise manage their financial resources. Accordingly, firms seeking to improve their resource allocation may find building a risk culture a worthwhile endeavor.

Figure 3.1 summarizes the key forces that may motivate a company's decision to build a strong risk culture.

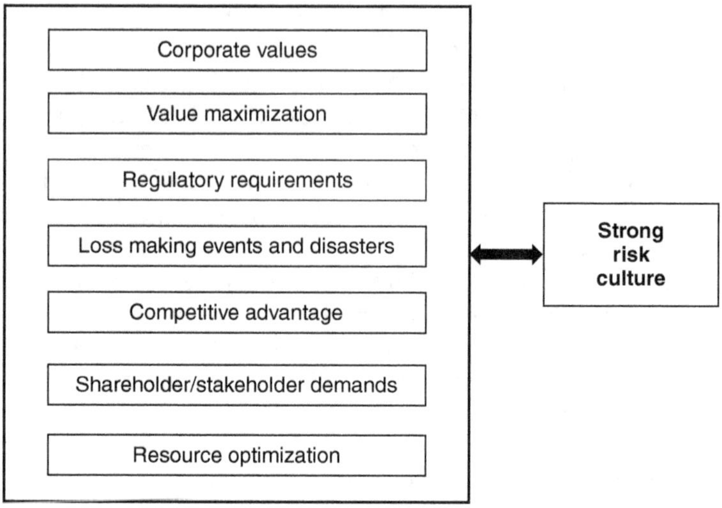

Figure 3.1 Forces influencing a strong risk culture

Studies of risk culture

Over the past few years a number of consultants and industry groups have conducted studies and surveys of risk culture, in an attempt to gauge how it is perceived and practiced. In this section we shall consider the results of some of these studies, highlighting key themes that have emerged. Given the fact that there has not yet been a great deal of rigorous research into risk culture, such studies and surveys help fill the information gap by providing an overall framework for analysis and discussion. Coupled with an examination of examples from different industries and regulatory bodies, they can help us build up a picture of how risk culture works (or does not work) in practice.

Let us begin with an early (2006) survey conducted by the Risk Management Association (RMA, a global industry group representing the field of risk management), which examined the views of 31 regulators and financial intermediaries on the topic of enterprise risk management – a holistic view of risk and approach to its management within an organization.[1] Among the key benefits of implementing an enterprise-wide approach to risk management cited by survey participants were an improved understanding of risks and controls (cited by 48% of respondents as important), establishment of a common risk culture (48%), identification and assessment of all risks (45%) and consistency in policy and standards (45%). It is interesting to note that, even in advance of the devastating financial crisis of 2008–2009, some firms were already focusing on the importance of a risk culture in their processes.

It comes as no surprise that various studies were commissioned in the aftermath of the financial crisis to help firms (and regulators) understand how so many in the financial industry failed to properly manage their risks. Although the causes and transmission effects were varied and complex (e.g., poor governance, concentrated risks, lack of understanding of stress scenarios or correlations or lack of liquidity, misaligned incentives), it has become clear that the absence of a risk culture at many of the largest institutions played an important role in at least some of the problems.[2]

Let us first consider the results of consulting firm KPMG's 2009 study of risk management.[3] Some of the most interesting findings relate to risk culture, the perception of risk management within an institution and the qualifications and knowledge of board members with regard to risk. Many of those surveyed felt that the absence of a proper risk culture was a key driver in the credit crisis: risk culture ranked third (48%), behind only governance (50%) and incentives (52%) in terms of importance. Given this fact, it is little wonder that so much attention has been directed toward the establishment of more robust risk cultures. In terms of "fixing" risk management, 45% of respondents felt the need to improve technical skills, 40% communications, 35% top-level awareness of risk, 29% management support and 20% risk culture.

Separately, 77% of those responsible for risk were committed to creating a risk culture, although many still felt the process was being driven by external parties (e.g., regulators) rather than internal ones (e.g., directors or executive managers). This is a powerful, yet mixed, message: risk culture is seen as important, but it is not necessarily driven organically by those who should be most interested in its successful implementation. This means, of course, that the exercise can degenerate into a box-checking or compliance task, rather than one truly meant to alter the character of the firm. In addition, 76% of KPMG's respondents felt that the risk management function was stigmatized as a support function. Recall from our earlier discussion that when risk managers are viewed not as partners, but as controllers or cops, there may be a tendency to see them as second-class citizens or to adopt an "us versus them" mentality – which can further imperil communication and cooperation. In terms of future enhancements, the largest categories of "most" and "next most" significant changes were related to risk governance (77% total) and risk culture (77% total). Most of the desired changes were said to be required from the "C" suite (CEO, COO, CFO, CRO). In order for risk managers to become more meaningful partners, 60% of respondents wanted to see the CRO function more involved in strategy, and 50% wanted more responsibility assigned to the function. From a knowledge perspective, some 45% also felt that board members were lacking in their knowledge of risk and risk matters. This again points to a critical deficiency: if the truly sustainable risk culture is meant to be driven from the top, then ensuring the top is sufficiently knowledgeable about risk issues is a prerequisite.

Let us next consider a general risk management survey conducted by consulting firm Deloitte.[4] Although this broad-based study was about risk management in general, the results reveal some important issues related to risk culture. In the first instance, approximately half of the respondents felt that risk management was not fully integrated into their respective firms, a stunningly high number considering the focus was on financial institutions, whose business is the management of risk. Respondents also concluded that creating a risk-aware culture was essential for navigating future challenges, and the majority felt that risk managers should play a key role in driving business strategy and should get involved in important business decisions. Most stated that it would be important, in the future, to infuse risk considerations into the fabric of the organization, and that risk management should be a central responsibility of executives throughout the firm. Finally, respondents felt that greater risk awareness would be established through a combination of communication, enterprise risk management approaches, explanation of risk principles and rotation between risk and business personnel – many of the issues we shall consider in Chapters 5 and 6.

Finally, a 2010 study by McKinsey examined 20 individual case studies of risk culture failure across a variety of industries, including healthcare, finance and energy.[5] McKinsey concluded that risk culture (success and failure) is built atop four pillars, namely transparency, acknowledgment, responsiveness and respect. Problems associated with a culture can be broken down into issues of communication, tolerance and insight (together constituting transparency); confidence in the power to challenge and freedom to be open (together constituting acknowledgment); care and speed (together constituting responsiveness); and cooperation and adherence to rules (together constituting respect). In McKinsey's view, risk culture failures can be traced to one or more breakdowns in these areas, suggesting that fixes or preventive measures should be focused on strengthening these four pillars.

There are other studies of risk management and risk culture that we could point to, but the ones mentioned above give some indication that risk culture is beginning to seep into the mindset of corporate leaders. While the process is still in its infancy – certainly when compared with established risk management practices – the trend toward acknowledgment and acceptance is strengthening.

The influence of stakeholders

While it might seem obvious that a firm would want to create a risk culture, sometimes external pressure can add momentum and a sense of urgency to the process. Indeed, we might argue that the institutionalization of a risk culture can be assisted by the efforts of various stakeholders, including shareholders, creditors, clients, rating agencies, industry groups and regulators. To be sure, these stakeholders cannot force an institution to adopt a risk culture in the same way they might be able to influence it to achieve certain leverage targets or hold a certain amount of capital or use certain models to assess risks – mostly because we are dealing primarily with human behaviors, something which can be difficult to assess and control from the outside. But these stakeholders can play an important role in guiding the right behaviors by directly or indirectly rewarding or penalizing.

Shareholders

While various external stakeholders are vital to a company's initial and ongoing success, only shareholders have the direct interest and power to shape that success. In the standard corporate construct, shareholders, as providers of capital, are granted both rent rights (e.g., a share in the profits, through either dividends or capital gains) and voting rights (e.g., the right to vote on a set of issues important to the company's progress). In exercising these rights, shareholders can help shape a company's destiny.

In terms of voting rights, shareholders typically have the opportunity to vote annually in the election of directors, who are meant to serve and protect their interests.[6] If shareholders are satisfied with the job the current directors are doing, they can vote to keep them; if they are somehow dissatisfied, they can vote them out and replace them with others. Reasons for voting directors out vary, but they are typically related to poor financial performance of the company, flawed business strategy, failed acquisitions or outright losses due to bad decisions, fraud and so on. Although it may be unusual for directors to be removed because a company does not have a risk culture, it is not at all unusual for directors to be removed if the company makes large mistakes in risk management – which may be caused, or exacerbated, by a weak risk culture. We need not look very far for examples of this: directors at the helms of many of the financial institutions that suffered large risk-induced losses during the financial crisis of 2008–2009 were summarily removed and replaced with others believed to have a stronger grounding in risk. Similarly, directors have been replaced when companies have suffered instances of internal fraud or other control problems (UBS, Société Générale and Olympus, to name but a few). The pressure brought to bear by these actions is clearly medium-term in nature, but it exists as a powerful lever.

A more immediate action occurs when shareholders who are dissatisfied with a company's performance (including for risk-related reasons) simply withdraw their capital. By selling shares, investors effectively exercise their option to redeploy capital into more profitable or balanced risk/return opportunities. If enough investors sell shares because they are disappointed with the company's performance – including, in the context of our discussion, for reasons related to risk-induced losses that might have been avoided through strong controls and culture – they will put extreme downward pressure on the company's stock price. That might be sufficient to induce changes in the management team or on the board of directors; it might also, of course, make the company vulnerable to a takeover or to some form of financial distress.

The main point is that shareholders can influence a company to improve or strengthen its management of risks, including by making changes related to a risk culture. The most effective manifestation of this occurs when shareholders act in unison, either through voting or by redeploying capital.

Creditors

Creditors to a company come in various forms: banks as direct secured or unsecured lenders, institutional and retail investors as secured or unsecured bondholders, and suppliers as trade creditors. Each of these creditors supplies short- to long-term financing to a company in exchange for what it considers a fair rate of return (i.e., some credit spread over a risk-free benchmark). While some lending is secured (i.e., with collateral taken in the form of physical or financial assets), a great deal occurs on an unsecured basis – certainly where investment-grade companies are concerned. In fact, unsecured creditors have the more interesting role to play, as they should logically take a keen interest in precisely how a company is operating; secured creditors can rest relatively easy in the knowledge that although they are getting a lower rate of return than their unsecured counterparts, they do not have to worry if something goes wrong.[7]

The issue to consider, then, is the kind of influence unsecured creditors can have on a company. In other words, we are interested in knowing whether these creditors can use their funding lever to move a company in a specific direction. In the first instance, it should be clear that creditors are unlikely to have as much direct influence on a company as shareholders, for the reasons noted above.[8] That said, there is evidence to suggest that creditors might have some indirect impact on a company's future strategy by acting as a source of discipline. For instance, if a firm is perceived as performing poorly, taking too much risk, failing to control its operations or pursuing a questionable strategy, unsecured creditors may simply choose to withdraw their capital, either by cancelling unused facilities (e.g., bank lines) or by not renewing or rolling over maturing obligations as they come due (e.g., notes and bonds). In this way a company receives a strong signal from its creditors that they do not believe the returns being earned (e.g., the credit spread) are sufficient to compensate for the actual or perceived risks. When a company's leaders receive this signal they may choose to listen rather than risk a funding or liquidity crisis; that is, they may redirect some aspects of the company's operations that are deemed to be faulty or questionable. This influence and response cycle happens periodically when a company runs into financial trouble for one or more reasons that cause investors or lenders to pull back on lending, which can lead to a liquidity crisis and even deeper problems.

Tying this to our discussion, we can imagine instances when the corporate problems that concern creditors are related to a poor risk culture. Thus, if a company has a weak culture that allows excessive risk-taking, which in turn creates massive, albeit authorized, losses, creditors may balk at further lending until controls are tightened and risks are reduced to more acceptable levels, which are then constrained by a formal risk appetite – the very features one might find in a company with a strong risk culture. In fact, this pressure may be exerted in concert with the actions of credit rating agencies, as noted below. We may therefore consider creditors to have some indirect ability to influence a company's risk culture, when the current culture is deemed to be the cause of other problems. However, they are at best an indirect source of pressure.

Clients

Clients can decide which companies they want to deal with, and on what basis. In most cases they are free to choose among different firms to obtain the goods and services they require. The free market allows competition and, in the main, offers clients a broad range of choices. Regardless of the specific industry, product or service, decisions on whom to deal with are typically made on the basis of pricing, availability, efficiency, financing terms (if applicable) and after-market service. To some extent clients may also decide on the basis of a company's reputation for fair treatment and ethical behavior.

If a company's clients are dissatisfied with any of the key factors noted above, they can move their business elsewhere. And, while such decisions are typically made on the basis of very tangible economic measures such as pricing and support, on occasion a company's failure to act properly or its contravention of prudent norms may be enough to cause clients to leave (or threaten to leave). For instance, if the culture of an insurance company is to charge disproportionately for particular insurance or annuity products because it believes it can get away with doing so, it may lose customers who do not appreciate this philosophy. Similarly, a bank that sells its corporate customers unnecessary or overly complex derivative products in order to maximize (unfairly) its returns will soon see clients disappear.[9] When a firm's culture is not about doing the right thing, the firm may alienate its client base – to the detriment of its revenue generation capabilities and, ultimately, the returns it can create for its shareholders. In this sense, clients can exert some indirect influence on a company to practice the right behaviors, including those that necessarily stem from having a good risk culture.

To be sure, clients do not have the same leverage over directors and management as shareholders: they have neither rent nor voting rights, and so cannot hope to apply the same level of direct pressure if they are dissatisfied. However, the withdrawal (real or threatened) of clients may in some cases be enough to cause a company's leadership to reconsider the way the company conducts business. Indeed, if enough clients voice similar concerns they can jointly act as a powerful, though still indirect, source of influence.

Rating agencies

Rating agencies occupy an interesting and important position in the global financial markets. The major agencies (including Standard and Poor's (S&P), Moody's Investors Service and Fitch) provide an assessment of the credit-worthiness of institutions, assigning rating scores that are designed to reflect the probability of default. While the primary focus of the major agencies is on the financial structure and outlook of a company's balance sheet, income statement and cash flows, they also consider external factors related to the industry, competition and the macro environment. In recent years they have also focused quite heavily on governance, management and culture. Indeed, the assessment of the enterprise risk management capabilities of both financial and non-financial firms, which includes an examination of risk awareness and risk culture, has become a more explicit element of the rating process.

Let us begin with a brief review of some key points raised by Moody's regarding risk awareness and risk culture. Moody's uses its risk management assessment (RMA) as part of the overall process applied to a firm seeking a rating. The RMA is broad-based and covers various aspects of risk management, including the relationship between risk appetite and risk controls and the degree to which a firm's risk philosophy and risk practices relate to daily operations. These are, of course, essential components of a risk culture. Within the analytical RMA framework, Moody's explicitly quantifies different elements of the target company's risk process across various categories (including those we outlined in Chapter 1). Of specific interest to our discussion is Moody's declaration of the importance of the "collective and individual responsibilities of and awareness by executive management on risk matters, integration of risk considerations in budgeting, capital allocation, and determination of capital adequacy."[10] This is, of course, the essence of a risk culture. Moody's has also weighed in explicitly on the role of a company's board with regard to risk management. In particular, it cites five central functions of the board with respect to risk:

1. Approve the firm's risk appetite as a component of its strategy
2. Understand and question the breadth of risks faced by the company
3. Ensure robust oversight of risk at the board committee and senior management levels
4. Promote a risk-focused culture and open communication across the organization
5. Assign clear lines of accountability and encourage an effective risk management framework[11]

While all five points speak to the themes we have developed so far, point 4 is of particular interest to us. More specifically, Moody's notes that "the support of the board is key to creating an overall culture that promotes decision-making at all levels of the firm that is sensitized to risk matters and risk-adjusted performance. This culture feeds from well-established business and ethical principles emphasizing openness in communication and the right to fail."[12] This quotation illustrates the importance of risk culture with respect to the responsibilities of directors and the rating ultimately assigned to a company.

Standard and Poor's also regards risk culture as a central factor in the ratings process, and evaluates its existence when reviewing a company's approach to enterprise risk management. The S&P rating process looks at both risk management culture and strategic risk management, which it believes are fundamental to ERM. From a culture perspective, S&P has noted that the most important dimensions include communication, frameworks, roles, policies, metrics and influence, while the strategic elements focus on identification and decision impact.[13] S&P's formal assessment of culture began in 2008, when it "started to look at how a firm's culture (communications, structures, incentives, and risk appetite) affects the quality of its decisions and at the role risk considerations play when making strategic decisions."[14] In order to gauge the presence of the culture (and strategy), S&P conducts management interviews and reviews ERM-related documentation to see how risks are defined and communicated, and how directors and executives figure in the process. Importantly, S&P reviews management's approach to this issue over time, to see how (or whether) it becomes embedded.

While this approach applies to both financial and non-financial firms, it is useful to look, as an example, at how S&P has incorporated the concept of risk culture into its assessment of the credit standing of insurance companies – presumably on the basis that insurers, which are in business to manage the risks of others, ought to feature prominently a culture which lets them properly manage their own risks. S&P defines the issue thus:

> in a positive risk-management culture, risk and risk management are important considerations in the everyday aspects of corporate decision-making. To evaluate the strength of an insurer's risk-management culture, we look at organizational and governance structures for the management of risks, and at communication of risk and risk management. The risk-management culture and size of the group will influence the staffing and organizational structure of the people who are charged with executing the risk-management function. They will also affect governance structures for risk management. An insurer with a strong risk-management culture will have a very transparent risk-management process within the company and with other interested parties through their public communications.[15]

So, an insurer that is rated by S&P will be judged in part on the existence of a risk culture; if the culture is deemed to be weak or deficient, the agency will lower the credit score it assigns. The lever, in this instance, is quite clear.

In both of these examples we should emphasize that while the agencies can attempt to evaluate a firm's risk culture and use that information in assigning a rating, they cannot directly force a firm to adopt a risk culture. Again, the influence must be seen as indirect.

Industry groups

Industry groups, including lobbyists that represent particular sectors in the political process, can also exert influence, typically by helping establish mutual goals which can be represented uniformly in connection with legislative or regulatory matters. Let us consider two examples.

First, we examine the observations of the IIF, which, as a political representative of the global financial industry, is well placed to understand the meaning of risk culture in the financial sector. In the aftermath of the 2008–2009 financial crisis an IIF working group spent considerable time analyzing the problems and their causes and effects, many of which ultimately centered on risk management issues.[16] The IIF concluded that the "cultivation of a consistent 'risk culture' throughout firms is the most important element in risk management."[17] The IIF also concluded that "management should take an active interest in the quality of the firm's risk culture ... [which] should be actively tested and objectively challenged in a spirit of fostering greater resilience and ensuring continuous improvement, reflecting the strategic aims of the organization."[18] These are powerful and telling statements. If, after analyzing all of the forces that contribute to risk management success and failure, the leading financial services industry group determined that the most critical element of the risk process is based on risk culture and that management must be a driving force, then we have surely discovered an important element of corporate governance in the real world – one worthy of analysis and implementation.

Another example comes from the Committee of Sponsoring Organizations (COSO) of the Treadway Commission, a voluntary US organization created in 1985 in the wake of financial fraud and certain financial reporting and governance failures. COSO comprises various accounting and audit groups, so it is logically focused on internal controls and enterprise risk management. In its key directives, COSO recommends that public companies adopt a holistic approach to risk management, with the board of directors playing a major role. Furthermore, directors should be able to understand and guide the company's risk philosophy and appetite, understand the degree to which risk processes are embedded in the firm and regularly consider exposures in relation to appetite. More broadly, the emphasis should be on creating the right internal environment (itself a combination of a clear risk philosophy and a risk culture: "COSO

ERM Framework components include[e] the establishment of the tone or the 'risk culture' of the organization"[19]), setting risk objectives, identifying and assessing risks, creating proper response and control mechanisms, communicating key information and monitoring exposures. Aspects of the COSO framework, which was refined in 1994 and again in 2001, ultimately had an influence on Sarbanes–Oxley, which is discussed below.

These two brief examples of industry groups recommending certain actions or behaviors to firms within their sphere of influence illustrate the focus these groups can bring to risk management and risk control. While it is again true that groups such as the IIF and COSO cannot enforce a particular mechanism that enhances risk culture, they can indirectly push firms in that direction. After that, it is up to individual firms to adopt what industry groups may have developed as best practices.

Regulators

Industry regulators also have a role to play in risk culture – either directly through rules or indirectly through legislation enacted by lawmakers. The existence of an overarching regulatory framework that recommends or demands attention to the elements of risk culture can be helpful. Naturally, such recommendations or requirements are not a panacea, and are not guaranteed to work in every instance: as we have said, corporate behaviors and cultures are dynamic, even mercurial, and depend in large measure on the nature and quality of directors and executives and their willingness to press forcefully for a risk culture. But regulatory recommendations or rules can foster stronger risk cultures. In fact, given the position of authority regulators occupy, we might argue that their influence in forcing changes to risk culture (among other things) is on par with that of shareholders. Given this influence, we shall cover the issue in more detail by reviewing overarching regulatory frameworks from selected industries that attempt to address issues of corporate culture generally, and risk culture and risk awareness specifically. We consider Basel II and III (banking), Solvency II (insurance) and Sarbanes–Oxley (US listed companies). Of course, frameworks exist for other industries, too.

Basel II and III

Basel II and Basel III are major regulatory frameworks agreed by national regulators and then applied to banks within each national jurisdiction. The Basel agreements (including the original Basel Accord from 1988, amendments of the 1990s, and the Basel II and Basel III iterations since the turn of the millennium) have been guided by the Bank for International Settlements (BIS) in its role as "central bank of the central banks." Under the BIS's consultative process, members contribute commentary on new regulatory recommendations during the comment and drafting stage. Once finalized, the recommendations are devolved to local institutions through each member country's central bank or banking regulator, which is responsible for local oversight.

Basel II, which was developed through consultation in the late 1990s and early 2000s and put into practice in 2004,[20] is focused on creating minimum capital and risk standards. The general intention behind Basel II is to ensure that banks have adequate risk management and capital management processes and resources to protect against the risk of insolvency. Banks with riskier business profiles must hold more capital than those with less risky profiles. Importantly, Basel II also focuses on the managerial aspects of risk and capital processes, which ties in neatly with our discussion of risk culture.

Basel II has three pillars:

- *Pillar 1 – minimum capital requirements*: this section of the accord covers minimum acceptable quantitative methods for computing credit, market and operational risks, which can be used to determine the appropriate capital allocation. The main focus is credit risk models, which an institution can implement with varying degrees of flexibility and sophistication (e.g., the so-called standardized approach and the two internal ratings-based (IRB) approaches – foundation and advanced). Market risks are determined using value-at-risk (VAR) models, which were introduced in the 1996 Basel Market Risk Amendment. Operational risks are computed using one of three approaches: the basic indicator approach, the standardized approach or the advanced measurement approach. The result of Pillar 1 is an estimate of the minimum capital an institution needs to support the risks inherent in its businesses.
- *Pillar 2 – supervisory review*: the second pillar covers the supervisory and capital aspects of the framework, giving local supervisors flexibility to deal with additional dimensions of residual risk (e.g., reputational, concentration, liquidity, legal) and to review the risk management processes of their local banks. This review process is important for our discussion, as it concerns not only risk and capital management governance and structure, but how these are embedded in an institution's management activities.

  Pillar 2 requires banks to demonstrate that they have in place the appropriate systems and processes to ensure sufficient capital to support their risks. Demonstration is via the internal capital adequacy assessment process (ICAAP), which is described in greater detail below. (The ICAAP requires consideration of all risks, including those that are not explicitly covered under Pillar 1.) The national regulator examines a bank's ICAAP through the supervisory review and evaluation process (SREP), which compares the bank's ICAAP results with its own assessment. At the conclusion of the review the regulator decides whether the bank's capital is adequate or whether some additional amount is required (over and above minimum requirements). While the bank retains responsibility for implementing risk and capital allocation processes to manage its capital position prudently, supervisory authorities must be prepared to act in a preventive manner. Since the ICAAP is so vital, and since it contains important information on risk appetite, let us consider it in more detail.

As noted, the ICAAP requires, among other things, that a bank consider how much capital is required to protect debt holders while at the same time achieving an adequate return on equity for its shareholders. However, the ICAAP is not simply about reflecting a sufficiency of capital. It is also about ensuring that a process exists to embed the right capital-setting discipline, which brings us to process and behavior. A bank must typically demonstrate that multiple management layers, including board directors, executive managers and senior managers of both the holding company and its major legal entities, share an awareness of risk, a knowledge of the risk management process (e.g., identification, quantification) and an understanding of the capital-setting process. Managers must show that the ICAAP is an integral part of the bank's business and risk strategies, and must demonstrate that senior management supports and is engaged in the ICAAP. Furthermore, banks must be able to explain how they use the ICAAP in steering business.

Importantly, the ICAAP is intended to be forward-looking, examining how risks and capital requirements might evolve over time. It is intended to be a predictive tool, rather than a backward-looking exercise. Thus, banks that have historically calculated capital levels by reviewing previous events and extrapolating must now integrate forecast views of risks (including those identified through strategic reviews of its business and those evident in stress testing and scenario analysis). While the ICAAP is customized by each bank to account for its specific risks and businesses, as well as the views of local regulators, the general process consists of the following stages:

- Identifying risks affecting the bank in all major categories (credit, market, liquidity, operational, concentration and so on)
- Using relevant models to determine how much capital is required to support these risks
- Planning capital needs on a forward basis through strategic analysis, stress testing and so on

During the SREP regulators typically focus on:

- The background of the ICAAP process within the bank
- Risk philosophy
- Business strategy

  - Risk assessment, including stress testing
  - Capital planning
  - Adoption of the ICAAP

  While the ICAAP is relatively new to the industry, some of its central tenets – including those related to board awareness of risk and capital requirements – coincide with issues related to risk culture. It is worth emphasizing that while Pillar 2 gives banks a certain degree of freedom in creating the processes to allocate, control and monitor risks and capital, these processes must fall within overarching regulatory imperatives and interpretations.
- *Pillar 3 – market discipline*: the third pillar of Basel II concerns transparency, ensuring that participating institutions develop and adhere to a minimum set of disclosure items that allow the market at large to determine risk and capital adequacy. More specifically, a bank must provide sufficient information to allow a range of stakeholders to consider its internal capital and capital adequacy planning, risk exposures and risk assessment processes, and senior management and board awareness of these issues. This pillar again includes elements which are relevant to our discussion of risk culture, especially regarding transparency for external stakeholders. In particular, Pillar 3 requirements allow external parties to better judge whether a bank's processes ensure the proper application of risk strategy, risk appetite and risk/return tradeoffs.

While aspects of Basel II must be seen as useful and effective (and a step forward compared with previous regulatory efforts), certain portions were somewhat flawed. This became particularly apparent in the lead-up to the financial crisis of 2008–2009, when many institutions found themselves short on capital after suffering significant losses (despite adhering to the tenets of Basel II). Some institutions were also affected by tight liquidity, excess leverage and high funding costs. Accordingly, in the aftermath of the dislocation, regulators set about closing loopholes and fixing rules that clearly did not work as intended. Basel III (which is being rolled out in stages through 2019) focuses on several key points:

- Improving the quality of capital by disallowing certain forms of previously allowed subordinated equity-like instruments (Tier 3) and increasing the proportion of retained earnings and common equity (Tier 1) in the total capital calculation
- Increasing the minimum capital standards for all banks and giving national regulators powers to impose surcharges for systemically important financial institutions (those considered too big to fail) and for counter-cyclicality (building up capital in good times for use in bad times)

- Requiring banks to manage their counterparty and derivative exposures more actively through better integration of market and credit risk, incremental risk charges, credit value adjustments, netting, use of clearinghouses and so forth
- Introducing certain standard leverage and liquidity ratios
- Reinforcing measures that can help banks build up capital during periods of strong credit growth (e.g., better provisioning discipline, more use of long-term data and downturn-based loss predictions given default estimates, stress testing)

Most of these Basel III prescriptions relate to risk process and methodology, rather than to behavior, culture or awareness. However, to the extent that banks are required to adhere to these new directives, they will certainly find it easier to do so by taking advantage of the features of a strong risk culture, including governance, strategy and appetite, communication, partnership, efficiency and expertise.

Solvency II

Just as global banks must adhere to Basel II and Basel III rules regarding capital and risk, European Union insurance companies – as well as certain "third-country equivalents" (in Switzerland, Japan and Bermuda) – must adhere to Solvency II directives. Solvency II is an insurance regulatory framework that builds on the original Solvency I directive introduced in 1973, placing greater emphasis on the important risk management advances of recent years.

More specifically, Solvency II focuses on minimum requirements for an insurer regarding governance, risk management processes, disclosure and transparency, and capital adequacy (in particular, ensuring sufficient capital to meet claims and promote the stability of the sector as a whole). Like the Basel regime for banks, Solvency II has three pillars:

- *Pillar 1*: this pillar covers quantitative requirements for the amount of capital an insurance company must hold in support of its risks. These include the solvency capital requirement (SCR) and the minimum capital requirement (MCR). The SCR is a risk-based measure that sets the main solvency level for an insurer. It can be calculated using the European Standard Formula or a model developed by an insurer, and is the amount of capital needed to cover all of an insurer's risks, taking into account any risk mitigation (e.g., reinsurance). MCR is a lower capital threshold that serves primarily as a trigger for supervisory intervention.
- *Pillar 2*: the second pillar centers on governance and risk management process requirements. Pillar 2, similar to Basel II's Pillar 2, looks for evidence that an insurer has integrated the risk management process into the governance

of its business. This again ties aspects of the regulatory framework into risk culture.

Specifically, when regulators examine an insurer's compliance with Pillar 2, they are looking at the robustness of its risk management process, which includes a defined strategy, policies, processes and internal reporting. Of particular interest to us is the strategy, which must reflect sufficient details about the objectives of risk-taking business, implementation principles, the nature of the risk appetite and how the governance process assigns risk management responsibilities and authorities.

Beyond this, the insurer must prove that policies are properly documented and followed, and show how risks are identified, quantified, managed and monitored (this with regard to both current risks and future or anticipated risks, enterprise-wide and in detail). Pillar 2 also requires an insurer to demonstrate a strong internal control framework (audit and compliance, and mechanisms to implement and track both activities). It is worth noting that the regulatory expectation regarding internal controls is much like that regarding risk management: the organizational culture must accept and embed these controls, and rely on them to manage the business. The key control functions (risk, audit, compliance) must demonstrate full capabilities to assess, monitor and manage relevant risks and controls within the authorities granted them through the governance process.

The actuarial function, which is of unique and special interest to insurers, must demonstrate a high degree of technical proficiency in ensuring appropriate use of methodologies and assumptions, indicating whether premiums will cover future claims and providing opinions on underwriting policies, reinsurance agreements and whether the firm's infrastructure is sufficient to carry out the actuarial function. Finally, and of interest to us from a technical or expertise perspective, Solvency II requires an insurer to demonstrate that all professionals in key managerial roles are "fit and proper" with respect to professional qualifications, experience, knowledge, reputation and integrity. Note that, similar to Basel II's self-assessment process, Solvency II requires an insurer to perform an Own Risk and Solvency Assessment (ORSA), which focuses on risk, process and capital management. The results are reviewed by the local regulator.

- *Pillar 3*: the final pillar covers the minimum standards for disclosure by insurers to the public (summary information) and to supervisory authorities (detailed information). The intention of the disclosure pillar is to ensure sufficient transparency for the public and regulators to analyze, monitor and oversee insurers' activities.

While much of the regulatory focus of Solvency II is rightly on the minimum capital requirements and technical issues embodied in Pillar 1 (which speaks directly to the issue of risk appetite and risk capacity), the main elements of Pillar 2 spotlight some issues common to risk culture. As we noted earlier, the most effective form of risk management is one that is embedded in daily behaviors and actions, and Pillar 2 essentially recommends change management by leadership so that risk awareness permeates the organization. It is worth noting that Solvency II also emphasizes the desirability of having multiple lines of defense to deal with risk-related matters, including risk management (daily duties of directors and managers), risk oversight (board, governance, committees) and risk assurance (audit). This corresponds with some of our comments in Chapter 1.

Sarbanes–Oxley

The Sarbanes–Oxley (SOX) Act represents the culmination of the US legislative process that followed the accounting and financial scandals at companies such as Enron, WorldCom, Adelphia and Tyco. Under the 11 sections of SOX, any company that is publicly listed on a US exchange must have in place financial controls and governance structures sufficient to prevent internal control failures.

While the quantitative and compliance measures are rather detailed and prescriptive (and have been the target of criticism for imposing excessive cost and reporting burdens), some aspects are more qualitative in nature and focus on corporate culture and risk awareness. In fact, SOX internal control measures require companies to create an enterprise-wide risk culture that is driven by directors and executives – which is consistent with the themes we explore in this book. Let us briefly review the 11 sections of SOX, adding commentary where they are relevant to our discussion of risk culture:

- *Public Company Accounting Oversight Board (PCAOB)*: the first title concerns the creation of the PCAOB, which is responsible for reviewing the public accounting firms that are meant to independently audit the financial controls and statements of listed companies.[21] The PCAOB also sets minimum standards for public accounting firms with regard to compliance audits, quality control and enforcement of SOX requirements. This section and the one that follow are relevant to our discussion because they reinforce the concept of a diligent review of controls and financial statements by auditors. To be sure, the focus is external, rather than internal, auditors, but the end result is another line of defense through which to avoid surprises.
- *Auditor Independence*: the second title goes to the heart of establishing the independence of external auditors and minimizing potential conflicts of interest (such as combining audit and consulting services, or hiring of auditors by the company being audited).

- *Corporate responsibility*: the third title relates to the individual responsibility that senior executives must take with regard to the accuracy of the company's financial statements (including a quarterly signoff by the CEO and CFO declaring that the items presented are complete and accurate) and the limits they face regarding certain corporate behaviors (including conflicts of interest). This title links with aspects of corporate culture generally and risk culture specifically, where accountability and responsibility for decisions and actions by leaders are essential, and where doing the right thing at the top sets the tone for the rest of the firm.
- *Enhanced financial disclosures*: the fourth title, which again links to risk culture, covers minimum reporting requirements for financial transactions, including off-balance-sheet transactions, special purpose entities and stock transactions for designated corporate officers. This title also requires the establishment of robust internal controls sufficient to ensure the accuracy of financial reports and disclosures, and mandates both audits of and reports on those controls. Finally, the title sets requirements for the timely reporting of material changes in financial condition. Of course, the entire topic of transparency of financial operations is central to our discussion of risk culture, as is the concept of robust internal controls.
- *Analyst conflicts of interest*: this title speaks directly to the elimination of conflicts of interest between security analysts and investment bankers.
- *Commission resources and authority*: like the fifth title, the sixth defines minimum practices related to security analysts in order to restore investor confidence.
- *Studies and reports*: the seventh title details studies required by the Comptroller General and the Securities and Exchange Commission relating to the effects of consolidation of public accounting firms, the role of credit rating agencies in the operation of securities markets, securities violations and enforcement actions.
- *Corporate and criminal fraud accountability*: the eighth title describes specific criminal penalties that can be imposed for manipulation, destruction or alteration of financial records or other interference with investigations. It also specifies certain protections afforded to whistleblowers, which are relevant for those seeking to challenge unacceptable behaviors.
- *White-collar crime penalty enhancement*: the ninth title imposes greater criminal penalties for white-collar crime and conspiracies.
- *Corporate tax returns*: the tenth title simply indicates that the company's CEO should sign the official corporate tax return.
- *Corporate fraud accountability*: the eleventh and final title defines corporate fraud as a criminal offense and proposes certain specific sentencing penalties.

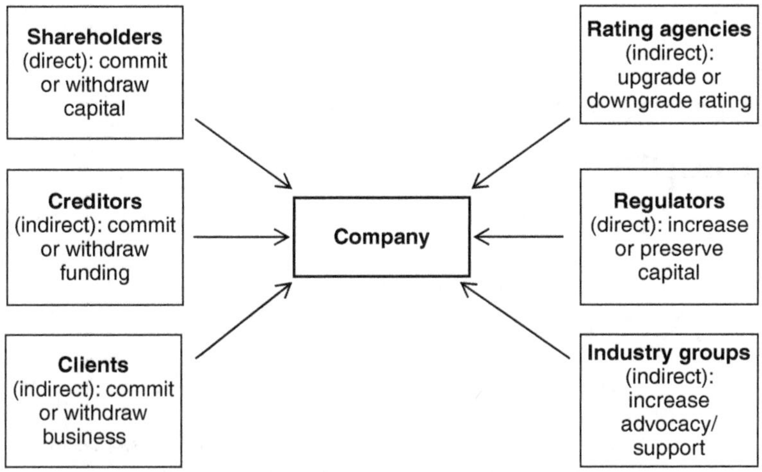

Figure 3.2 Stakeholders exerting influence on a company

As we can see from this brief overview, some aspects of SOX relate centrally to risk culture – in particular those titles that require or emphasize transparency and accuracy in financial reporting, strong internal controls, the prevention of conflicts of interest, and accountability at the top levels of the firm, which are strands that support and sustain risk culture.

Interestingly, although aspects of SOX have been criticized as heavy-handed and as costing companies extra resources for compliance, similar legislative steps have been taken for listed companies in other countries, including Australia, India, Japan, Germany, France and Italy. Thus, we can expect a similar focus on corporate governance, internal controls, oversight and culture to apply to listed companies in some of the world's largest economies.

Of course, various other regulatory frameworks have been created in recent years to reinforce the concept of corporate controls, such as the Dodd–Frank financial reform act in the US. The main point here is that regulations can be an effective means of influencing certain types of behaviors to strengthen the risk culture. Given the power of regulators to enforce specific actions, their influence can be considered rather more direct than that of some of the other stakeholders mentioned above.

Figure 3.2 summarizes the key stakeholders and the actions through which they can exert direct or indirect influence on a company with regard to risk-related matters, including the creation or strengthening of a risk culture.

4
Deficiencies and Problems I: Concepts

In the previous chapters we have outlined the risk process, presented some definitions of risk culture and its practical manifestation when successfully implemented, and considered why a firm might move toward the establishment of a risk culture. In this chapter we shift our focus slightly to explore the causes of a weak risk culture and the problems that surface when a risk culture is not part of the corporate fabric. We also consider the ultimate consequences that can befall a firm in this state. We shall drive home the key points in the next chapter by referring to examples from the real world where a flawed or deficient risk culture created an environment where losses (or worse) became a reality.

One point to bear in mind in this discussion is the difference between cause and effect: in some cases a problem may create certain negative effects which in turn reinforce the causes of that problem, in a continuous feedback loop. For instance, if two-way communication between revenue generators and risk managers is flawed or absent, this will lead to poor decision-making, misunderstandings and mistakes – possibly even financial losses. Each of these consequences may then create further strains and conflicts, leading to even less communication, and so on, in a negative cycle. The same vicious cycle can occur with other essential characteristics of risk culture, including respect, accountability and escalation.

Why weak risk cultures appear

Let us begin our discussion by understanding why weak risk cultures exist. We can divide the essential causes into three broad segments:

- Lack of awareness or ignorance
- Willful disregard or neglect
- Insufficient resources

First, a company's management may not be aware of, or understand, the importance of a risk culture. It may not realize that the lack of a risk culture, or reliance on a flawed or weak risk culture, can lead to larger problems with dire consequences. The fact that a firm's leaders are unaware of the benefits of a strong risk culture (or the destructive power of a weak one) necessarily indicates some management shortcomings. It should come as no surprise that risk culture can be an important, value-added element of corporate operations, so for directors and executives to be ignorant on this point is unsatisfactory. The lack of awareness needs to be corrected through some of the actions noted in Chapters 6 and 7.

The second reason a company might have a poor or non-existent risk culture is rather more dangerous, as it relates to willful disregard or neglect. In this case the firm's leaders may fully understand what a risk culture is and how it can help, but choose to disregard the concept and practices. In other words, they simply choose not to invest any effort in building a risk culture – perhaps believing that the concept does not apply to their own operations or that time is better spent on other initiatives. They make a conscious decision to sidestep or avoid the process. The ultimate costs of taking this approach may be paid in a more expensive form at some future time.

In the third instance, a company may lack the resources to improve or strengthen a weak risk culture. Directors and executives may be aware of the need for a robust culture and may understand the many benefits it can bring, but they are unable to resource the effort properly. As we shall see in subsequent chapters, improving the risk culture takes a certain amount of time, effort and resources. Some initiatives are capital intensive; others are people intensive – meaning that a minimum level of resources is required. If a firm cannot afford to implement these improvements, it will be unable to take advantage of the benefits delivered by a strong risk culture.

As we can see, the causes of a weak (or non-existent) risk culture are quite straightforward. Let us now look at some of the practical problems that arise from a weak culture.

Practical manifestation of a weak culture

In Chapter 2 we considered the practical manifestation of the successful risk culture. In this section we consider the flip side of the coin: not every institution has a strong risk culture, and we are interested in understanding some of the warning signs which might indicate that all is not well.[1] Ultimately we know that firms that lack a strong risk culture may be at greater risk of suffering difficulties or unexpected losses, so identifying and paying attention to these warning signs is important. As we shall see in the following sections, some of these issues are related to governance, structure and management approach, while others are more closely associated with the behaviors of individuals.

Governance, structure and management approach

- *Ignoring risk issues at the top*: the job of directors and executives is to create strategy that is aligned with risk capacity and to pay attention to both the risk process and significant risk exposures. Firms that lack a strong risk culture may find that directors and executives disregard or ignore these issues. When this happens, the message sent to the balance of the organization can be extremely damaging: other employees will believe that the same disregard is acceptable behavior, which will result in further destruction of any risk culture that exists or in a complete inability to take seriously the initial creation of a culture.[2] Take the example of a global pharmaceutical company that is involved in research into and production of new medicines. If the company's directors and executives do not enforce a strict culture of risk awareness and risk management, if they are willing to take unwise risks without regard for consequences, if they look the other way when it comes to research and development rigor, then employees running sensitive R&D and production operations may not take their own duties seriously. The end result could be flawed research leading to the production of unsafe drugs, to the detriment of external and internal stakeholders.
- *Allowing inconsistent messages on business and risk strategies*: weak risk cultures are affected by a lack of synchronicity between business and risk plans. When these plans do not coincide, several factors may be at work: lack of knowledge regarding risk issues, lack of awareness of how revenues are generated, dysfunctional relationships between business and risk managers (lack of respect, poor communication and so on) or fundamental disregard for or disagreement about the business and market outlook. This divergence can create broader problems related to risk management and surprise losses. Consider a large securities firm that has established a risk appetite through its governance processes; unfortunately, as a result of bad coordination and communication, the appetite has been isolated from the business and revenue strategies of the firm. As the year wears on and the firm tries to remain on budget, it may find that it is having to take much more risk than the appetite has indicated. Management may, at this point, ask the board to increase the appetite in order to remain on budget. If the directors support this request then two key messages emerge: the firm's management has been unable to relate appetite to revenues, and the appetite is effectively meaningless, as the figure can be moved as needed to accommodate business. Both messages reflect a fundamental misunderstanding of the importance of synchronizing risk and business parameters.

- *Not linking risk and return*: the fundamental rule for any risk-taking firm is to ensure a direct relationship between risk and return. In other words, risky business must generate a return that is commensurate with the risk being taken, or else isolated or widespread risk mispricing will ensue. A firm that consistently misprices risk is not treating shareholders fairly and may find it difficult to remain solvent if risk markets or events worsen. Firms with a weak risk culture often lack the discipline and knowledge to price their risks correctly, and may eventually be left with portfolios which are completely misbalanced. Let us return to the example of a bank that is heavily involved in granting loans to the large corporate market. Since this market is very competitive, risk pricing has historically been tight, with the bank's lending officers generally trying to subsidize the loan business through more lucrative fee-based transactional advice (e.g., M&A) or capital markets deals (e.g., derivatives, capital issuance). Unfortunately, the bank more often than not loses out to its competitors in realizing these additional high-margin cross-selling opportunities. This essentially means that the bank's loan portfolio as a standalone risk block is severely mispriced: the bank is not earning what it should to cover its cost of risk, because it is unable to cross-sell and refuses to price in the true cost of risk.
- *Encouraging directors to be "yes" men (and women)*: directors serve to protect the interests of a firm's shareholders. In order to perform their job well, they must at once be independent (able to steer clear of any undue influence from executive management) and knowledgeable (able to understand and challenge executive management). In some (perhaps many) firms, directors do not exhibit such independence or expertise, suggesting that shareholder interests may not be adequately protected. In fact, some of the most dramatic failures of corporate risk governance can be traced back to directors who did not have the fortitude or knowledge to challenge executives on key risk matters, did not promulgate risk strategies or appetites and failed to deliver the correct oversight. They preferred to simply go along with whatever executive managers recommended – arguably doing little to support prudent risk management. Let us consider a large investment bank whose CEO is also chairman of the board of directors. The company's 12 directors come from different backgrounds, and only one has had some experience with risk matters. The CEO, under the influence of his business leaders, wants to increase the bank's exposure to a risky asset class – well above what might normally be prudent. Since the CEO also happens to chair the bank's risk committee, he votes in support of the increase, and then conveys the same message to the board during the quarterly meeting. The majority of the directors, who have no background to challenge the proposal, quickly agree; the sole director with risk experience, feeling outnumbered, simply acquiesces and goes along with the proposal. The

end result is a potentially dangerous increase in risk because these directors have failed to challenge.

- *Failing to understand risk*: it seems odd to think that in this day and age a company would actually attempt to take or preserve some risk without fully understanding what it is, how to value or manage it or how it might affect operations. And yet some firms continue to enter risky businesses or transactions without a complete understanding of what they are doing and why. This is a recipe for broader problems and surprises, and may eventually lead to financial damage. A company can find itself in this position for any number of reasons, including lack of awareness or ignorance, poor identification processes, overly complex businesses and under-resourcing of the risk function (together with its demotion or subordination in the governance chain). Regardless of the reason, this is a clear sign that a firm is lacking in terms of risk culture. Take the example of an industrial company that has operations in various countries, indirectly creating exposure to currencies and interest rates in those countries. If the company is not aware or concerned that it is creating those exposures as a by-product of its industrial operations, it may suffer from surprise losses if rates move against it.
- *Ignoring the power of risk or displaying overconfidence in risk skills*: a company that has little respect for the benefits and damage that can be created by risk is clearly not considering or managing risk properly. This behavior is indicative of risk awareness not being properly embedded in the firm's operations and can again lead to surprises and losses. Similarly, a firm might believe it understands risk so well that it can make no mistakes or bad calls. This hubris can be just as damaging as pure disregard; it can cause a firm to take decisions or actions that would be unthinkable for firms that have a healthy respect for risk – taking risks that are too complex to price or manage or too large to be handled properly in the face of a dislocation. Consider a diversified insurance conglomerate which believes that, because it has expertise in insurance and reinsurance risks, it can easily step into the derivatives market and take complex, long-dated derivative risks – as if the derivative and insurance risks were fungible. The organization may soon discover that the confidence it has in its risk skills is misplaced, and not immediately transportable to the derivatives market.
- *Playing follow the leader*: it is not unusual for a company without a defined risk philosophy or risk strategy to approach risk-related opportunities on an ad hoc basis, often following the lead of peers or competitors. As more competitors enter the space, the company may feel increasing pressure to do likewise – the classic herd or lemming mentality. The thinking behind this approach is that if a firm's competitors are profitably engaged in some risk-related business, then a similar strategy should work for the firm itself. This is precisely the wrong way to think about risk matters, and

again indicates a weak risk culture. A firm that fails to apply a coherent risk strategy to its own business and client activities and prefers instead to mimic other firms is missing a key element of risk discipline and risk culture. For instance, because its competitor across the street has already created a nice business doing the same thing, a bank may decide to offer its retail depositors capital-protected certificates of deposit that provide upside on an index and protect the downside. But the new product may not fit within the retail bank's strategy; the bank may be ill equipped to manage the attendant risks and it may not have the technology to support the offering. In short, it may be chasing the new product simply because it wants to present the same sophisticated offerings as its main competitor – even if the decision is not strategically sound or operationally possible.

- *Tolerating bureaucratic decision-making processes*: one key to effective risk governance is to assign decision-making authorities to professionals with the skills to evaluate risk and decide quickly and correctly. We can easily imagine that a firm characterized by bureaucracy (e.g., multiple sign-offs even for mundane, low-risk business) and committee-driven decision-making, rather than delegation of authority and an efficient decision-making chain, is effectively reflecting a weak risk culture. In fact, it may have no confidence in its risk process or risk managers, and it may not be interested in focusing on efficiencies. Extending the example above, we can imagine that the bank makes decisions solely by committee. Individual risk managers lack delegated authorities, forcing even the smallest credit decisions to be considered through a formal, time-consuming committee process. This will have the effect of driving good business away and of widening the chasm between bankers and risk officers.
- *Allowing weak, passive or ineffective lines of defense*: as we noted earlier, the successful organization relies on multiple lines of defense to help control risks. This approach implies shared responsibilities (with clear accountabilities) and shared views on the ideal evolution of risk. Firms with a flawed risk culture are likely to allow weak, passive or ineffective practices in one or more lines of defense, with the result that the full power of the risk management process is not available. Ineffective lines of defense allow risks to go unchallenged, violations to proceed without consequence, the risk appetite to be breached with impunity, business to be booked regardless of return and so on. In the worst case, when all lines of defense are ineffective in fulfilling the risk control mandate, no one is truly accountable for the firm's risk, and losses are almost a certainty. Take the example of a commercial bank that manages a large book of commercial and industrial loans and leases. The loan officers responsible for originating loans are meant to be a first line of defense, ideally refusing even to consider granting loans that do not meet strict risk/return criteria. However, they fail completely in that

duty, seeking instead to generate as much loan volume as possible, regardless of the underlying quality or return. The credit officers managing the process – ostensibly the next key line of defense – are technically inadequate and managerially weak, approving loans that really should not be made. Finally, controllers and auditors, responsible for ensuring a secure environment for booking loans and collateral, verifying loan documentation and transaction pricing, and allocating capital, also fail in their duties – permitting poorly documented loans to be booked, wrong or insufficient collateral to be posted and so forth. In short, all aspects of the bank's defenses are compromised, leading ultimately to excessive credit losses.

- *Relying on ineffective rules and policies*: good risk governance, and hence good risk culture, depends on meaningful and substantive rules and policies that provide necessary protections and ensure that a firm's risk philosophy and risk tolerance are properly communicated, understood and followed. When rules and policies are not effective in providing these essential protections, the risk culture is weak. Ineffective rules create the opportunity for confusion, internal arbitrage and even losses, and thus fail to reinforce the essential control environment that is needed to protect a firm. Imagine a savings and loan (S&L) in business to take retail deposits and grant home mortgages and small commercial and industrial loans. While the S&L's credit committee has developed certain general credit policies, these are not detailed enough to prevent certain risky behaviors. For instance, while the policies require a "sufficient" down-payment on a home mortgage, the loan officer has discretion in deciding what constitutes "sufficient." With such a general rule in effect, the S&L may eventually find itself extending mortgages on the basis of a 5% or 10% down-payment, moving it (unintentionally) in the direction of becoming a risky subprime lender.
- *Following a seat-of-the-pants, rather than deliberate, approach to risk management*: risk management is part science and part art, but its practice requires a consistent level of discipline. Calling on history, experience, judgment and other qualitative factors is perfectly acceptable – and, indeed, desirable: numerical methods are not the only way to consider risks. However, some basic institutional framework for the disciplined consideration of risks is still required. Firms with a weak risk culture may lack such a framework, relying more on intuitive than deliberate approaches to risk management. This may lead to inconsistency or subjectivity, as well as a general lack of clarity among risk takers, none of which benefits the wider acceptance and establishment of a risk process. Consider a global retailer which sells apparel and other goods through a large network of stores. The retailer sources its inventory from the Far East, where production costs are low. Unfortunately, the company has experienced inventory supply disruptions in the past as a result of lack of raw materials, labor disputes or other factors.

These disruptions had a negative impact on revenues. While most companies in this situation would develop a contingency plan (e.g., carrying additional inventory, identifying suppliers in a different region, taking out business interruption insurance), the retailer may decide to ignore such contingency plans, perhaps believing that the disruptions will not happen again or that, if they do, it will come up with a solution on the spur of the moment.

- *Failing to see the whole picture*: a firm that is unable to capture and understand the entirety of its risks cannot be said to have a robust risk culture; indeed, operating with blind spots is the antithesis of prudent risk management. One of the important characteristics of a risk culture is transparency, and a firm that is struggling to understand its risk profile has not achieved this essential element. In all likelihood a firm in this position has not invested enough in the skills, resources and infrastructure required to produce a true picture of risks. Let us consider the example of a diversified industrial conglomerate that operates a large financing subsidiary. If the company has not planned for, and invested in, an enterprise risk management platform and mindset it will have a piecemeal approach to risk. It may have separate risk reporting for the industrial and financing businesses, making it difficult to set a comprehensive risk appetite and to make coherent and consistent decisions regarding a range of risk exposures. If the company cannot see the whole picture, it may also suffer from internal arbitrage, with risk takers trying to book risk in the center which gives them the most flexibility.
- *Underinvesting in control resources and infrastructure*: following from the point immediately above, a firm that is unwilling or unable to make the necessary investments in control resources and infrastructure will not be able to build a strong risk culture. An effective risk management process relies on skilled professionals and high-quality data and IT infrastructure for measurement, monitoring and management. A company that cannot fund such essential investments is in a dangerous state: it may find itself taking risks which it cannot manage and which could imperil its stakeholders. By extension, it will be unable to create a meaningful risk culture, as risk takers and risk managers will be flying blind. We can imagine an insurance company that underwrites property and casualty policies, covering automobiles, residential homes and commercial buildings. The insurer grew rapidly, and it neglected to invest adequately in technology and data management. These deficiencies may lead ultimately to flaws in the insurer's ability to track and price risks, manage its portfolio, properly reinsure portions of its portfolio and efficiently service its customers – any, or all, of which can result in lost revenues or outright losses.
- *Failing to delegate clear risk responsibilities*: firms that do not define risk responsibilities and accountabilities properly, or do not clearly delegate these to the relevant professionals, are effectively suffering from a weak risk culture. We

have already noted that governance is a key feature of a strong risk process, and any structure or action that impedes good governance stands in the way of strengthening the risk culture. When professionals cannot take risk decisions or exercise judgment effectively because they are not given the correct authorities or are unaware of their authorities, they do little to protect or advance the interests of the firm. Take the case of a commercial bank that provides loans and credit services in the middle market and the large corporate market. The bank's governance setup requires that all loan requests above $1 million be approved by a risk committee rather than a credit officer. Since 95% of the bank's loan volume comprises transactions of more than $1 million, this governance setup effectively prevents the bank's risk experts from exercising any judgment or authority, meaning that the risk process will be bureaucratic and inefficient – and rather demoralizing for those in the risk management chain.

- *Not questioning profit sources when budgets are being met*: many companies have a tendency not to diligently question the source of profits as long as budgets are being met or surpassed. To be sure, most firms are quick to question and scrutinize losses, and this is an important part of the financial discipline that characterizes a good risk culture. But if the same discipline is not extended to an examination of profits, then a firm cannot be said to have the strongest possible culture. It is important to emphasize that while a company may be generating profits from some risky business, the quality of those profits cannot be fully known without an in-depth examination. It is quite possible that profits being booked today are being exchanged for risks that may appear over a long horizon, or that do not adequately compensate for potential losses. Budget scrutiny in all environments is essential in building the right behaviors. Imagine a large mining and resource company with operations in 20 countries. The company is exposed, through its operations, to a host of different risks: currency and interest rate risks from its overseas subsidiaries, property and casualty risks from the mining operations, business risks from the overall economic climate, operational risks from its daily activities and so forth. The company does not have a holistic view of its risk profile, which, as we have mentioned, can be a source of problems. As a result of this deficiency it may also be unable to explain how it makes and loses money: with so many risk factors at play in so many subsidiaries, it may be hard to understand how revenues are actually generated. As long as international managers are delivering on budget, executive leadership in headquarters is not too concerned with how the earnings are being created. However, if half of the subsidiaries are meeting their budgets by trading in financial risks, management will be in for a surprise if these activities tail off or produce losses. If management simply assumes, without questioning, that most revenues are coming from core mining operations, then it is misinformed and may be making erroneous decisions.

- *Allowing misaligned incentive mechanisms*: incentive mechanisms, particularly in financial services, are a key element in reinforcing desirable (or undesirable) behaviors. Incentives guide how people act and perform, and thus factor heavily in determining a firm's fortunes. When incentives are focused primarily or exclusively on profit generation at the expense of prudent risk management, wrong behaviors will necessarily be instilled. Such misaligned incentives are indicative of a weak risk culture: proper risk behaviors are sacrificed in the search for near-term profits which maximize compensation. While some firms (and regulators) have certainly increased their attention to the discrepancies that can arise from misaligned incentives, and have enacted changes accordingly, this practice is far from uniform. Weakness of this type can be seen as a failure of executives and directors to manage incentives appropriately. Consider the case of a global insurance company that has a large book of property and casualty policies and also operates a derivatives and financial engineering subsidiary that specializes in long-dated derivatives. If the insurer lacks policies that tie compensation to risk, return performance and time horizon, it will soon find that its insurance underwriters try to write as many policies as possible (volume growth) rather than analyzing whether the risks of those policies are acceptable. Similarly, those operating the derivatives business will have every incentive to write as much complex long-term business as possible, since such contracts carry much larger margins. If the revenue streams are present-valued to determine today's bonuses, the derivatives specialists will have little concern about the long-term tail risk they have created.
- *Being unable to attract external talent*: a dynamic, forward-looking company tries continually to attract talent from outside. Indeed, an infusion of fresh ideas and new views on both business and risk can provide valuable forward progress, and must be seen as part of the ongoing evolution of the institution. However, when a firm is perceived as being weak in risk management or as lacking a risk culture, its ability to attract the talent it wants may be limited. In-demand professionals seeking to make a move may not want to work in an environment which is dysfunctional, or where risk issues are disregarded or downplayed. Losing access to this talent pool can be a big disadvantage and may further stall the formation of a true risk culture. Consider a large energy company that is active in both upstream and downstream operations, and runs a substantial energy trading and financing business. As a result of a series of mistakes, surprises and accidents over the years, the company is regarded as a weak manager of risk without a coherent risk strategy or meaningful risk culture. As it tries to bring new talent into the risk organization, particularly at senior levels,

it may encounter difficulties in attracting the candidates it wants. On the basis of the energy company's history and reputation, the preferred external professionals may believe that it is not serious about risk management and risk culture. This will leave the company routinely trying to hire its second or third choices.

Individual behaviors

- *Permitting communications to break down*: we have indicated at various points that communication is essential to create an atmosphere of cooperation and trust, to reinforce transparency and to build partnerships. Communication is the lifeblood of any company. Firms that lack a strong risk culture may be experiencing a breakdown in communications: executive management may not be conveying required information on strategy, risk appetite or other corporate imperatives and may be ineffective in explaining the risk profile and other risk issues to the board of directors; business producers may not be discussing risky transactions with their risk management partners on a timely basis; and risk managers may not be communicating risk issues to their business colleagues or to other control managers (e.g., finance, treasury, audit). Any such failure of communications protocols may be sufficient to render the risk culture ineffective. Consider a multinational pharmaceutical company that has production and distribution subsidiaries in 15 countries. As a consequence of this global footprint it takes currency and interest rate funding risks in each country, where local treasury centers are charged with managing their positions. As part of the process, the central treasury at headquarters must be apprised of all positions and decisions being taken and kept abreast of sensitive market information and forecasts. If some of the subsidiary operations fail to communicate properly, on a timely basis, the risks that are being run, there is no way for the company to review its risks holistically. The situation becomes even more critical if all 15 centers fail in their communications responsibilities, as this could lead to significant confusion, perhaps even losses.
- *Finger-pointing or lack of accountability when losses occur*: any institution whose executive managers, business professionals or risk professionals do not accept accountability when things go wrong has little or no risk culture. When experienced, well-compensated professionals shirk their responsibilities, or are willing to be seen and heard only when things are going well, the environment is at least partly dysfunctional. Such behaviors can be very destructive, and may lead to significant surprises as a result of bad decision-making. Perhaps even worse than shirking responsibility is deflecting blame to others – classic finger-pointing. Bad blood is almost certainly going to be generated between the parties, leading to any corporate value system being further undermined. Imagine a shareholder-owned

quasi-governmental finance agency that is responsible for providing funding to certain local housing markets, under the umbrella of enabling legislation. Within this framework the agency has its own credit underwriting standards, but these can be overridden by political intervention. In the event that unwise loans are granted as a result of political pressure and losses ensue, the management of the finance agency may seek to blame politicians for forcing the firm to extend the unwise loans, while politicians may criticize the agency's leadership as incompetent. In either event, stakeholders will have been ill served.

- *Lacking mutual respect, and creating second-class citizens*: lack of respect between business leaders and risk managers (and other control managers) is a common symptom of firms with a poor risk culture, and can be particularly divisive. When the two groups exhibit overt or covert disdain for each other, a whole series of problems can accrue: poor communication, lack of transparency, unwillingness to act as partners, destructive actions and, ultimately, bad risk decisions. Importantly, it is not unusual for those generating revenue to believe they are superior to those managing risks (who may be regarded as support or corporate overhead or cost centers). This leads to the emergence of multiple classes of employees, dividing the organization and culture. Consider a large commercial bank that has a strong revenue base and a reasonably aggressive stance toward risk. If the bankers and risk managers have a divisive relationship and lack respect for each other's functions, it is easy to imagine a whole host of problems appearing: bankers will fail to bring their risk colleagues into the loop on deals, believing that they are simply a box to check; risk managers will seek to impose all manner of red tape on the approval process to frustrate their banking colleagues; bankers will ignore risk/return considerations, portfolio stress results and other information proffered by their risk colleagues and so forth. These attitudes and behaviors will eventually lead to loss of business or to the booking of bad business which generates risk-related losses.
- *Escalating negative decisions in hopes of their being overturned*: we have already indicated that a mature governance structure allows periodic appeal of risk decisions to the next managerial level. This is both appropriate and fair, as there are times when a second consideration can benefit all parties. However, when escalation becomes frequent and routine, something is wrong with the risk process, organization and culture: either risk managers are perceived to be so unskilled that business managers will simply not take "no" for an answer – even when that is the correct answer – or senior risk executives are regularly overturning decisions made by subordinates, which effectively undermines and demotivates the rank and file and generates doubts about the strength and capabilities of the risk organization. Continuing with the example immediately above, we can easily imagine

that, in a weak risk culture, bankers will escalate all negative decisions to the head of risk or simply go direct to the head of risk for all decisions – in contravention of governance policy and process. An even worse outcome would be the head of risk frequently deciding to overturn the decisions made by subordinates or to rule on individual cases without involving the responsible risk experts.

- *Attempting to arbitrage decision makers*: a confused organizational structure, multiple risk policies and an aggressive business team that seeks to generate as much business as possible regardless of its risk merits can lead to internal arbitrage – another symptom of a weak risk culture. In this situation business managers seeking to transact risky business will play off different parts of the risk management function against one another in hopes of getting an affirmative answer. That is, if an initial request to approve risky business is declined by a risk manager, the business manager may attempt to take advantage of policy loopholes or organizational differences to seek an alternative, affirmative, answer from another risk manager. This has the effect of creating embarrassment, confusion and lack of discipline and control. Consider a global reinsurance company that operates in multiple jurisdictions and has specific policies governing its underwriting standards. If governance is weak or is flouted because there is no risk culture, the firm may find that individual underwriters present new reinsurance business to the jurisdiction which has the most favorable terms (e.g., the best pricing or the largest capacity or the greatest degree of risk flexibility). This may lead ultimately to a misbalanced risk profile and loss of credibility for the risk management function, which will be seen as incapable of policing internal policies related to underwriting.
- *Trying to browbeat risk managers*: an associated practice in firms that lack a strong risk culture is for business managers to regularly bully, harass or browbeat risk managers into providing the "correct" (affirmative) risk decisions. Such a power structure can arise when the risk culture does not provide the seniority, authority or resourcing required for risk professionals to challenge their business colleagues. This type of interpersonal behavior will engender a destructive relationship between the two groups, and may ultimately lead to a questionable risk-related portfolio. Consider the example of an industrial company with a treasury function that is responsible for managing liquidity and rate risk for the entire firm. On occasion it also takes some speculative risk positions in financial assets as a form of revenue enhancement and diversification. If the treasury function is very aggressive and the risk management function is especially weak, treasury officers may take advantage of this fact by trying to force through increasingly speculative trades in a bid to create a bigger bottom line for the treasury center, and thereby increase their own compensation. The treasury officers may

be harsh and abusive in their treatment of risk colleagues – and if their risk colleagues are not up to the job, they may get their way.

- *Promoting a silo mentality between risk management and business functions*: a firm with a flawed risk culture is almost certain to exhibit a silo mentality where risk and other control functions are isolated from business functions, with little or no opportunity for constructive dialog, relations or rotation. The existence of these silos – which may be the result of an attitude of superiority on the part of business managers (as the revenue generators) or of actions by top management that create a multi-class system – can squelch any meaningful communication and exchange of information and any attempts to build a partnership approach. When this compartmentalization occurs, bad risk decisions and lost business opportunities may follow. Imagine a government housing agency, charged with financing home mortgages, that has a weak risk culture. Its business leaders, responsible for purchasing mortgages from mortgage originators and repackaging them in pools, want to take a great deal of risk in order to boost revenues and bonuses. They may have little regard for the risk function, and prefer to keep information regarding mortgage origination deals and block purchases to themselves, seeking only final approval through a risk committee. The risk management function, isolated in this manner, may be limited in its ability to influence risk discussions and risk evolution; it may be able only to analyze the portfolio, run stress tests and consider deals coming through the risk committee. While this activity provides a surface review of risk matters, it is not going to advance the idea of a business/risk partnership, and all the attendant benefits of such an approach.
- *Hiding problems or losses*: one of the most damaging signs of a weak risk culture is that some people in the organization perpetuate a practice of covering up problems or losses, refusing to be forthright about the true risk management situation. Common examples are trying to hide losses by falsifying values, taking advantage of known control flaws, booking deals in unauthorized vehicles and postponing problems to the future by not reporting accurately the nature of a deal. Such behavior does little to advance the transparency and integrity that are essential to a strong risk culture. Interestingly, while these actions are most often associated with the business side, they can also appear in the risk management function when it fails to challenge bad situations or convey negative information. This is particularly dangerous, as the control functions are meant to be a key independent line of defense. Consider a large investment bank that takes a great deal of market risk across a number of products and asset classes. It runs a fairly sophisticated book of exposures which can be complex to track and understand. It also has a complex and poorly designed infrastructure that has evolved over time and lacks robust controls. It is possible, in this scenario, that a senior trader or

head of trading could take advantage of the complexity of the risk profile, the breadth of risk-taking activities and the weakness of the infrastructure to disguise any losses accruing from bad trading decisions. This may carry on for years, until some auditor or controller is able to discover the problem; by that time the firm will have lost even more money.

- *Punishing whistleblowers, or shooting the messenger*: a firm with a strong risk culture supports the idea of internal whistleblowers – good corporate citizens who are on high alert for any mistakes or misbehavior regarding risk or other control issues. It also supports the idea of clear and honest communication, including when bad news must be delivered and acted on. When the risk culture is weak, there may be a tendency for senior managers to discourage whistleblowers from coming forward with revelations, perhaps even punishing them for doing so (which links to the problem noted immediately above). Or senior managers may engage in a practice of shooting the messenger – blaming those who deliver bad news regarding risks or losses as if they were responsible for such losses, regardless of the facts. In either case employees may see little upside in being forthright about what they see and know, which does little to strengthen the risk culture. Consider an automotive company that is primarily engaged in the design, production and distribution of cars, but also runs a large treasury operation that is responsible for currency, liquidity and interest rate management to support the company's global operations. Suppose further that the treasury department decides to take some additional market risk (perhaps in excess of its approved authorities) and posts a large loss as a result. When they notify top management of the loss, the risk managers responsible for overseeing treasury activities may be sanctioned by executives, who may view the loss as the fault of the risk department rather than the treasury officers. This may cause others in the company to suppress bad news in the future.
- *Ignoring and failing to escalate violations*: as noted in Chapter 1, part of a proper risk process is the development and use of risk limits, which control risky activities within the framework of an overarching risk appetite. When risk limits are regularly breached without consequence, or when multiple instances of violation are not escalated up the management chain for relevant action, the firm is again suffering from a weak risk culture. The notion of controlling risks is clearly missing, suggesting that the broader risk governance structure is dysfunctional. We can again use the example of an international bank that has a team of aggressive risk takers in the proprietary market risk arena, who actively take positions in equities, currencies, credits and interest rates. Although the traders are governed by a series of risk limits that devolve from the risk appetite, they breach these limits from time to time. These violations may not be diligently followed up by

the risk management function, which looks the other way. Furthermore, although governance rules require escalation when a trader violates limits for a second time, the risk managers may again ignore such rules.

- *Imposing no penalties for bad behavior*: to extend the previous point, one of the most telling signs of a bad risk culture is that those taking risks are not liable for any misbehavior, including violating limits, not seeking prior approval for complex risky deals, not adhering to explicit risk policies and not following client management rules. Such behavior may be accidental or willful; the main point is that in a weak risk culture, such transgressions are ignored by those in control functions and in the management hierarchy. This does little to strengthen risk management practices and may, in fact, embolden those who have violated firm rules to repeat their offenses or take them even further as a way of testing the boundaries. To continue the example above, the proprietary traders responsible for violating limits escape unscathed as a result of the inaction of the risk management team. This means they have no incentive to correct or improve their behaviors in the future – which could lead to larger problems.
- *Leaving the rainmakers alone*: in some firms, so-called rainmakers – those who generate a great deal of revenue or bring in important clients – may be regarded as exempt from the normal rules of the company, precisely because they are critical to furthering the fortunes of the firm. People in this protected class may be given greater flexibility to deal in risky business or to violate policies and rules (per the point above) without consequence. Such a multi-class regime is again indicative of a poor risk culture. Imagine an investment banker who is responsible for bringing in large merger deals that generate hundreds of millions of euros in fees for the bank. Given his importance as a deal maker and revenue generator, he may be treated differently by management. Thus, if the banker decides to commit the bank to an underwritten capital raising to support a merger he has negotiated – and does so without going through the risk approval process – management may protect him from any disciplinary action because he is so important to the revenue of the franchise.

As we can see from this overview, the characteristics of a weak risk culture are numerous and varied. Naturally, not every firm that has a poor risk culture will experience all (or even most) of these problems simultaneously. The point to emphasize is that the weaknesses can have serious consequences: financial or reputational losses, inefficiencies, bad decisions and bad behavior.

The next logical step in our discussion is to consider the consequences of having such a poor risk culture. In other words, we want to understand what can happen if a firm is burdened by the practical problems we have just outlined.

The potential consequences of a weak risk culture

Firms that are plagued by some of the deficiencies noted above create an environment where bigger issues can emerge. We must remember that risk culture is not an abstract concept without practical consequences. Firms that cannot build the right fabric of awareness and control will suffer from broader problems. Of course, not all of these problems will occur in every instance, and not all of them will lead to the direst outcomes. But the mere potential for larger consequences means the topic is worth exploring in more detail.

- *Surprises or unacceptable losses*: for executive managers, stability is a prized commodity. In an operating environment characterized by competition, internal and external pressures, market volatility and other complications, lack of internal surprises must be seen as a positive. When a company lacks a risk culture and is thus susceptible to some or many of the problems noted above, the chance of negative surprises increases dramatically. In most cases these surprises come in the form of unacceptable losses. To be sure, we know that any firm which takes risks will sustain losses; this is perfectly acceptable provided the potential for losses is well understood ex ante. This awareness is possible with a rigorous risk management process which identifies, quantifies, manages and reports exposures. When the risk process is not rigorous and does not make clear the potential for certain types (or magnitudes) of losses, surprises arise and the firm cannot claim to be in control of its risks, which any management team should see as unacceptable. (Importantly, such surprises can erode confidence, as we shall discuss in the next point.)
- *Damaged reputation*: a firm's reputation is an important asset that should be valued and protected; for many firms, it is a source of business and revenues. When a firm has a weak risk culture and is susceptible to the problems we have noted, its reputation is likely to suffer as a consequence. The degree to which a company's reputation is called into question by external parties, and for how long, depends on the nature of the problem: the more difficulties the company has as a result of risk culture flaws, the greater the damage. Any reputational damage is likely to lead to loss of business and to draw the scrutiny of shareholders, rating agencies, creditors and investors, who may wonder whether further problems will arise in the future. Reversing reputational damage is difficult and time-consuming; the integrity, trust and value associated with a company and its history cannot typically be restored overnight, so the loss of business and share value may last for months or even years.
- *Loss of market faith or confidence*: an associated point relates to loss of market faith or confidence in a firm's management team, and perhaps also its directors. This loss can occur directly or indirectly. Directly, the problems

noted earlier in this chapter as manifestations of a weak risk culture can create the negative perception in the market that a firm lacks the character and behaviors to keep its risks under control. Indirectly, a weak risk culture can lead to surprises that can, in turn, reduce market confidence. In either event, the consequences may be the same: lack of faith in the company and its management (and directors) can create downward pressure on the share price or result in other negative consequences (e.g., a ratings downgrade, withdrawal of funding). Loss of market faith or confidence in the company can also be reputationally damaging, a process that can take years to reverse.

- *Liquidity problems*: while a company may have sufficient capital to remain a going concern, a lack of liquidity can lead to a short-term crisis – which may ultimately prove fatal. Once again, the absence of a strong risk culture can have a direct or indirect effect on a firm's liquidity position (indeed, the point immediately above can play a key role in any potential liquidity crisis). We can imagine a scenario where a weak risk culture leads to (potentially large) surprise losses, which lead to loss of market faith or confidence, which leads to the withdrawal of liquidity facilities or other sources of funding, which creates financial distress. This chain of events may seem like a theoretical discussion, but it is unfortunately not theoretical at all: history reveals that liquidity-driven problems at failed firms have originated at least in part as a result of failed risk cultures (e.g., Lehman Brothers, Enron, Swissair).
- *Higher funding costs*: there is little doubt that a company that faces significant risk problems caused by a poor risk culture will be regarded in the market as financially weakened. For at least some time, investors or financial institutions that act as de facto lenders to the firm will almost certainly demand a greater premium when providing debt capital. Higher funding costs will, of course, reduce overall profitability, placing greater stress on financial operations. The duration and magnitude of higher funding costs, and whether the company's weakness is temporary or permanent, will depend on the nature of the initial problems and the action plan put in place by the firm.
- *Ratings downgrades*: we noted earlier that some credit rating agencies focus on the importance of risk culture in the definition of a robust risk process. Thus, severe risk control problems that create losses or otherwise weaken the financial standing of a company may lead to one or more of the established credit rating agencies downgrading the company's rating. Of course, the consequences of a downgrade are well known: higher funding costs (as noted immediately above), downward pressure on the stock price and further regulatory review.
- *Regulatory scrutiny*: problems created, or exacerbated, by a weak risk culture may draw the scrutiny of regulators (particularly in industries where regulations are strictly enforced, such as financial services, housing, energy and

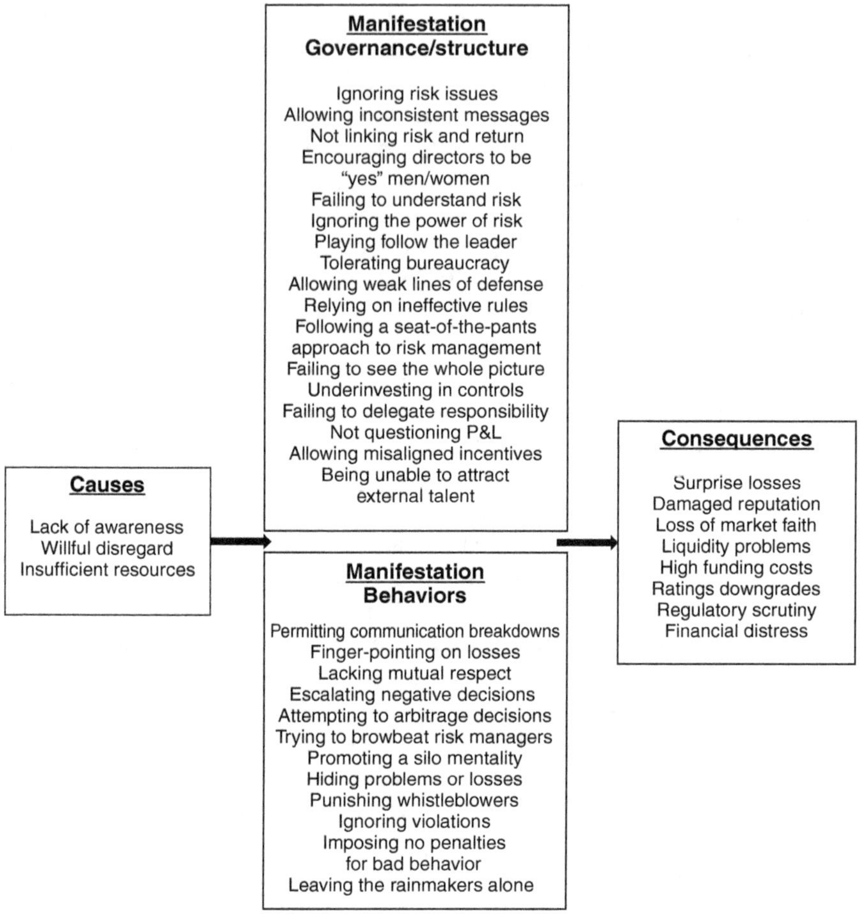

Figure 4.1 The causes, manifestation and consequences of a weak risk culture

construction). While regulatory review is part of the standard operating environment for many firms, it is generally limited to periodic reporting and perhaps an annual inspection or review of certain risk-related operations or techniques. While such periodic review may be considered quite normal and tenable, excessive scrutiny is seldom appreciated by firms, which would rather be left to manage their affairs in an orderly and prudent fashion. When problems arise, a firm can expect additional (sometimes intensive) inspection, and possibly a request for enhancements or investments to ensure a risk-related problem does not recur. Inspections may include continuous on-site monitoring and review until actual or perceived problems have been resolved. Importantly, news of additional regulatory scrutiny can swiftly move into the public domain, placing additional reputational and financial pressure on the firm.

- *Financial distress and bankruptcy*: the direst endgame of a failed risk culture is, of course, financial distress that leads to bankruptcy. To be sure, this is an extreme point, and certainly not the most likely outcome for institutions that have a weak risk culture. But the possibility exists, and should serve as an important reminder that deficiencies in the risk culture can have serious consequences. In this extreme scenario, as a result of the deficiencies outlined above, a company may suffer significant losses (financially, reputationally or both) which deplete its financial resources, leading to a rapid sharp reduction in its liquidity and the flight of its customers, investors and other creditors. In the end, these forces may be enough to push the firm into an irreversible state of distress, leading to bankruptcy. This bleak scenario is not, unfortunately, entirely theoretical, as we shall see in the next chapter.

Figure 4.1 summarizes the key issues associated with a weak risk culture. In the following chapter we shall move on to real examples of firms that have succumbed to some of the larger consequences noted above as a result of weaknesses in their risk culture.

5
Deficiencies and Problems II: Cases

To throw some practical light on our discussion from the previous chapter, it will be helpful to examine real-life instances of weak risk culture in financial and non-financial companies and certain quasi-public agencies. This will give us a better appreciation for what can go wrong when a risk culture is ineffective. Some of these cases center on failed risk management processes that led to large, and often surprise, losses; others demonstrate how failed internal controls, internal fraud and misrepresentation also led to losses. In the extreme cases, the problems resulted in financial distress and bankruptcy. Of course, even those situations that did not result in severe financial damage still led to reputational damage. And, since reputation is a valuable asset for any company, although its loss can be considered to be different, it is potentially no less damaging.

Unfortunately, the global business landscape is populated with many examples from different sectors. Tables 5.1–5.3 report a small sample of incidents from recent years that arguably had their origins in a weak or non-existent risk culture. This list is not exhaustive; it is intended only for illustrative purposes. The tables categorize examples into three distinct groups: financial companies (Table 5.1), non-financial companies (Table 5.2) and quasi-governmental or public sector institutions (Table 5.3).

In order to get more insight into the dynamics of weak risk cultures, let us examine a handful of examples from these tables in greater detail.

Barings (1995)

We begin with a popular case study that represents an important milestone in the history of risk management and controls and internal fraud. Interestingly, although the Barings episode is now well over a decade old, institutions continue to suffer from the same problems, as if lessons have not been adequately learned. In 1992, Nick Leeson, a back office manager for the British

Table 5.1 Risk-related problems: financial sector examples

Institution	Issue/problem
Barings plc	Internal fraud in Singapore subsidiary led to massive losses and eventual takeover
Daiwa	Internal fraud and unauthorized trading led to large losses
LTCM	Disregard for risk and overreliance on models led to massive losses and wind-down
Allied Irish	Internal fraud and unauthorized trading in the US led to large losses and dismissal of top executives
Bankers Trust	Unethical treatment of clients led to financial and reputational losses and eventual takeover
Bear Stearns	Disregard for risk led to large losses, liquidity problems and eventual takeover
Lehman	Disregard for risk and lack of risk appetite led to massive losses and bankruptcy
Société Générale	Internal fraud in HQ led to massive losses and dismissal of top executives
CIT Financial	Disregard for risk led to funding problems and eventual restructuring
Merrill Lynch	Disregard for risk and lack of robust risk appetite led to massive losses and takeover
Northern Rock	Disregard for risk led to large losses, funding problems and eventual government takeover
Washington Mutual	Disregard for risk led to large losses and eventual takeover
Countrywide	Disregard for risk led to large losses and eventual takeover
Bradford & Bingley	Disregard for risk led to large losses, liquidity problems and eventual takeover
AIG	Disregard for risk and lack of robust risk appetite led to massive losses and bankruptcy
Dexia	Disregard for risk and lack of robust risk appetite led to massive losses and government takeover
RBS	Disregard for risk and ill-advised acquisition led to massive losses and government takeover
UBS	Internal fraud in London led to massive losses and dismissal of top executives
MF Global	Disregard for risk led to large losses, funding problems and bankruptcy

Note: Most financial institutions operating during the financial crisis of 2007–2009 suffered excessive losses as a result of very similar problems: unclear or asynchronous risk appetites, build-up of concentrated positions in illiquid assets, misbalanced risk/return tradeoffs, risks which were not well understood, model-related problems, unrealistic planning for downside scenarios and so forth. All of these problems are symptomatic of weak risk culture; the companies and outcomes listed in the table are simply a cross-section of some of the largest problems.

Table 5.2 Risk-related problems: non-financial corporate examples

Institution	Issue/problem
Hanwa Steel	Disregard for risk led to massive losses and dismissal of top executives
Metallgesellschaft	Internal fraud and unauthorized trading led to large losses
Enron	Internal fraud and an unethical culture led to accounting irregularities, losses and bankruptcy
Sumitomo Corp	Internal fraud and unauthorized trading led to large losses
WorldCom	Internal fraud and accounting irregularities led to losses and bankruptcy
Parmalat	Internal fraud led to massive losses and eventual bankruptcy
Tyco	Internal fraud and accounting irregularities led to losses and bankruptcy
Global Crossing	Accounting irregularities led to losses and bankruptcy
Adelphia	Accounting irregularities led to losses and dismissal of top executives
Swissair	Accounting irregularities led to liquidity problems and bankruptcy
Lernout & Hauspie	Accounting irregularities led to losses and dismissal of top executives
Siemens	Accounting and compliance failures led to losses and dismissal of top executives
BP	Lack of strong safety and risk processes led to environmental disaster and large losses
Olympus	Accounting irregularities to hide losses led to dismissal of top executives

Table 5.3 Risk-related problems: quasi-governmental/public institution examples

Institution	Issue/problem
Orange County	Excessive, leveraged risk-taking led to massive losses and bankruptcy
Fannie Mae	Disregard for risk led to massive losses and eventual government takeover
Freddie Mac	Disregard for risk led to massive losses and eventual government takeover
German state banks	Disregard for risk led to massive losses and government bailouts

merchant bank Barings, moved to Singapore to continue his operational career. Soon after arriving, he took the opportunity to move to the front office as a trader responsible for executing Barings' Nikkei futures trades on the Singapore International Monetary Exchange (SIMEX, now part of the broader Singapore Exchange). Futures execution is a low-risk business that involves buying and selling contracts on behalf of trading desks within a bank, without taking outright risk views. Unfortunately, Leeson executed some bad trades in 1992 and put them in an error account to hide the small losses, apparently intent on making them good through additional unauthorized trading.

This marked the beginning of a nearly three-year period during which Leeson traded aggressively, typically on a losing basis. By manipulating systems and reports, he showed growing profits to superiors in London and Tokyo, but in reality he posted a £3 million loss in the error account in 1993 and a further £4 million loss in 1994. Since he was familiar with back office processes and had good relationships with Barings' treasury function, he was able to continue hiding the bad trades, booking phantom profits and sourcing more margin to post with the exchanges to support the illicit trades. Indeed, he secured £144 million in margin financing in 1994, seemingly with no questions asked by the treasury, audit or risk management functions. By late 1994 he was increasingly desperate to make back the money and began very aggressively selling "straddles"[1] on the Nikkei and Japanese government bonds – a strategy which required very quiet markets for him to retain the premiums earned from the sales. Unfortunately, in mid-January 1995 (when he had secured another, somewhat staggering, £750 million in margin financing, with few questions asked), the Kobe earthquake struck, causing the Nikkei to plunge and volatility to spike. That placed Leeson's total losses at £860 million, compared with £440 million of group-wide capital. Barings was insolvent. Leeson fled but was eventually apprehended and sentenced to prison. Barings was purchased by Dutch bank ING, which assumed its liabilities. In the aftermath of these events, the complete absence of a risk culture at Barings became obvious: the bank suffered from massive internal control failures, including unclear divisions between front and back office duties; controllers, treasury officials and risk managers did not query multiple demands for funding; P&L explain was missing, and the source of the "profits" from Leeson's low-risk strategies was never questioned; the board set no risk strategy or risk appetite; head office did not regularly review risk reports from Singapore or question the nature of profits; and local risk controllers were too junior to question or challenge the business.

Enron (2001)

The spectacular history of energy company Enron has been the subject of many books and analyses since it filed for bankruptcy in 2001. The company, which was founded in the mid-1980s through the consolidation of various US natural gas pipeline companies, became the embodiment of the "new economy" trading firm – appearing more like a Wall Street trading house than an energy player. By the late 1990s Enron had shed much of its energy distribution capability and had become an aggressive trader of energy products, electricity, pulp and paper, weather risk and even bandwidth (a nascent market), taking advantage of deregulating markets to become the seventh-largest US company by revenue. Unfortunately, much of Enron's dealing was based on an aggressive business stance that paid little heed to risk management and internal controls. There is no evidence that the board of directors had any notion of what executive managers were doing; they blindly supported entry into new markets and approved no formal risk strategy or risk appetite. Problems began to surface when a whistleblower made it clear that the very functions (CFO, treasurer) meant to scrutinize and control the activities of business managers were actually engaged in financial statement misrepresentation, fraud, self-dealing and conflicts of interest. Much of the financial chicanery was directed by the CFO and selected associates through offshore special purpose vehicles which were not scrutinized or challenged by Enron's risk managers, internal auditors or external auditors. Furthermore, the compensation of key executive managers, including the CFO and treasurer, was intimately tied to the performance of these vehicles, in a flagrant example of conflict of interest.[2]

By October 2001 Enron was forced to restate earnings for 1997–2001, which decreased equity by $2.1 billion and brought an additional $2.6 billion onto the balance sheet. These restatements, along with growing news reports of irregularities, caused various large creditors to pull back on lending, which placed a funding and liquidity squeeze on the company. A failed attempt at a merger with cross-town rival Dynegy spelled the end of the road for Enron. In November 2001 it filed the largest corporate bankruptcy in US history until that time. The CFO, CEO and others were indicted and convicted on various charges. In addition, Enron's external auditor, Andersen, ultimately filed for bankruptcy as a result of its mishandling of the Enron account.

The story of Enron is one of an absolutely non-existent risk culture: directors had no conception of marrying business strategy with risk strategy or setting a risk appetite; executive managers set a destructive tone and were never challenged by directors; risk managers were routinely disregarded and overruled by executive managers, and no constructive partnership developed between the business and risk functions; infrastructure was insufficient to reveal problems; financial positions and risks were completely opaque; and internal controls (in the form of finance and audit) either proved ineffective or actually aided and abetted in the problems.

Parmalat (2003)

Parmalat was founded as a regional Italian dairy producer in the early 1960s by Calisto Tanzi. It grew into a large multinational company with a dominant position in UHT milk and its derivatives. During the mid- to late 1990s Parmalat's management led the company on an acquisition spree around the world that was heavily financed by debt. At its peak in the early 2000s Parmalat had operations in Europe, the Americas and Asia and had diversified into football clubs and other non-commodity-related ventures. Unfortunately, many of these operations were loss-producing and cash flow negative, and some senior managers within the company tried to disguise the deteriorating financial condition using special purpose entities and financial derivatives (including credit derivatives written on the company's own creditworthiness). This scheme continued until 2003, when CFO Fausto Tonna decided to try to raise funds in the bond market, to the surprise of Tanzi. Tonna was fired and replaced by a new CFO, Alberto Ferraris.

In what should have been a serious warning signal, Ferraris' access to the company's official books was blocked by head accounting officer Luciano Del Soldato. Ferraris soon began to fear that Parmalat had a great deal more off-balance-sheet debt than it was disclosing, and as more information came to light (including a fake €3.9 billion deposit held at Bank of America), Ferraris left the company – jolting the markets, which quickly suspected all was not well. Del Soldato became CFO and tried desperately in late 2003 to raise funds through a Cayman vehicle to cover upcoming debt payments, but failed. That brought down the house of cards built by Tanzi, Del Soldato and other senior executives. As a result of the financial fraud, Parmalat was forced to file for bankruptcy, and with nearly €14.3 billion in debt outstanding (eight times the amount reported in its official financial statements), it became Europe's largest-ever bankruptcy. The company's trademarks and main assets were preserved in the restructuring (with the milk operation being purchased by French firm Lactalis in 2011), but most of the non-core subsidiaries in Europe and the Americas were liquidated. Tanzi and some senior executives were charged with fraud, money laundering and other financial crimes.

It is clear from the evidence of the Parmalat case that the company suffered from a weak risk culture: senior executives had no sense of ethics and established a corrupt ethos at the top that cascaded to other key executives; control functions, including risk management, financial control and audit, were completely ineffective in identifying or preventing questionable transactions (including all of the derivatives and offshore vehicles) and obviously did not challenge senior management; and Parmalat's directors were also completely ineffective in discharging their duties, failing to protect shareholders by challenging, probing and questioning business operations. In short, all of the defenses that a risk culture is meant to build were completely absent.

Lehman Brothers (2008)

US investment bank Lehman Brothers, which collapsed in 2008 as a result of a combination of large losses from overly concentrated risk positions, liquidity problems and excessive leverage, suffered from a weak risk culture. Lehman had been a successful fixed-income powerhouse before its acquisition by Shearson/American Express and after its spinoff, but it began drifting into larger and more illiquid risks during the 2000s. In the lead-up to the crisis Lehman had large and growing exposures in increasingly illiquid mortgage-backed securities and commercial real estate – risks that were well in excess of what could have been regarded as prudent. It eventually became clear that the bank also had flawed governance, organization and processes.

As the financial crisis took hold, Lehman was forced to write down the value of its enormous securities holdings, a process that occurred throughout 2007 and the first half of 2008. In the second quarter of 2008 the bank posted $2.8 billion in losses, and its stock price plummeted because the market suspected further write-downs were inevitable. The losses led to increased pressure for management to raise additional capital to shore up the bank's liquidity position. Unfortunately, by early September 2008 potential deals to sell portions of the company and to raise capital appeared increasingly untenable. The bank was forced to announce a further $3.9 billion loss and the sale of a stake in its asset management arm. The end was in sight. After further withdrawal of funding from counterparties and a decision by US government officials not to support Lehman, the firm filed for bankruptcy – becoming the largest filing in US history, leaving behind more than $600 billion in debts and a massive off-balance-sheet book of derivatives.

Ex post analysis of the Lehman collapse revealed a whole host of problems: directors who failed to challenge CEO Dick Fuld; a risk function that had no direct reporting line to the CEO, lacked true authorities and was regularly overruled; a risk committee that was headed and structured by the CEO – allowing little scope for independent challenge; a fluid risk tolerance level that increased constantly at the behest of the CEO; continual limit violations that were not dealt with forcefully; and an accumulation of concentrated risk positions in mortgage, real estate and credit-related risks.

RBS (2008)

RBS, a UK banking conglomerate that grew rapidly through acquisitions in the 1990s and early 2000s, was unfortunate in attempting to conclude the largest-ever banking acquisition (of Dutch retail/commercial bank ABN Amro) just as the financial crisis was coming into full force. Worse, RBS paid much more for ABN Amro than originally anticipated because cross-town competitor Barclays temporarily participated in a bidding war. Despite the bank's many years of success in executing its strategy and becoming a dominant player, these two events revealed a series of flaws and problems, at least some of which were rooted in a poor risk culture.

As the crisis unfolded, RBS's management was distracted by the process of integrating the newly purchased ABN Amro – a non-trivial task during good times, and an exceedingly difficult one when the financial markets are in turmoil. Perhaps more importantly, the bank was burdened by a large portfolio of risks in various problem sectors. In the second half of 2007 the bank had to write down the value of its US mortgage-related and leveraged finance exposures, booking a £1.1 billion loss. This marked the first of several successive quarters of large losses, underscoring the bank's risk management weaknesses. During the early part of 2008 RBS wrote off another £5.9 billion from its mortgages, leveraged finance and other credit activities and was forced to raise an enormous £12 billion of capital; unfortunately, a second £7 billion issue could not be placed, leaving the bank vulnerable. The mounting losses and weak capital position forced the UK government to take a 70% stake in the bank to keep it from going under.

A series of management changes soon followed as the government tried to right the institution. Stephen Hester, the new CEO, declared a full-year 2008 loss of £9 billion and availed himself of the government's Asset Protection Scheme to backstop some of the bank's bad assets. Hester was candid in his assessment of the bank's problems and its flawed risk culture, noting that in addition to the botched ABN Amro acquisition (too expensive, too unwieldy, not properly challenged by directors, poorly timed), the bank's risk management process and systems had failed: the bank had entered the crisis period with too much concentrated risk in its investment banking unit, had inadequate risk monitoring and valuation systems, lacked a good grip on the downside that could affect the bank, had no formal sense of a risk appetite or strategy and suffered from risk mispricing.

Fannie Mae (2008)

Fannie Mae (the US Federal National Mortgage Association) has historically occupied a somewhat unique, if uncomfortable, position: from its creation in 1938 until 2008 it operated as a NYSE-listed company accountable to shareholders, while simultaneously trying to foster growth in the US residential mortgage market – a decidedly political role. In its original function Fannie Mae (and its twin, Freddie Mac, or the Federal Home Loan Mortgage Corporation) was responsible for purchasing mortgages from banks, savings and loans, and other mortgage originators on the basis of certain conforming standards (e.g., maximum loan amount, loan-to-value ratio, tenor, rate). It repackaged them into pools, which were used to create mortgage-backed securities (MBSs). The MBSs were then sold to global investors, who would gain the benefit of the monthly principal and interest pay-downs on the mortgages. Fannie Mae used the money from the sale to purchase more mortgages, in a never-ending cycle, and through this mechanism was able to help the home mortgage market grow at a reasonable rate. (Fannie Mae also purchased MBSs from investors, thus helping ensure ongoing secondary liquidity.) The key problem came when politicians decided to push for an expansion of home ownership to individuals with much weaker credit standing and to those unable to put down more than 5% equity (rather than the more typical 20%). These changes, which started in the 1990s, required Fannie Mae (and Freddie Mac) to loosen their underwriting standards, accepting so-called subprime mortgages into the pools.

It comes as no surprise that when the housing market collapsed in 2006–2007, Fannie Mae was in a vulnerable position. During the course of 18 months Fannie Mae and Freddie Mac lost tens of billions of dollars on their massive leveraged inventories of subprime mortgages and secondary market securities. Indeed, with housing prices falling 20–30% in most US markets (and even more in a few others), causing delinquencies and defaults to soar, there was little way for Fannie Mae (or Freddie Mac) to escape the damage. Unfortunately, the agency had long believed that the importance of its role and the implicit government guarantee on its operations meant that it could take risk seemingly without end: it was leveraged more than 50 times, even as its executives testified before Congress that the little sliver of capital it had to support its massive balance sheet ($2.8 trillion of mortgage securities plus more than $800 billion of secondary investments) was sufficient. In fact, it was wholly inadequate. During 2008 the company lost billions of dollars, and by September 2008 it was technically insolvent. The company was taken into conservatorship, posting a full-year loss of $58 billion. The problems continued into 2009–2011, as Fannie Mae's total losses closed in on $100 billion. (Note that this fiasco followed an accounting scandal earlier in the decade, when Fannie Mae executives falsified $6.3 billion in profits. The agency was eventually forced to restate its earnings and institute new controls.) A similar set of problems and losses occurred at Freddie Mac.

Fannie Mae obviously suffered from a poor risk culture, as evidenced by directors who failed to guide or challenge executive management, and who lacked a basic understanding of risks; a risk appetite that was wholly inappropriate for the size of the firm's capital base; an ineffective risk management function that allowed the accumulation of a large amount of concentrated risk in illiquid assets; an apparent lack of understanding within the risk function of the potential downside of a sharp decline in housing values; and poor controls that did little to provide transparency – and, indeed, allowed for earnings manipulation.

AIG (2008)

AIG, a US insurance/financial supermarket founded in the 1920s, was one of the largest casualties of the financial crisis, winding up as a "ward of the state."

The cause of its problems dates back to 1987, when then CEO, Hank Greenberg, created a derivatives unit outside the core insurance business to diversify revenues and capitalize on a growing business in debt, equity, commodity and, eventually, credit derivatives. By all accounts this unit was given tremendous latitude and flexibility, and it soon become known in the financial industry as an aggressive player in difficult-to-price long-dated derivatives. Greenberg was ousted in 2005, after the attorney general questioned earnings manipulation relating to finite reinsurance contracts. His successor, Martin Sullivan, ostensibly put in additional controls and made governance changes, but these had no impact on the derivatives unit's business, which kept on getting larger and riskier.

In the lead-up to the financial crisis, AIG had a great deal of illiquid, long-dated credit derivative risk on its books, a fact that was well known to many in the industry (although apparently not to regulators, who were busy examining the main insurance companies but not the rather toxic derivatives subsidiary). The business leaders managing the credit derivative book stated publicly in 2007 that they could not envision a scenario where they would lose money on the book – hardly a signal that they were in control of the business.[3] In fact, as the crisis took hold and AIG began to revalue its risky derivative positions, it had to write down the value by $11.5 billion, causing a bottom-line loss of $3.5 billion. Sullivan was ousted, and board member Robert Willumstad took over as CEO, effectively overseeing AIG's sale to the government. In the third quarter of 2008 the company lost an amazing $62 billion from its derivative, credit insurance and financial product operations (an amount that increased to a total of $100 billion for all of 2008). The US government decided to intervene at that point as it could ill afford another enormous bankruptcy after Lehman. It injected $85 billion for an 80% stake in AIG, and eventually added another $40 billion.

Although the company eventually regained its footing and went public again (repaying the government in increments), it serves as an interesting example of a financial institution that should have known better. Its business was (and is) risk management, and yet it violated all of the principles of good risk management and had no semblance of a risk culture that could protect it from making the wrong decisions and taking bad risk. By all accounts the firm had directors with no strong knowledge of risk; there was no formalized risk appetite (certainly not one governing the derivatives operation); there was little knowledge in the executive suite of the large risks being run; risk managers were apparently unable to stop the worsening risk profile; the firm had a very misbalanced risk/return profile; and risk reporting surrounding the subsidiary was less than transparent. All of these characteristics point to a weak, arguably non-existent, risk culture.

BP (2005, 2006, 2010)

We shift focus slightly in this example, moving from finance-related risk matters to operational and infrastructural ones. Global energy giant BP (formerly British Petroleum) has a history of difficulties with regard to safety and control, at least some of them stemming from a lax risk culture. To be sure, the company has operated many projects in many parts of the world very successfully for several decades, helping build its brand name and reputation in the process. However, it has stumbled seriously in recent years with respect to its internal control and risk management methods, and the result has been injury (in some cases death) to employees, environmental damage, financial losses and reputational damage – the very things that a strong risk culture seeks to minimize or avoid.

The first episode that seems indicative of a poor appreciation of risk occurred in 2005, when an explosion at the company's Texas City oil refinery (the third largest in the state, acquired but not properly integrated some years before) killed 15 people and injured 170 workers. Various investigations were launched, which eventually led to the company being charged with criminal violations and paying fines related to safety violations. Further fines were later levied after the company reportedly failed to put in place safety improvements. Without getting into the technical engineering details of the explosion, we can note that the post-accident reports indicated failure by responsible parties to take appropriate actions in the ongoing maintenance and repair of an isomerization unit. The detailed critique of the company focused on failings relating to operational risk management, maintenance, inspection, and health and safety. There was also a significant criticism of the management culture at the site, and BP's internal reported noted that Texas City exhibited "a culture that evolved over the years [which] seemed to ignore risk, tolerated noncompliance, and accepted incompetence."[4] Furthermore, "site leadership had, in part, started to recognize this poor working environment and culture, but had not influenced the workplace culture quickly enough to avoid the incident on March 23."[5]

Unfortunately, this was only the first of three major incidents to occur at BP. The second involved a 6,500-barrel oil spill in Alaska's Prudhoe Bay as a result of corroded pipes. The spill was the largest on record on Alaska's North Slope, and resulted in the company suffering further reputational damage, pleading guilty to misdemeanors and paying millions of dollars in fines. Importantly, and consistent with the 2005 Texas City incident, it appears that repeated warnings (from inside and outside the company) regarding growing corrosive damage were ignored by management. These included findings collected by union workers in 2004 and 2005 and forwarded to management for action. Nothing was done in response, which led ultimately to the spill in 2006. In addition, and illustrative of the problems that can be associated with risk models, BP's own rather complex suite of risk models failed to properly model the effects of corrosion on the pipeline – meaning that a further mechanism to prevent or minimize damage failed.

The 2006 spill, while damaging, pales in comparison to the third incident: the 2010 explosion of the Deepwater Horizon oil rig atop the Macondo well in the Gulf of Mexico, which took the lives of 11 workers and led to an environmental disaster. It was the largest accidental aquatic oil spill in history, with crude flowing from the ocean floor for a good part of 2010. An estimated 4.9 million barrels spilled between the time of the explosion and July 2010, when a temporary cap was placed over the well head; smaller amounts then flowed until a permanent cap was created in September. By that time, widespread damage had been done to the Gulf ecosystem, fishing industry and tourism – which eventually cost the company tens of billions of dollars in restitution, along with further damage to its reputation. The Deepwater spill also led to changes in the executive suite, with the CEO and various other senior executives departing. The inevitable post-mortem (focused primarily on BP, but assigning some blame to rig operator Transocean and well construction firm Halliburton) revealed what has become a recurring theme: poor risk controls, a focus on profits and cost-cutting rather than prudent operational risk management, a management culture which did not respond to bad news properly, poor communication and so forth. One member of the independent panel reported that "a large number of decisions were made that were highly questionable and potentially contributed to the blowout of the Macondo well. ... Virtually all were made in favor of approaches which were shorter in time and lower in cost. That gives us concern that there was not proper consideration of the tradeoffs between cost and schedule and risk and safety."[6]

While these operational incidents can be viewed separately, driven by unique dynamics and conditions in each location, it is also possible to view them collectively, as part of a pattern: a company without a risk culture to support diligent operational risk management, the proper investment in risk controls and safety measures or an environment that permits challenging of authority. Perhaps the worst part of this neglect is that in these instances we go beyond financial and reputational losses into human tragedy.

UBS (1998, 2007, 2011)

UBS, the Swiss banking giant, has a history of risk control problems which seem indicative of a perpetually weak risk culture.[7] We can point to various instances over more than a decade which speak to a risk function that lacked authority to enforce limits or policies, a risk profile that was poorly understood and that allowed concentrated risks to be taken, and poor internal controls that permitted fraud to be perpetrated.

In 1998 the bank suffered massive losses as a result of its exposures to troubled hedge fund LTCM and the Russian markets. The losses drew the ire and scrutiny of various stakeholders, including shareholders and regulators, and led to changes in both the executive team and the risk management function. Unfortunately, similar problems occurred during the credit crisis of 2007, when the bank suffered significant losses on its internal hedge fund (which took risk positions that effectively doubled those taken by the official trading desks). In 2007 alone the bank announced CHF4.4 billion in net losses, which included CHF20 billion in losses from US mortgage assets and other real estate deals. These losses were just the tip of the iceberg; excessively large risk positions in credit, foreign exchange and fixed-income markets within the rest of the bank were so damaging that it had to be bailed out by the Swiss government in a multi-billion-franc capital infusion. In addition, through an asset guarantee program UBS was effectively backstopped on a rather substantial CHF40 billion of bad assets. The size and scope of losses led to a veritable revolving door in the executive suite between 2007 and 2009.

As if to add insult to injury, the bank again demonstrated its weak risk culture when it was announced, in 2011, that a rogue trader on its equity desk had gamed the system, booking unauthorized trades that eventually cost the bank more than $2.5 billion and led to the third management shakeup in a decade.

In each instance, the publicly released post-mortem documents point to many of the issues we raised in the previous chapter, including a weak risk management function; inadequate infrastructure; lack of proper management tone on risk issues; poor risk transparency; an ill-defined, and poorly enforced, risk appetite; and a divisive business-versus-control attitude.

MF Global (2011)

In late October 2011, MF Global, a publicly listed US broker-dealer, was forced to file for bankruptcy after suffering massive losses on leveraged bets in European government bonds. Prior to achieving this notoriety, MF (which was part of the Man Financial Group until 2007) operated as an over-the-counter derivatives dealer that executed proprietary and customer trades in the exchange-traded and OTC derivative markets, and in global foreign exchange and bond markets; it was also a primary dealer in US government bonds. In March 2010 former Goldman Sachs head and New Jersey politician Jon Corzine assumed the helm, with a mandate to increase revenues and expand the firm's footprint. Unfortunately, in the span of little more than a year Corzine and his management team opted to make very aggressive, risky bets in European sovereign debt, essentially betting that Eurozone pressures associated with Greece would ease and that the prices of Italian, Spanish, Irish and Portuguese bonds would rally in response. According to records, MF took a $6.3 billion position in these bonds, funding them in the reverse repo market. The total exposure was well in excess of prudent leverage levels.

When European bonds weakened during the third quarter of 2011 MF suffered losses and was unable to renew its funding. This resulted in the firm posting negative net worth, forcing a Chapter 11 filing. It soon became clear that customer funds had been comingled with the firm's own funds, in violation of securities laws. In fact, after MF declared bankruptcy, it became evident that customer funds were missing, and in early 2012 the trustee reported being unable to find more than $1.6 billion in customer funds.

After the collapse (the eighth largest bankruptcy in US history), it became clear that MF suffered from myriad risk management problems, many indicative of a weak risk culture. For instance, the board of directors apparently had no specific risk strategy or risk appetite in place, which was one reason why Corzine was able to accumulate such a large position in European sovereign bonds. In addition, the CRO's concerns regarding the riskiness of the positions were largely dismissed by Corzine and the board, until it was too late. In fact, the CRO was in such strong disagreement that he resigned six months before the losses and bankruptcy. Furthermore, the firm's internal controls were so weak that management was able to access client funds and use them for proprietary risk purposes. Not only was this reflective of a poor control system; it was also an enormous ethical and legal breach – the kind that is evident when a firm has no true risk culture.

Olympus (2011)

Olympus, a Japanese manufacturer of optics and photographic equipment, is a further example of how the lack of a risk culture and a culture of doing the right thing can lead to corporate misdeeds. The Olympus governance scandal came to light in October 2011, although its roots go back some 25 years. During the 1980s Olympus, like other Japanese companies, engaged in "financial engineering" – a convenient euphemism for speculation – to supplement earnings (which were being pressured by the surging yen). This strategy worked reasonably well until the collapse of the Japanese stock market in the early 1990s, at which point the company suffered an estimated $1.5 billion of losses. Rather than reflect these losses in the relevant income statements for the period, management began a multi-year cover-up scheme, initially disguising the losses through derivative contracts and structured products. These were followed by other accounting schemes over the years as Japanese accounting rules changed. So-called tobashi trades – effectively manipulation based on transferring bad assets to affiliated, but unconsolidated, trusts and companies – became part of the process. Ultimately the company tried to pass some of the losses against M&A fees.

In 2011, Michael Woodford, Olympus' first non-Japanese CEO, made it known through queries to board members that he had concerns the company had covered up bad investments by disguising unrealized losses on securities positions as fees and payments on four M&A transactions (three unlisted companies and one public UK acquisition, Glyrus Group) – in contravention of ethical behavior, corporate governance standards, accounting standards and securities laws. For instance, in the $2 billion acquisition of Glyrus, Olympus reported paying $687 million in fees. This figure is well in excess of any standard M&A fee structure, which typically calls for a payment of between 1% and 5%. A further $800 million paid for the three unlisted acquisitions – which were written down by 75% within the first year – also appeared suspicious.

Shortly after this disclosure, the board sacked whistleblower CEO Woodford and the company's share price plunged by 75%, threatening a delisting action. The disclosure also led to the resignation of company chairman and president Tsuyoshi Kikukawa. Successor president Shuichi Takayama came out with the usual corporate apology for "misreporting," and with promises of a full investigation. In fact, a 200-page independent report confirmed all of the facts, noting that "the core part of the management was rotten, and that contaminated other parts around it."[8] Three successive presidents (Shimoyama, 1984–1993; Kishimoto, 1993–2001; Kikukawa, 2001–2011), as well as numerous other senior executives and outside consultants, all had a hand in the cover-up.

The episode was one not of simple misreporting, but of a completely dysfunctional corporate risk culture, which brought reminders of corporate accounting scandals of the early 21st century (e.g., Enron, Tyco, WorldCom, Global Crossing). The available information makes it clear that some directors were privy to the misstatement and de facto condoned the unethical behavior and cover-up. (The independent report noted that "there were a lot of yes-men among the directors."[9]) In addition, it seems evident that the firm's internal controls and accounting processes were insufficient to reconcile the differences on the financial statements and that lower-level managers who might have been able to raise a flag failed to do so or felt they had no power to do so. These symptoms are, of course, evidence of a non-existent risk culture, where a company's leadership would sacrifice the corporate reputation to protect against bad news. In fact, the independent report noted that "the head of the company ran an autocratic regime over a long period, generating an internal atmosphere in which people hesitated to disagree."[10]

The examples above are dramatic and help reinforce the point that the lack of an effective risk culture can be a significant factor in creating, magnifying, accelerating or otherwise contributing to a range of problems that can culminate in massive losses, financial distress and even bankruptcy. However, it is important to emphasize that not every problem associated with a weak or non-existent risk culture need be so dramatic. Every day, week and month many firms suffer small problems, inefficiencies and confusion that disrupt the smooth functioning of operations without leading to the spectacular disasters cited above. In other words, risk culture weakness can create small, as well as large, problems. But these small problems should also concern a firm's directors, executives, employees and stakeholders, as they indicate a lack of proper appreciation for the essential management imperatives required to steer a firm.

6 Building and Strengthening I: Structure and Organization

At this stage in our journey we have covered certain basics of risk culture, including definitions, institutional and regulatory considerations, deficiencies and flaws. The next step brings us to the key elements that a firm can implement to build or strengthen its culture. Of course, building and strengthening is a firm-specific exercise: what works for one company may be inappropriate or ineffective for another, and vice versa. The program of change, the pace of change and the metrics of change will necessarily vary by firm. That said, there are certain common imperatives for any company to consider, adapt and then implement. Given the importance of this exercise – which attempts to address some of the serious flaws noted in Chapters 4 and 5 – we shall divide the matter into two chapters: in this chapter we shall consider structure- and governance-related prescriptions,[1] and in the next we shall focus on knowledge and behavioral imperatives. In both chapters we shall emphasize that the enhancements a firm undertakes to boost risk awareness in all of its dimensions should ultimately create an environment where ideas, behaviors and structural changes lead to practical actions.

One important point to emphasize in these building and strengthening chapters is that the issues raised are intended to be prescriptions for creating, fixing or enhancing; they are decidedly *not* checklists for a firm to implement point by point and then expect to have created a robust risk culture. We have stressed repeatedly – and do so again – that the success of a risk culture is predicated on gradual, organic adoption of these points by a firm's leadership and its employees. Those seeking quick-fix solutions to their risk culture problems will be disappointed.

Before we begin, it is worth noting that many companies have focused their risk management improvements on risk processes and risk metrics, rather than risk culture, for at least two reasons. First, a culture can develop only after processes and metrics are in place. For instance, there is little point in building risk awareness if the basic blocking and tackling is missing. Second, a culture is more difficult to build, and takes longer to instill, than process-oriented tasks: things that are difficult sometimes get pushed aside in favor of those that are relatively easy to deal with. But while companies may have been able to ignore or delay implementation of risk culture until now, there is a growing realization that they no longer can: internal and external stakeholders generally expect a culture to be embedded within the firm so that the positive benefits can start to accrue. Indeed, delaying any further seems unwise.

Structure and governance

Our examination of structure and governance prescriptions focuses on the following key areas, each of which we shall discuss in greater detail:

- *Imperative 1*: defining a common risk philosophy
- *Imperative 2*: formalizing the risk appetite
- *Imperative 3*: assigning accountability
- *Imperative 4*: developing the correct incentives
- *Imperative 5*: building operational sophistication
- *Imperative 6*: rotating personnel
- *Imperative 7*: injecting new blood from outside the firm

Imperative 1: defining a common risk philosophy

A firm must have a clear understanding of its view on risk and what it wants to do with risk. Accordingly, directors and executive management need to define a risk philosophy, which should be a function of:

- *What businesses the firm wants to be in*: in the first step a firm should state clearly, and in detail, which businesses it wants to operate and what risks might affect such businesses.
- *What kinds of risks the firm wants to take*: once the businesses have been identified and designated, the firm can then specifically define the risks it wants to take or accept, as well as those it would prefer to avoid, cede, hedge, transfer or eliminate.
- *How revenue generation and risk are linked*: the final step lets the firm explicitly link its business and risk strategies, at least conceptually. This linkage provides critical synchronicity, ensuring clarity of purpose and goals. The firm can deepen the business/risk linkage when considering its risk appetite, as we shall discuss below.

The risk philosophy, which we can view as the key conceptual or aspirational document, can be converted into an action plan, which we term a "risk strategy."

The strategy contains specific implementation steps that make the philosophy practical. The philosophy and practical strategy should be approved by relevant governance bodies (e.g., the governing risk committee, the board of directors) and should be communicated, in simple and unambiguous terms, to all business and control personnel: everyone must be on the same page.

Importantly, while we see the risk philosophy as dynamic, it must also feature a degree of stability. A firm should revisit its philosophy and its approach to risk-taking periodically, but should plan only on making small adjustments from time to time, as corporate goals and the operating environment change. The key is to avoid sudden changes in approach or scope, which lead to confusion, mistakes or other managerial or control breakdowns. Figure 6.1 summarizes this process.

Let us consider a few simple examples. In the first case, a bank determines that it wants to focus its risk business on serving loan clients, and therefore to either limit or eliminate pure proprietary trading activities. While market risks need to be assumed periodically in order to service client needs, it should be clear under the bank's strategy that positioning simply for the sake of generating a proprietary profit is incongruous with the business and risk goals and is therefore disallowed. We can say that the bank favors client-based credit risk to generate its revenues and that it avoids (or at least minimizes) proprietary market risks. This strategy may lead to lower earnings volatility, though perhaps also to larger losses or reduced business volumes when the economic cycle is in a downturn.

In a second example, a US-headquartered multinational industrial company with operations in Indonesia, Brazil and Germany decides that it will permit its local operations to manage their currency and funding risks independently, without ex ante head office consultation. This philosophy allows a degree of

Figure 6.1 The definition of a risk philosophy

autonomy and flexibility, which the firm's management may feel comfortable granting because of the maturity of the local management teams or the on-the-ground expertise that exists in each local marketplace, say. By adopting this philosophy the firm is essentially indicating that it is comfortable running certain decentralized financial risks (in addition to its core operating risks) and that it views such risks as consistent with, and central to, its revenue-generating activities.

As a third example we take an insurance company that is primarily in the business of writing auto insurance policies – what we term "high-frequency, low-severity" risks, since auto accidents and claims happen every day, but tend to be small amounts (thousands of dollars or euros per episode, at a maximum). From time to time the company also underwrites certain property and casualty risks related to damage to commercial buildings by fire, natural disasters and so on. These risks are of a different character: low frequency, high severity – just the opposite of the auto portfolio. While the insurer is quite comfortable managing and retaining its close-to-the-mean auto risks, since it believes it has the correct actuarial skills to manage these with a modest amount of capital on a portfolio expected loss basis, it does not want to actively pursue or retain the catastrophic property and casualty risks, as these involve a different set of skills, pricing and capital. Accordingly, the firm's philosophy is to retain its auto risks and cede or transfer the property and casualty risks to a reinsurer.

In these brief examples we can also imagine that the philosophies and resulting actionable strategies are well controlled through relevant constraints and limits, as discussed below.

As we have indicated, after defining the risk philosophy, the firm's management must communicate its parameters clearly to all those involved in risk-related businesses and to the control functions. In line with a strong communications effort and an emphasis on transparency, the company might issue risk mandates which specifically delineate the kinds of risks that can be taken within a given unit or business center (we shall discuss this in more detail in relation to imperative 5). These mandates reinforce the concepts and ensure everyone is aligned. It should be understood that the creation of a risk philosophy is very closely tied to a firm's risk culture; the philosophy serves as a central mechanism for defining the firm's operations and risk-taking beliefs, and acts as a vehicle for consistent and understandable communication on the topic.

As we consider this and other imperatives, let us also briefly mention who must be held responsible for implementation in each case. In this instance the responsibility rests with board directors and executive management, who must take the time to analyze and discuss the particulars of the philosophy as it relates to business strategies, skills and shareholder expectations, and then approve it through formal governance mechanisms. Only directors and executives have the power to define the philosophy.

Imperative 2: formalizing the risk appetite

The concept of a formalized risk appetite has gained considerable currency in recent years, as both market circumstances and stakeholder demands have forced firms to explicitly state, in financial terms, how much they are prepared to lose in pursuit of risk-related business. There are various ways of defining the risk appetite. For instance, in the financial sector, the IIF's Committee on Market Best Practices (CMBP) has defined risk appetite as "a firm's view of how strategic risk-taking can help achieve business objectives while respecting constraints to which the organization is subject."[2] COSO has indicated that risk appetite "is the amount of risk, on a broad level, an organization is willing to accept in pursuit of stakeholder value."[3] The US-based Institute of Internal Auditors has noted that it is "the level of risk that an organization is willing to accept."[4] The Society of Actuaries considers risk appetite to be "the level of aggregate risk that an organization can undertake and successfully manage over an extended period of time."[5] These definitions have a similar thread: willingness or ability to take risk. For our purposes we shall define the risk appetite as *the amount and type of risk a company is willing to accept in the pursuit of a stated business strategy.*

Risk appetite must be closely related to the firm's financial capacity to support risky business, consistent with its stated risk philosophy. In other words, risk appetite should reflect risks that the company has indicated it wants to take, so long as those risks fall within its financial ability to bear losses. Obviously, a firm would not choose to risk more than its financial resources allow, as it would quickly find itself in a precarious financial position (and would almost certainly incur the ire of its stakeholders). In this light, we can think of *risk capacity* as an absolute outer boundary of risk a firm could take, but one that it would not want to test under normal circumstances. *Risk appetite,* in contrast, is the "comfortable" amount that a firm can put at stake – an amount that is well within the outer boundary. Put another way, risk capacity might be regarded as a stress test function of the risk appetite, essentially factoring in a buffer over and above the appetite.[6] Since a stress test to crystallize the buffer can be driven by any number of scenarios, this is a somewhat subjective exercise.

The financial resources available to support a company's risk capacity are typically defined to include earnings and capital. Capital is of particular interest, because it is the core buffer used to absorb risk-related losses. The amount available will depend on the contributions of external shareholders: they will subscribe capital coincident with the return they can expect to receive. Accordingly, there must be some alignment between shareholder expectations and the amount of capital available in support of risk-taking operations. Thus, shareholders providing capital to a very risky firm will do so because they expect to receive a higher return than they would from one that is less risky, *ceteris paribus*. In terms of earnings, if these are not paid out in the form of dividends, they add to the capital buffer and are thus part of the capacity equation. As we shall note below, certain other factors – including leverage, liquidity and ratings – are also used in the determination of capacity.

A risk appetite, which lies within the company's risk capacity, is obviously highly dependent on quantitative characteristics. However, it should also include some qualitative considerations, such as the strategic importance of individual risk-taking centers within the firm, the existence of any difficult-to-quantify or complex risks, the firm's experience and expertise in dealing with particular classes of risks and the firm's institutional memory from past crises. The risk appetite should therefore go beyond a simple numbers game.

Two other areas can be considered when establishing the risk appetite: zero-tolerance risks and dynamic "no-go" risks. Zero-tolerance risks are those that a firm wants no part of: they are often catastrophic risks which it is better to transfer or otherwise avoid or eliminate. Reputational risk is often classified as a zero-tolerance risk, as few firms are willing to place their names and reputations on the line in exchange for economics or market share associated with a risky deal or business line. Dynamic no-go risks are those which a firm does not want to deal with at a given point in time, but may consider as circumstances or market events change. They are thus considered to be temporarily, rather than permanently, off limits. For instance, during a downturn in the economic cycle, a firm may withdraw from certain risk businesses because it prefers not to run the chance of additional losses; when the cycle turns, the firm may be willing to re-enter that market.

Let us consider a simple example of risk capacity and appetite. Assume a company has \$100 million in capital and generates \$25 million of earnings per year. Consistent with its philosophy and resources, it may determine that its risk capacity over a one-year horizon cannot exceed total earnings plus 25% of capital, or \$50 million; any amount above that figure could put it in financial jeopardy and should therefore be avoided. We can interpret the \$50 million as a stress loss boundary, meaning that the risk appetite – the prudent level needed to support business – will necessarily be less than \$50 million. Depending on the firm's strategies, the appetite might be set at \$35 million, say. This is an amount that the company feels comfortable putting at stake in support of its business plan, and should the worst come to pass its loss will not place the company in financial jeopardy.

Risk capacity can also be expressed as a probabilistic measure. For instance, a company might indicate that it would be willing to lose \$20 million in a given risky business area with a 10% probability of occurrence, or \$75 million across all businesses with a 1% probability. The probabilistic approach must be rescaled into real numbers to make it comprehensible to the relevant internal audience.

It is worth noting that when setting its risk capacity ($50 million in this example), a company must take account of its leverage position, its access to liquidity and its credit rating, as all of these can affect ongoing operations. Liquidity, the lifeblood of any company, is a particularly important consideration and must be factored in explicitly. Unlike other risk factors, a liquidity risk appetite can never be set at zero: a firm will always have to take some amount of liquidity risk, as it can never perfectly match its inflows and outflows. That said, it can manage the position very conservatively. To return to our example, the company cannot simply set the $50 million risk capacity in a vacuum; it must understand the dynamics of its leverage (because a loss of capital will leave it overleveraged or needing to quickly shrink its balance sheet), its access to liquidity and funding (because a loss may make its liquidity and funding providers nervous) and its credit rating (because, once again, a loss plus either an overleveraged balance sheet or a strained liquidity position could result in its debt being downgraded). Thus, risk capacity is influenced directly by available financial resources and the demands of capital providers, and indirectly by bank lenders, other creditors and credit rating agencies. In some industries (e.g., banking, insurance) regulators may also place direct or indirect constraints through capital and leverage requirements. It should also be clear that every firm will have a unique risk capacity and risk appetite. These individual characteristics will appeal to different types of capital providers (e.g., bond holders or equity holders).

While the risk capacity and appetite represent macro boundaries of risk-taking comfort, practical risk management calls for a certain amount of granular operative capability. Thus, operationally, it is common for a firm to take its overarching risk capacity and parcel it into narrower, more granular, risk metrics which conform to the specific kinds of risks being run and the business and profitability opportunities. This approach to risk capacity allocation through limits can help control the risk profile more effectively (while remaining within established boundaries); it can also be an effective way of reallocating capital from one business to another, as opportunities or circumstances warrant. Standard lower-level metrics include sensitivity and value-at-risk limits (for market risks), risk equivalent exposure (exposure at default and probability of default – for credit risks) and maturity gaps (for liquidity risks).

It is worth noting that the allocation of risk appetite at the operative level can be top-down or bottom-up. The top-down approach begins with the establishment of the outer boundary through the mechanisms noted above, and then proceeds with a suballocation of that capacity to individual risk-taking centers, perhaps on the basis of a risk-adjusted profitability hurdle. The bottom-up approach is precisely the reverse: each risk-taking center submits its desired capacity (consistent with an approved business strategy), and these individual requirements are summed to a figure which must then be reconciled with the firm's total risk capacity or appetite – with adjustments back to the operative level being made as needed. Figure 6.2 summarizes the key points of the risk appetite concept.

The practice of setting and monitoring the risk appetite must be continuous and dynamic, because business opportunities and market circumstances are constantly in flux. Directors and executive managers must actively drive the process; it is advisable to institutionalize an annual review of the risk appetite and monitor its implementation and usage regularly during the course of the year (e.g., quarterly). The annual review lets directors and executives take stock of the operating environment, the business strategy, desired returns and available financial resources to ensure full synchronicity with the risk plan.

Let us return to our primary theme by relating risk appetite to risk culture. It should be clear that the establishment of a concise and prudent risk appetite makes it easy for all of a company's employees to understand its risks more readily, and to communicate using a common language. It also ensures synchronicity between the business strategy and the risk strategy, which is often a source of confusion. Accordingly, clearly defined risk appetite not only provides for prudent financial control, but also serves as a vital link in promoting the kind of understanding and behavior that is fundamental to a risk culture. Importantly, there exists a symbiotic relationship between the two: the risk appetite is critical to reinforcing the risk culture, and the risk culture makes the risk appetite meaningful and actionable. Naturally, it is incumbent upon executive management and risk management to disseminate details of the risk appetite to those who must be aware of the metrics and principles.

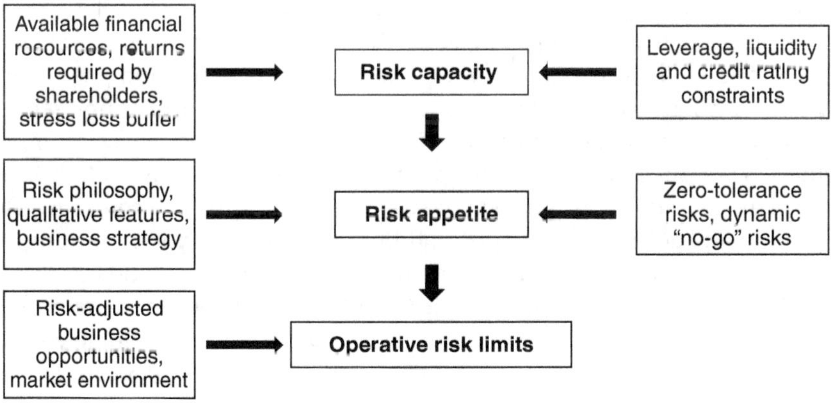

Figure 6.2 Setting a risk appetite

This is primarily an internal exercise, although at least the general concepts behind the risk appetite (if not the specific figures themselves) can also be released to certain stakeholders (e.g., regulators, rating agencies). Note that an additional risk culture benefit can be gained from setting a risk appetite: the process can help build the partnership between business leaders and risk managers. If the two groups can use the process to agree on what makes sense from both a business strategy perspective and a risk capacity or tolerance perspective, they will have a vested interest in trying to make it work: each is a stakeholder, working in concert with the other. If, in contrast, the setting of a risk appetite (before it is sent to the board of directors for scrutiny and approval) is seen as solely or primarily the work of just one group, there will be no shared vision and little concept of a partnership.

Implementing the risk appetite is more complex than implementing the risk philosophy. It requires the active participation of different parties, depending, in some measure, on whether the firm elects to use a top-down or bottom-up approach. In the top-down approach, the directors, having received relevant data and a framework from the key "C" executives (CEO, CFO and CRO), must consider and approve the figures through standard governance processes. Thereafter, the risk management function must translate the appetite into operational limits and devolve those limits to each risk-taking business unit. Under the bottom-up approach, business managers and risk managers should collate the operative risk profile and convert individual limits into higher-level metrics, forwarding them to the executive suite for discussion, adjustment or concurrence. In the final step the board should review the proposed appetite and pass judgment.

Imperative 3: assigning accountability

Professionals working in an institutional environment typically seek fulfillment by accepting and exercising certain authorities and responsibilities. Indeed, this is precisely why many people enter the corporate or governmental world: the exercise of decision-making power, based on experience and judgment, is very motivating. And, of course, proper governance of any institution requires the delegation of authorities from directors to executive managers, middle managers and the rank and file. It would be unrealistic (and highly inefficient) to force all decisions to be made at the top levels of the firm. Accordingly, clear definition and delegation of responsibilities to the proper experts must be seen as essential in building and strengthening the institutional foundation.

Under this construct, managers with relevant professional experience must be empowered to make decisions and they should be held accountable for the decisions they take. (For the purposes of our discussion, we regard this as being applicable to both risk management and business management.) The delegation of responsibility in this manner generates a high degree of professional satisfaction or motivation, which is important in getting employees to do the right thing and take pride in the organization and in strengthening the corporate culture. Clear accountability also reduces the inevitable finger-pointing when something goes wrong.

For example, if the chief risk manager of an industrial company is hired to design an enterprise-wide risk management program to identify, quantify and manage financial, commodity, and property and casualty risks, he or she must be assigned explicit accountability for implementing the program. Implementation may include hiring professionals, building a risk appetite for consideration with business managers and executives (to be approved by the board), investing in the proper risk technology, creating relevant policies (again for consideration and approval by the board or risk committee) and approving certain risk-related transactions within the operative limits set under the risk appetite. If the board and executive managers grant the chief risk manager (and his or her delegates) the mandate and authority, they can demand accountability – and the parties will work toward a common goal.

Let us consider the flip side. When professionals can hide behind a diffuse committee structure which makes all significant risk decisions, or when all decisions are ultimately taken at a higher managerial level, no one is likely to feel responsible or accountable. Decision-making that is diffuse or concentrated at higher managerial levels is at once demotivating and unclear, and may increase the chance of bad decisions.

From a risk culture perspective, the organization that chooses to delegate authority and hold those with such authority to account (whether the consequences are positive or negative) strengthens its governance and reinforces its culture. For example, risk management professionals at designated levels of seniority can be given approval authorities and be measured on the basis of the decisions they take; they, and not a diffuse committee, can be unambiguously accountable. (This does not remove the committee structure, but reserves its role for large risks, policy considerations and so on.)

Implementing this imperative is, in the first instance, the responsibility of executive management, who must define the authorities that different units, departments, individuals and committees are to be accorded. When these authorities have been defined, they should be passed through the formal governance checks, which in most cases will include consideration and approval by the board of directors. After approval, the appropriate authorities should be clearly communicated by executive management to the relevant professionals, directly or through a human resource function.

Imperative 4: developing the correct incentives

Incentives motivate people to work. While incentives come in different forms (e.g., titles, flexibility in work scheduling or location, opportunity for promotion), the single most powerful incentive tends to be compensation. In some industries compensation can be particularly significant and may be tied to achieving specific performance targets, such as revenue growth, net profits, market share, cost efficiencies, operating margins and share price performance. When compensation mechanisms create the right sorts of behaviors, the corporate culture generally, and the risk culture specifically, benefit greatly.

Of course, as we noted in Chapter 4, bad compensation mechanisms can have exactly the opposite effect – creating perverse behaviors such as taking too much risk or taking ill-advised risks (e.g., long-term, complex, concentrated, mispriced) in order to meet some performance goal. When compensation metrics are focused primarily, or exclusively, on profit generation rather than risk-adjusted profit generation, misbehaviors will almost certainly arise.

Thus, the goal must be the creation of the correct incentives. Firms operating in different industries may choose to apply their own unique approaches; this is certainly the case for private companies, which operate outside of the scrutiny of public shareholders. But for public companies operating in both financial and non-financial industries, certain standard approaches can be considered. Let us review some of the most common approaches.

- *Risk-adjusted performance metrics*: in the first instance, metrics which are used to determine compensation should not be based on volume measures such as revenues, gross profits, total sales, loan volume and gross premiums written, as these fail to take account of any dimension of risk. If risk does not figure into a performance metric, those responsible for generating business have no incentive to consider risk in their activities; their only aim will be to book as much business as possible, with no regard for the consequences. Clearly this will not motivate the right risk-related behavior. Accordingly, a firm does well to dispense with volume metrics and to replace them with metrics that factor in the level of risk being taken. This is most commonly done by looking at risk-adjusted returns, economic value-added and other revenue or sales measures from which risk reserves have been deducted. Firms can also use a risk-adjusted return on the capital supporting the specific business, under the assumption that riskier business draws a higher capital charge (and must therefore deliver a higher return in order to justify the use of capital). Any metric that properly takes account of dimensions of risk will emerge as a more powerful behavioral mechanism.
- *Long-term performance metrics*: the second key dimension of performance evaluation relates to time horizon. Historically, it has been common for companies to reward employees for the profits generated in a given year, even when revenues are actually created over a period of time. In essence, this present value approach takes future revenues and discounts them

back to today (typically at the risk-free, rather than credit-risk-adjusted, rate); compensation is then based on that present value calculation. This approach has the disadvantage of allowing the company and the employee responsible for the future stream of revenue to ignore what happens in the "out years." In other words, if the revenues are generated from a risky activity that remains on the books for the next *x* years, but the compensation is paid on a present value basis today, the responsible employee has little incentive to worry about the risk in the remaining years: that will be dealt with in due course, will become someone else's problem or else will drop off the radar screen entirely. Again, the correct behavioral incentives are missing from this scheme. In order to avoid this problem, a company can design its compensation program to defer, rather than present-value, the incentive payments to match the revenue inflows as they are realized over time. This is likely to make the employee more sensitive to the term risk horizon that characterizes a piece of business, ensuring that it is properly considered, monitored and managed over time. This program is operationally more complex, but it certainly creates a more powerful positive behavioral mechanism.

- *Clawbacks*: another mechanism that can be used to promote correct behavior is the clawback. As the name suggests, a clawback is a feature of a compensation mechanism that allows a company to take back some amount of previously granted cash or equity in the future if problems arise or if a risk-related transaction does not work as anticipated. The clawback is a means of controlling tail risks, and can help ensure that employees responsible for committing the firm to a medium- or long-term transaction have some skin in the game, even after incentive compensation has already been received. Like the long-term performance mechanism detailed immediately above, the clawback can attune an employee to doing the right thing for the firm and its clients on a continuing basis.
- *Ties to group performance*: many incentive schemes correlate compensation with the financial result achieved through an employee's own efforts (e.g., his or her own sales or revenue targets, hopefully risk-adjusted), as well as the efforts of a business unit or division. While the focus on performance metrics that are closest to the employee's daily responsibilities certainly makes sense, it can result in skewed behavior if metrics are not tied to broader group-wide performance. For instance, a revenue generator might do very well in his or her own business area but care little for what is happening elsewhere in the firm. This does little to promote a shared sense of the organization and places too much emphasis on individual results. When incentives are linked to both individual results and group performance two benefits appear: employees have a stake in ensuring the broadest possible success of the firm, and the sole focus on individual P&L is diminished (as are the

sometimes questionable behaviors this can lead to). If, for instance, incentives are structured so that a minimum group target must be reached before individual targets come into play, employee behavior can be reoriented in support of the company at large.

- *Less cash, more equity*: in the past it was popular to award cash bonuses to employees who met their targets. Cash allows instant access and use, and is very appealing from an employee's perspective. In the 1980s and 1990s the turn toward including an equity component started to become more widespread, with employees in various industries receiving stock and stock options as part of their incentive compensation. This had the great benefit of tying an employee's personal fortunes to those of the company – creating an alignment of incentives, to the extent that stock and options could be converted into cash only after some multi-year vesting period. One powerful mechanism for promoting a stronger culture is to continue down this path, de-emphasizing the cash component (with its immediate conversion) and emphasizing the equity component (with its alignment and deferral characteristics). Thus, if a previous compensation regime called for 70% cash and 30% equity, perhaps the more relevant mix would be precisely the reverse.
- *Bonus deferrals*: following on from the previous point, another important alignment mechanism is bonus deferral, where the incentive package (in whatever mix of cash and equity) vests over a period of time – perhaps 25% per year for four years, or 20% per year for five years. This deferral mechanism brings us back to the same principles discussed under long-term performance metrics and clawbacks, and ties an employee more firmly to the medium- and long-term success and goals of the company.
- *Separate policies for risk managers and controllers*: finally, we must make the obvious, if sometimes overlooked, point that compensation policies for those in a risk management or control function must be structured and considered separately from those used for revenue generators or front-line business managers. The reason should be obvious: a control professional should never be evaluated against profitability measures that are linked to risk-taking and risk capacity, as this might unduly tempt them to grant more risk capital to business colleagues seeking to maximize revenues. Of course, risk managers and other controllers should be able to benefit from the success of the company at large, and their incentives can therefore be linked to group performance metrics. They should not, however, have any stake in the success of businesses they are charged with monitoring. In addition, the long-term performance and clawback mechanisms described above should also apply to the control functions, as these provide the powerful medium- and long-term thinking that is so critical to a strong culture.

Figure 6.3 summarizes these compensation schemes.

Each of these mechanisms has the effect of tying performance to the long-term success of a company, and reinforces the idea that sensitivity to risk issues and prudent approaches to risk management (including tail risk) can benefit the entire company over time. They also ensure that the operating view throughout the firm becomes medium- to long-term, rather than very short-term (as has traditionally been the case with present-valuing of profits in order to calculate current compensation). While such realigned compensation will not, by itself, guarantee good behavior by everyone at all times, it can certainly help create a new way of thinking about success, and must be seen as a driver in the creation of a stronger culture.

One caveat must be emphasized: in a competitive environment, the search for talent often allows competing companies to buy out the long-term, deferred compensation packages of top employees; this renders the deferral somewhat meaningless, as a top employee knows he or she will be cashed out by a competitor. This situation is unavoidable, as competing companies are generally free to offer whatever they please. That said, the likelihood of being bought out by a competitor is probably reserved for a small handful of top talent, rather than the organization at large, so the points we have made about incentive compensation hold true as a mechanism for building a culture.

Responsibility for implementing a comprehensive package of incentives rests initially with the human resource function, which must benchmark current practices against industry norms and some desired goal that has been discussed with executive management (indeed, the risk-adjusted metrics should be agreed

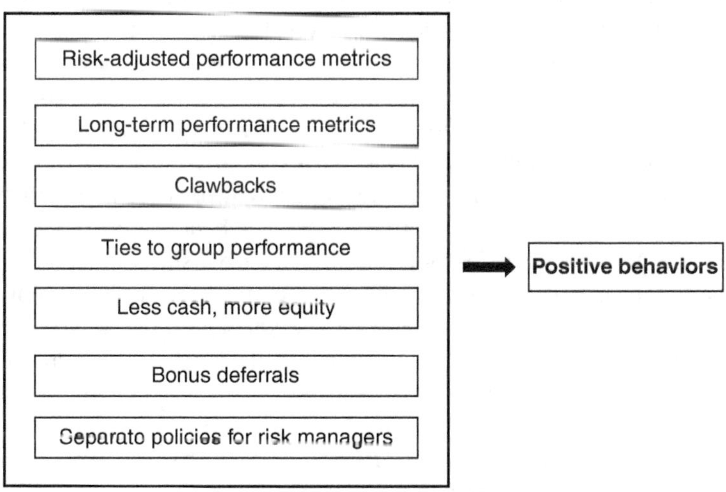

Figure 6.3 Compensation mechanisms to reinforce positive behaviors

between the chief risk officer and business leaders). Once the particulars of the new incentive program have been detailed they must be approved by the board of directors. Thereafter, human resources must create a clear communication and education program for all employees so that the details of the incentive structure are well understood.

Imperative 5: building operational sophistication

A company with scope or scale in its operations requires a minimum level of operating infrastructure and efficiency to help strengthen its culture. While the specific nature of the operating platform and processes will necessarily vary by company and by industry, a few common threads can be identified:

- *Creating the right structure, organization and governance*: it seems obvious that the fundamental definition of a company's structure, its organization and its governance rules must be clearly stated in order to ensure transparency, efficiency and integrity. However, things are sometimes not made as clear as they should be, which can lead to confusion, bottlenecks, internal arbitrage, inefficiency and operational threats. Accordingly, the operational sophistication of a company can be improved by focusing on the essential structure and governance issues that define organizational hierarchy, responsibility and authorities, accountability, policy, use of committee structure and other internal rules. With the correct prescriptions in place, other aspects of organizational efficiency can be introduced more readily.
- *Making the risk function prominent*: the location and prominence of the risk management function within the organization is another element of operational sophistication. In fact, the degree of prominence speaks volumes about how directors and executives perceive risk in the context of the company's operations. If the risk department is tucked away within the office of the CFO or treasurer, or is not represented on executive committees or other important firm-wide governance bodies, then the clear statement is that risk management is an afterthought that does not deserve a great deal of notice or say. This approach will, of course, do nothing to boost the firm's risk culture. If, in contrast, the head of risk reports directly to the CEO or president, is part of the executive suite, represents risk on relevant senior management governance committees and is a voice to be reckoned with, then the firm has already taken a vital step in strengthening its risk culture: the signal that is sent by directors and executives when they place the risk function in a position of prominence and authority is unambiguous.
- *Defining the mandate clearly*: everyone working in a firm (at a certain managerial level) must know what his or her responsibilities are and how these translate into an action plan or operating mandate. This defines the scope of

engagement, helping to promote accountability and reduce conflict or territorial encroachment. Importantly, as far as risk activities are concerned, a mandate specifies clearly what risk exposures may or may not be taken, and what risk capacity or limits are assigned in this regard. Thus, for instance, an underwriter of auto insurance should be limited by the operating mandate to underwriting auto policies and not catastrophic property coverage; a bond trader should be limited by the operating mandate to trading bonds, not equities and foreign exchange; and a corporate loan officer should be limited by the operating mandate to underwriting commercial loans, rather than debt or equity capital markets offerings. Similar definitional clarity should be developed for risk managers, controllers, and everyone else in the risk function.

- *Investing in a minimum level of technological infrastructure*: the modern company relies heavily on all manner of technology for most aspects of business, including production and inventory control, marketing, sales and client contact, funding and risk management, financial statement preparation and monitoring, human resource management, expense control and communication. Given the preponderance of technology in the corporate environment, it is obvious that some minimum standard of infrastructure is required to operate efficiently and safely. Such technology often represents a large investment, but it must be seen as an essential cost of doing safe and efficient business. In addition, while not all aspects of a firm's business might initially fit into a technology platform, the prudent approach is to attempt to move in this direction. Finally, all platforms should feature proper security and integrity, with fully auditable access and data trails; this can reduce instances of operational risk, which is a potential problem in any type of firm.
- *Using relevant and reliable data*: the infrastructure backbone noted above is only half of the equation. To be useful and effective, it must accept and output data that is relevant to a company's operations and secure and reliable enough to be used with confidence. This data can be used to report on internal and client activities, inventories and risk exposures, and to prepare essential management reports such as trial balance sheets, cash flows and income statements. When the technology and data combination is of the highest possible caliber, a firm will be able to close its books very quickly after every month end, putting it in a much better position to guide its business and to report to regulators, exchanges and other stakeholders.

Figure 6.4 summarizes these important elements of operational sophistication.

As noted, every company will have its own standards for creating the right environment, so the comments above must be seen as general and high-level, and must be supplemented by specifics for each firm. The main point is that

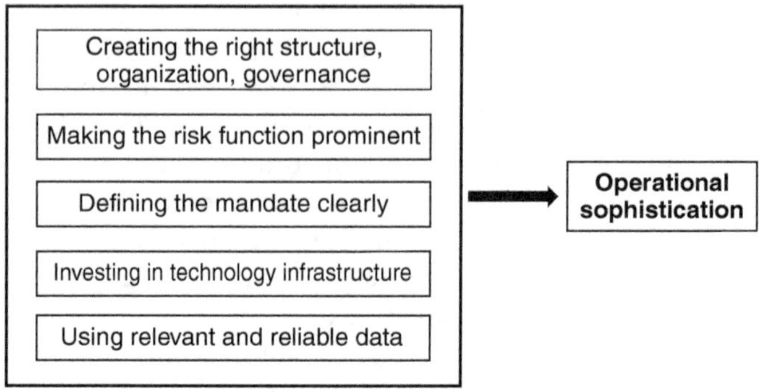

Figure 6.4 Elements of operational sophistication

operating integrity and efficiency go a long way toward helping a firm act on information and eliminate problems, and thus strengthen its culture.

Implementing operational sophistication is a complex task that involves a number of parties. To put it into proper context, let us break down the individual components and consider who must drive each piece. Creating the right structure, organization and governance – including, we might add, placing risk management in a position of prominence and authority – is a joint responsibility of executive management and directors. To begin, executives need to identify an organizational structure that will serve the firm's business and control purposes. They should also make explicit the role and authority of the risk management function. The board of directors must specifically approve this structure, thereby institutionalizing it within the corporate framework. Similar responsibilities should be allocated to the heads of risk, finance, audit and other control functions in defining roles and mandates for their own teams.

Defining the mandate is the function of executive management – both heads of business lines and the head of risk. These colleagues must define the broad operating parameters for each business and then devolve the field of play through the risk management group to each business manager, on an individual basis. Implementing a monitoring scheme to ensure adherence to the mandates is the function of risk management.

The technology dimension of operational sophistication is, again, a multi-part task that begins with executive management (including the head of technology or the chief information officer) analyzing and approving a multi-year technology plan and associated funding. Depending on the size of the investment, board involvement may also be required. Once the technology plan is in place – covering the joint requirements of business and risk, finance and operational control – the technology team must work on a detailed rollout, remaining in close contact with business and control colleagues throughout the process. The implementation of useful technology in a company of any size is a complex undertaking which demands a project implementation plan and steering committee (although hopefully one that is not bureaucratic). The same process can be used for those functions that already have pieces of a technology platform, but lack the complete architecture.

An associated implementation point relates to reliable data – which is intimately tied to the technology platform. The definition of what is essential data for management and regulatory purposes must be jointly created by business and control leaders, who must decide the specific requirements that will let them manage the business and its risks, and then communicate these requirements to the technology team for integration into the technology rollout. Like the broader technology footprint, the data streams are likely to be rolled out in phases and should follow a project management plan so that they remain on course. Finally, the integrity of the data sources and the output should be reviewed and verified by auditors before data becomes part of the official books and records of the firm.

Imperative 6: rotating personnel

When a company hires and trains professionals to do specific jobs, there is a logical tendency to try to keep those professionals in their areas of specialization for as long as possible, perhaps even permanently. On the surface this makes sense, as a great deal of time and resources will have been invested in developing specific skills, and keeping people in situ will pay continuous dividends. In addition, retaining professionals within their delineated spheres allows them to develop extensive networks and contacts, and to become truly expert in that area.

However, there is also something to be said in support of rotating personnel to other areas of the firm. Some companies do this as a matter of course, having realized the benefits of moving professionals into other areas to give them the broadest possible exposure to the company's total operations. While this can interrupt or perhaps dilute the concept of specialization, it can create a more well-rounded professional. In fact, the practice of rotating professionals with different skill sets can go a long way toward strengthening the fabric of risk culture. Such rotations can be arranged along two different axes:

- *Rotations within the risk and control functions*: first, internal rotations within the risk and control areas (e.g., finance, audit) should be arranged as a regular part of the management of human resources. While the process can be customized according to the needs of the company, the focus should generally be on seasoned professionals who can be rotated through multiple areas of risk (credit, market, liquidity, operational, legal) and control (finance, audit, compliance) to help them gain additional experience within the control universe and to provide a fresh pair of eyes in a particular area. In general, risk and control professionals should not occupy the same role indefinitely, as they can grow stale and "lazy." Separately, more junior professionals can also be rotated through multiple risk disciplines as a form of induction.

- *Rotations between risk and business functions*: the second step is to institute rotations of business and risk professionals. As we discussed earlier in the book, the first line of risk management defense resides within the business, so business professionals should be transferred (for a period) to the risk function in order to deepen their risk expertise. This knowledge will transfer back to the business units when the rotation ends. Of course, the infusion of business knowledge into the risk function is an important by-product, as it can help strengthen partnerships and the risk culture. Risk managers must also be part of this transfer process. They can gain a greater appreciation of the business (and its attendant challenges and pressures) by serving for some time within one or more business units. This mechanism also allows the dissemination of risk knowledge across the business.

The mechanisms for arranging rotations can be structured to suit the needs of the company, provided the goal of transferring knowledge and experience is successfully accomplished. Rotations must typically last for at least a few quarters in order to be effective; this is sufficient time to gain an awareness of the issues, build skills and make a positive contribution, but not so long that the employee becomes totally divorced from the functions and business of his or her "day job."

Implementation of the rotation process involves two parties. First, executive management must sponsor this type of scheme so that it is seen to carry the undoubted support of the top of the firm; this will ensure that both business and control leaders actively participate. Once this decision has been taken, it is the task of human resources to create the mechanisms that allow regular rotation to occur. This involves developing the rotation program, identifying and nominating professionals to participate in the program and then monitoring their progress and success over time.

Imperative 7: injecting new blood from outside the firm

A point closely linked to the one immediately above relates to regularly injecting new blood from outside the firm. Recruiting outside professionals (both business and risk) can be a valuable structural mechanism that not only adds important professional skills, but ultimately helps strengthen the corporate culture and risk culture. In fact, it is logical to imagine that a firm will be strengthened when it incorporates talents and experiences from many sources.

We know that there are many ways of analyzing and managing risk, and the experience of risk professionals from other institutions can strengthen a firm's own approach – essentially giving it the best of all worlds. Of course, bringing in such professionals is not intended to be hiring for the sake of hiring; it is targeted to fulfill three objectives:

- To bring in technical expertise in an area where the firm may be weak or lacking
- To gain a fresh perspective on risk processes (i.e., a different way of doing things, or things the firm might not have considered in the past)
- To create a new energy and sense of purpose that can help motivate existing staff

Similar approaches can be considered in the business and control areas, to meet the same objectives: improving skills, bringing in new thoughts and energies, and ultimately adding another important thread in the fabric of the corporate culture. As always, care must be taken to select the right individuals. This relates not only to technical expertise, but also to professional and cultural fit, which is essential for success. Note that such external hiring should occur at all levels, from the most junior to the most senior. Each level of experience will add different skills and benefits. Naturally, to enable it to accomplish this task, the company must have compensation policies that are competitive with the industry. In addition, its reputation must be strong, so that the company

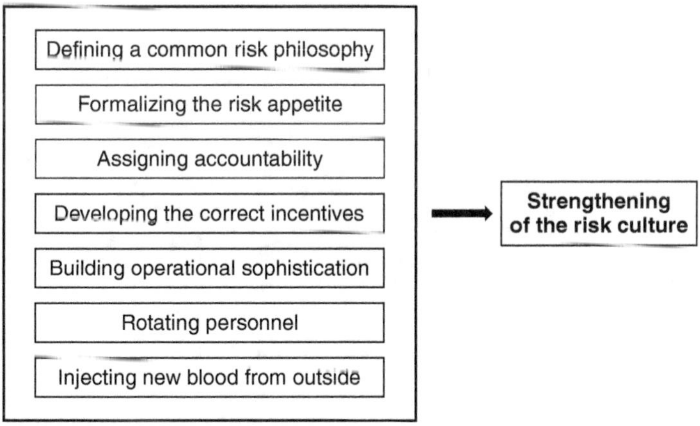

Figure 6.5. Structural and governance imperatives

is seen in the market as a preferred place to work and thus attracts the best possible talent.

Implementing the new blood imperative is the responsibility of senior human resource officials, working in concert with their business and risk partners. Open headcount or requisitions for talent, as well as the ideal candidate profile, should be identified by business managers and risk managers, who must then work with their human resource colleagues to find the right professionals in other organizations. Clearly, the more senior the talent being sought, the more senior should be the participation from human resources and the business or risk function.

In this chapter we have reviewed some essential structural changes (summarized in Figure 6.5) that a company can make to strengthen aspects of its risk culture. Some of these will be relevant to some firms; others, to other firms. To be most effective, they should be considered in conjunction with various knowledge and behavioral changes, which are the subject of our next chapter.

7

Building and Strengthening II: Knowledge and Behavior

We saw in the previous chapter that building and strengthening a culture relies in large measure on ensuring the right elements of structure and governance: the hard-and-fast rules and mechanisms that can be enacted through board resolutions, policy documents, corporate directives, human resource activities and other structural components of the corporate state. We now shift gears slightly, introducing imperatives that are primarily qualitative – specifically, knowledge and behaviors that can be instituted to help a firm build or strengthen its culture. It is worth reiterating the point from the previous chapter that these are general prescriptions that need to be believed, experienced and practiced so that they flow through the organization naturally.

Knowledge and behavior changes

In this section we focus on various qualitative elements of the improvement program, considering in detail the following:

- *Imperative 8*: establishing the right tone from the top
- *Imperative 9*: ensuring enough top notch risk expertise
- *Imperative 10*: ensuring proper business expertise
- *Imperative 11*: reinforcing the three Cs – communication, coordination, cooperation
- *Imperative 12*: demanding common sense, simplicity and clarity
- *Imperative 13*: building credibility
- *Imperative 14*: promoting mutual respect
- *Imperative 15*: developing a risk memory

Imperative 8: establishing the right tone from the top

A company or institution will ultimately succeed or fail based on the quality of its executive managers (who are there to guide and execute daily operations) and its directors (who are there to develop strategy and protect the interests of shareholders). There is, of course, a long history of corporate successes and failures, and the outcome in each case has almost always been determined by the actions and behaviors of executives and directors – in other words, how they performed in the face of adversity or opportunity and the example they set for the rest of the organization. Executives and directors who are skilled and transformational can take advantage of both positive and negative circumstances to come out on top; those who are out of their depth will fare less well, and may indeed jeopardize their firms.

In addition to professional acumen, technical skills and managerial and leadership experience, directors and executives must possess another key quality: the ability to set and reinforce the right tone on risk matters. A company with dozens, hundreds or thousands of employees requires leadership that personifies the character of the firm. Character is necessarily specific to a company's history, people and operations, and evolves over time. And although each company may have unique qualities, some universal concepts hold true for all of them: unwavering integrity and ethical behavior, respect for all stakeholders and a constant practice of doing the right thing. These key behaviors should extend to all aspects of a firm's operations, including its business and client strategies and its management of risks and controls.

Focusing specifically on risk, let us note that when executives and directors set the right tone with regard to the role and importance of risk management in advancing corporate and stakeholder goals, they are more likely to inspire similar participation from other managers and rank-and-file employees. Having leaders who are motivated to take accountability for risks and who understand the benefits risks can generate (and the damage they can do) increases awareness of the topic throughout the firm; others are likely to feel similarly accountable and may make extra efforts to become risk-aware. Such behavior can build on itself, creating a positive feedback loop that enhances and promotes risk awareness throughout the company. Note that multinational companies must take care to reflect the same tone across national boundaries, cultures and languages: it is important for a large, international organization to have a shared understanding of the message coming from the top.

The same behavior must also be exhibited by non-executive (external) directors. Although non-executive directors are sometimes seen as removed or exempt from the process because they devote only part of their time to the organization, they must be fully engaged in the process – as if they were full-time employees. So critical is the tone from the top that it emerges as *primus inter pares* of all the imperatives we consider.

Let us consider the example of a multinational corporation with industrial operations and sales in various countries. To implement this vital imperative, its executive and non-executive directors, along with the CEO, COO, CFO,

CRO and other members of the executive management team, must communicate through their daily actions the importance of risk in the operations of the company – regardless of the form of the risk, or the country in which it applies. They can do so through various mechanisms, including:

- Discussing the risk appetite, risk strategy and key exposures at every board meeting and executive meeting, releasing summary comments and notes to the company at large
- Leading the relevant internal risk committees in discussing new policies, deals, products, markets, clients and other elements of the risk profile
- Meeting with rating agencies, creditors and regulators regularly to review the key risk issues affecting the firm, again communicating the results to the company's population at large
- Discussing risk issues during internal and external quarterly earnings reports
- Enforcing disciplinary actions against those who chose to ignore risk policies or limits

The purpose of these practices is to demonstrate to employees that directors and executives are engaged substantively in risk topics, not just for show, and that they care about and understand the impact of risk on corporate operations.

Consider the flip side. Some years ago a colleague and I asked, "if the board and CEO do not take the process seriously, why should the CFO, head of risk management, accountants, or risk-takers?"[1] Indeed, they should not, and will not. If these leadership figures do not pay proper attention to risk and control, if they do not take the issue seriously and foreground it at every turn, then there is simply no incentive for others in the company to do so. Management defines the character of the company, and if the character is deemed to be risk-ignorant or risk-insensitive, then that same behavior will be manifested by every other employee, regardless of seniority or responsibility. That will deal a critical blow to the establishment of a strong risk culture.

Not surprisingly, implementation of this imperative falls to both directors and executives; they are solely responsible for ensuring that they practice and exhibit the right behaviors with regard to risk. If they are successful, other managers will follow their lead.

Imperative 9: ensuring enough top-notch risk expertise

A company that is in business to take risks cannot hope to have a strong risk culture if it does not have the best possible risk expertise. Indeed, a firm would be foolish to take risks when it does not have experts on hand to manage them, as it will find itself navigating treacherous waters. Risk expertise needs to be embedded in different parts of the firm, including with directors, executive managers, business leaders, risk managers and other control professionals.

Directors must have a good grounding in the essential components of risk, risk governance, the philosophy and appetite dimensions we discussed in the previous chapter, and the current state of key risk exposures. In short, directors must be armed with enough background to question and challenge executives and risk managers as needed. Unfortunately, there has been a general belief (borne out by survey results) that board directors too often have insufficient grounding in risk and risk management issues. While many may be conversant with business essentials, they may be less comfortable with risk issues, particularly those involving a degree of technicality. But some (if not most) board members must have a good grasp of the topic if they are to guide the company in a prudent manner. As we noted above, the creation of a proper risk culture begins with the correct tone at the top. If directors can display a sound understanding of risk issues and can both challenge and defend the risk philosophy and risk appetite in a meaningful way, they will more easily transmit the same respect for risk down through the executive and management ranks of the firm. This is not to say that directors must know every technical detail of how different risks are calculated, what models are being used and why, and how risks are transferred, hedged or otherwise mitigated. These are all granular risk issues, and gaining a reasonable understanding of them would certainly not be a productive use of time and energy by directors charged with leading the company strategically. However, a good understanding of the kinds of risks being run, how they generate revenues, what level of capital and financial resources are available in support of risk-taking and how the risk appetite is constructed and monitored must be seen as minimum requirements.

Executive managers must also have good knowledge of the essentials of risk, the philosophy and appetite, and the impact of risk on the business model and revenue streams. These professionals, who must of course deal with a whole host of additional issues, again need not be consummate technical experts; they can leave the most technically detailed topics to their business and risk leaders. But they should have enough grounding in the key concepts to make reasoned decisions regarding the strategic direction of the firm's risk activities and to speak knowledgeably about the issues to shareholders, bank lenders, rating agencies, regulators and other bodies.

Business managers running individual units that generate risk must have a much greater degree of risk expertise. In many firms these are the very professionals responsible for creating revenues that depend on accepting some level of risk. It would be unacceptable if a company were staffed by revenue generators who lacked rigorous knowledge of the risks they were creating through their business activities. Accordingly, some level of technical expertise that includes specific knowledge of the risks generated by the manager's own business line and a good grasp of risk appetite, portfolio risks and capital allocation must be seen as a minimum prerequisite. And while this level of expertise must be evident in business managers, it should ideally go into lower managerial levels as well; where the expertise does not go deeply enough, a company should ensure that proper risk training is available. In fact, in order to gain this expert knowledge it is advisable for business professionals to spend some time in the firm's risk management function as part of a rotation scheme (as noted in the previous chapter).

Needless to say, the most expert of a firm's risk experts will come from the independent risk management function, however it may be organized or constituted. This group should be the main repository of technical risk expertise, and must be staffed with professionals who are knowledgeable regarding all aspects of the risk process. The minimum technical expertise includes:

- Understanding of the essentials of risk governance (structure, authorities, policies, appetite, philosophy)
- Detailed knowledge of the different risk classes to which the company is regularly exposed (e.g., credit, market, operational, hazard, business, investment, liquidity)
- Solid grounding in portfolio risk management (as a complement to the growing use of enterprise risk management)
- Technical background in stress testing and scenario analysis
- Fundamental knowledge of capital allocation

Some of these topics require significant quantitative knowledge, and the staff may need to be PhDs from some quantitative discipline. In certain industries (particularly financial services), risk professionals must also have a strong grasp of the regulatory risk dynamics that can affect the firm, its risk processes and its exposures. Indeed, this requirement should not be underestimated in an environment where regulatory breadth and depth appear to be expanding. A further point regarding the depth of talent and expertise in the risk management organization is worth observing: if a firm invests wisely in securing the best possible risk talent it will have professionals who are deemed "worthy" of working with, and challenging, the business leaders: the two groups will be considered equals, which will go a long way toward reinforcing the partnership approach that is essential to a strong culture.

Internal audit must also have some minimum level of expertise regarding risk and control matters. These professionals have to be able to judge the efficacy of internal controls, including those forming part of the risk process and those extending into allied fields such as accounting and financial control, and they must therefore be sufficiently conversant with the main concepts and issues to know what to look for, what questions to ask and what issues to probe. If auditors do not have enough knowledge of this discipline, they will not be in a position to judge the efficacy of the risk management function and the internal control process, and may therefore miss opportunities to suggest improvements or avoid problems. Indeed, the importance of internal audit in an era of frequent, and sometimes large, internal fraud and control breakdowns also suggests that this team must be properly grounded in technical matters.

Consider, for instance, a global investment bank that is active in both advisory business and trading, across a range of products and asset classes. To be truly effective, risk managers must have a strong technical grip on the risks arising from underwritten capital markets offerings; the risks coming from directional, volatility and correlation-based traded products; the bank's liquidity profile and its leverage; how stress scenarios might cause the firm's risk profile to change; emergency actions that can be taken to deal with illiquidity, funding concerns and de-leveraging; the nature of the client base and potential legal issues affecting such clients; settlement and collateral procedures and the operational risks that may arise; the nature of the risk models being used to value risks and determine portfolio construction; the level of capital allocated to individual business; and so on. Business leaders, auditors and financial controllers must also be aware of relevant subsets of these topics.

While many within a firm may have the right risk-related expertise, some will not. To ensure that the correct base level of knowledge exists, a firm can sponsor formal training efforts, internal workshops, self-study and mentoring. Technical risk expertise can also be disseminated through regular internal forums sponsored by the business or risk functions. Working with their human resource partners, managers should establish minimum goals to ensure that such training opportunities are made available and completed successfully.

As a final point it is important to remember that in a strong risk culture, risk talent must be available in numbers sufficient to make a difference. Indeed, in a company of any reasonable scale, implementing the risk appetite at a granular level, creating risk models, keeping up with new business, responding to internal and external needs for risk information and commentary, avoiding or managing crises and so forth requires dozens, if not hundreds, of risk professionals. It is easy, in an era when cost control, margin growth and efficiency are the order of the day, to sacrifice proper resourcing – particularly in control areas, such as risk management, which are often seen as part of corporate overhead rather than corporate value. A strong risk culture demands strong, and sufficient, risk knowledge and risk resources. Table 7.1 summarizes some of the elements of risk expertise that a firm should have in order to boost its risk awareness.

Implementing this imperative is a joint responsibility. First, the head of risk and the senior-most executives of the company must support the notion that a certain level of risk expertise is desirable and should be budgeted for. Second,

Table 7.1 Summary of risk expertise by party

Party	Expertise
Directors	• Fundamental knowledge of risk governance, philosophy and appetite • Knowledge of key risk exposures
Executives	• Fundamental knowledge of risk governance, philosophy and appetite • Knowledge of key risk exposures • Awareness of how risks affect revenues • General knowledge of capital allocation and portfolio risks
Business managers	• Fundamental knowledge of risk governance, philosophy and appetite • Specific knowledge of risk exposures affecting relevant business line • General knowledge of capital allocation and portfolio risks
Risk managers	• Detailed knowledge of risk governance, philosophy and appetite • Specific knowledge of risk exposures by business line and of portfolio risks • Technical knowledge about stress tests and scenario analysis • Fundamental knowledge of regulatory risk issues and capital allocation
Other control professionals	• Fundamental knowledge of risk governance, philosophy and appetite, and capital allocation process • Knowledge of key risk exposures • Awareness of how risks affect revenues • Detailed knowledge of the internal risk control process and system

the head of risk and his or her risk managers should undertake a benchmarking exercise (which can be designed by senior risk and human resource professionals) to ensure their own staff are sufficiently qualified. They should then work with business colleagues on the same benchmarking task. Finally, for those individuals who are judged to be weak on risk skills, the head of risk and head of human resources should design and implement a risk training program that caters to specific functions within the firm, regardless of seniority. Naturally, this entire process must be ongoing.

Imperative 10: ensuring proper business expertise

A corollary to the point immediately above is that a firm seeking to build or strengthen its risk culture must employ professionals with a deep understanding of its business, its clients and the environment in which it operates. This again applies equally to directors, executives and line and control managers. The required depth of knowledge and expertise will obviously vary by role, but certain minimum standards must apply to all.

Let us again begin with directors. It is clear that these senior representatives of the shareholders must have a strong awareness of how a company's business lines generate revenues with the specific risks taken or created.[2] Directors should know the business strategy, its evolution, its sensitivity to different market environments and the role of clients in building market share and creating revenues.

Executive managers and senior business managers must, of course, have detailed operational knowledge of the technical elements of the businesses they run. Although we generalize somewhat to take account of the broadest range of industries, it seems logical that the management team of a company must be fully aware of:

- Businesses, products, deals, clients and competitors
- Business strategies and their sensitivity to changing market and client conditions
- Market environment – not just what is happening with a client or an industry, but what is happening in the financial markets at large
- Communication, leadership and management skills

Consider the example of an energy trading and distribution firm. In this case the business leaders – at both the executive and management levels – must have a good grasp on the range of energy products that the company deals in (e.g., electricity, petroleum and its by-products, natural gas, crack spreads, spark spreads); how these commodities and related products are priced in the market (e.g., supply, demand, transportation and distribution costs, insurance, disruptions, sovereign events); what major competitors are doing and how this may affect the revenue forecast; what end-use clients are seeking, both now and over a defined future horizon; how the revenue picture would change in the face of market supply disruptions, transmission problems, adverse weather conditions; how the state of the global economy may affect energy consumption; how alternative energy sources can be used to supplement the current energy portfolio and so forth. Obviously, the more expert the company's leaders are on these, and many related, issues, the stronger will be the competitive position and corporate culture.

We then come to risk managers and other control professionals. Too often their focus is on their own technical competencies rather than on the aspects of the business that create risks. This means they are operating in a partial vacuum, to no one's particular benefit. What separates risk managers from risk controllers, for instance, is a strong appreciation of how business works and how it can be made to work for the benefit of the firm and clients, without unduly exposing shareholders to unwise decisions. This ability comes only from sufficiently deep knowledge of the company's revenue-generating business lines. Thus, a risk manager who has enough knowledge of a product, client or market situation may be able to propose certain risk-mitigating solutions that allow good but risky business to be transacted safely. Absent this business knowledge, the easy default answer for a risk manager considering a new risky business proposal is "no." This may be a suboptimal response. To continue with our example above, risk managers (and other internal control professionals) working at the energy trading company should have a strong grounding in the essential revenue and P&L drivers of the business, how these can be affected by myriad macro- and microeconomic issues (as well as risk variables), how sensitive clients are to particular transactions or deals, whether any regulatory measures can affect business and so forth.

In relation to this point and the one immediately above (given their logical connections), it is worth emphasizing that a strong risk culture is built on a foundation of business management that is sufficiently expert in risk matters, risk and control management that is comfortable with business issues and details, and leadership that is comfortable with these matters as well as general issues related to management and communication. Not only does all of this lead to better decision-making in the long run; it also promotes a greater understanding between the risk and business functions (and can pave the way for future personnel rotations, as discussed in the previous chapter).

As with imperative 9, implementing this imperative is a joint responsibility. First, the senior executives of the company must support the notion that a certain level of business expertise is desirable and should be budgeted for. Second, the head of risk, the head of each control area and the head of each business line should use a benchmarking exercise to ascertain whether all staff members are sufficiently knowledgeable about the essentials of the company's business. (This test should be created by designated business experts and human resource professionals.) Finally, for those employees who are judged to be weak on business skills, the head of each business, working with the head of human resources, should design and implement a business training program. Again, this implementation process should be ongoing.

Imperative 11: reinforcing the three Cs – communication, coordination, cooperation

The next behavioral component that can positively influence risk culture centers on what we shall term the "three Cs": communication, coordination and cooperation. While each of these concepts is distinct, they have a common thread: human interaction. A consideration of human interaction is critical in any discussion of behavioral actions; indeed, there is little that is more important, and potentially more effective, than a robust regimen of communications, coordination and cooperation. This transparent partnership approach to doing business and managing risk can remove myriad hurdles and reduce the chance of problems or conflicts. Let us consider the three elements in more detail.

The first C, communication, is an essential ingredient in any corporate culture. Communication allows individuals to share information through formal or informal channels, thus arming them with facts needed for informed decision-making. Problems, misunderstandings, delays and general inefficiencies can be avoided when communication is regular and successful. As we might expect, there are different models of effective communication, and a detailed discussion is beyond the scope of this book. It is relevant, however, to note that from a risk perspective a multi-spoke approach can ensure proper linkages between all interested parties. Thus, risk managers should have multiple two-way channels that include business managers, executives, directors, regulators, financial controllers, auditors, compliance professionals and risk committees. If the communication links between these groups are strong, information will pass clearly and efficiently and concerns and decisions will be conveyed more accurately and rapidly.

A communications web comprises formal and informal channels. Formally, communication can occur through set meetings, committees, updates and presentations that require the attendance and participation of professionals from multiple areas. Since these are designed as standing meetings that occur at specific times, they can be used to facilitate the regular transfer of information – daily, weekly, monthly or quarterly. However, informal channels are just as important – perhaps even more so. These channels are often based on one-to-one relationships between business and risk professionals, and take care of the transfer of updates and awareness away from more formal settings. Informal meetings are often used to convey sensitive or confidential information that is necessary for management purposes, but not always relevant or available to a broader group. For instance, a global bank might manage formal communications via daily market and credit risk updates, bi-weekly risk committee meetings to review specific transactions, weekly portfolio risk committee meetings to consider the current construction of entire portfolios, monthly meetings to discuss new policy changes and quarterly meetings to consider the state of the risk appetite and business outlook. Of course, each of the bank's meetings might combine physical presence at the head office with tele-conferencing or video-conferencing that includes colleagues from offshore or subsidiary locations. But this is just the formal side of the equation: these scheduled meetings might be supplemented by dozens or hundreds of daily informal communications that take place via trading floor chats or phone calls and other electronic media. While this might sound like a lot of communication, it is critical to remember that these discussions form the backbone of effective business and risk management.

Of course, technology has been a great facilitator and enabler of communications. E-mail, text messaging, corporate intranets, multimedia content, remote conferencing and mobile devices are all part of the 21st century communications paradigm, and make it very difficult to argue against timely communication. In fact, the opposite may be true: such ubiquitous technology makes it almost too easy to share information, sometimes indiscriminately, and can result in some managers, particularly at the executive and board levels, being buried in information overload. Judgment must therefore be part of the discipline of communications: professionals must know what to communicate and when, and should avoid the buckshot approach of just spraying the horizon with all manner of information in hopes of hitting some (uncertain) target. The final note to make on this topic relates to the multinational footprint that many companies and organizations now enjoy. While this can pave the way for the broadest scope of business, it also requires extra effort in dealing with cross-border language and cultural issues. This is a separate, and sometimes complex, topic that is beyond our scope, but it is worth noting that the effective risk culture necessarily builds on an effective web of transnational communications.

Figure 7.1 summarizes this multi-spoke approach to risk management; similar multi-spoke models should exist for each division.

The next C is coordination. Although it might again seem self-evident that this form of corporate behavior is required to advance the interests of the firm, it is not a given for every firm: some perform this task very well, while others do not – to their detriment. A dedicated, institutionalized regimen of coordinating information dissemination, transactional consideration, client coverage, regulatory contact and other key elements of tactical operations can go a long way toward building the sense of partnership that is essential to a strong culture. Not only does coordination bring all parties into the know; it

Figure 7.1 Risk management communication channels

also promotes internally and externally the image of organization and control, with seamless understanding of all the main issues. This can build confidence and a sense of professionalism and respect.

A few practical examples can make the point obvious: a business leader coordinating with the relevant risk manager on a deal that might come to fruition in the future; several business managers coordinating their client calls through a centralized manager or process so that there is no confusion, duplication or misinformation; executives coordinating with business and risk leaders regarding important regulatory information in advance of a regulatory review in order to ensure consistency of message and views. It is easy to imagine how, absent this kind of coordination, some degree of internal chaos might ensue, including some of the surprises that can undermine confidence in risk management and business management.

The final C is, again, an obvious one: cooperation. Cooperation implies a collegial partnership rather than an adversarial relationship, and helps ensure proper understanding and communication between business and risk professionals. A spirit of cooperation is possible when different parties have a shared vision of the firm's ultimate goals. For instance, business and risk professionals at an insurance company may come to realize that by cooperating they can serve the interests of clients and maximize shareholder value while adhering to a stated risk philosophy and operating in a properly controlled environment. In practice this might mean making sure that new product requests are handled on a timely basis by risk professionals, who will have been given sufficient lead time by their business colleagues; that business professionals are willing and able to meet their risk colleagues' requests for additional data to evaluate an insurance proposal; that alternate risk-mitigating solutions are discussed constructively between business and risk professionals so as to deliver an appropriate client solution within prudent risk management parameters; and so forth.

To be sure, cooperation does not mean caving in to another party's wishes or somehow compromising on integrity. In fact, separation of powers and a healthy tension between business and risk or control professionals are essential. But operating in a collegial and coordinated fashion is at once efficient and productive, and serves as another thread in the fabric of the risk culture.

Implementing the three Cs is a complex undertaking because it is ultimately dependent on the interpersonal skills of individual employees. Business, risk and other control managers must be charged with managing the process: they should sponsor regular meetings and forums to disseminate key information, promote discussion and debate, and generally open up formal lines of communication. They should also encourage informal communication within, and between, different groups. In addition, these managers should conduct a 360-degree evaluation of the communication and cooperation shown by their own employees, and they should make it clear that a portion of every employee's annual review will focus on the effectiveness displayed in these areas. Professionals who need assistance with communications skills should have the opportunity of building these through a formal human resource-sponsored program.

Imperative 12: demanding common sense, simplicity and clarity

The next point to consider relates to common sense, simplicity and clarity in actions taken by a company's leaders, regardless of function or seniority. A risk-taking institution in general, and a risk function specifically, operates best when common sense is part of the construct. Firms in both financial and non-financial industries often operate with complex organizational structures, including market and client access and regulatory oversight that involve many parties. Given this complexity, there can be a tendency to create an equally complex map of internal interfaces and responsibilities that sacrifices common sense, clarity and simplicity. In fact, some firms may believe that by creating multiple layers of complexity they are somehow enhancing internal control and security – although the opposite might be the case. A firm should never choose to hide behind organizational or structural shields or barriers to preserve a status quo that is not infused with common sense.

To overcome this issue and move in the direction of strengthening the risk culture, managers should focus on two objectives: demanding common sense of team members in all aspects of risk management (including organization, governance, process, policy, transaction analysis, portfolio management and resource management) and promoting organizational and governance clarity and simplicity wherever possible, taking bold steps to remove excessive bureaucracy and rules. In aiming at these objectives, the emphasis should be on:

- Substance rather than form
- Added value rather than bureaucratic "make work"
- Simplicity rather than complexity
- Transparency rather than opacity

In the end, this imperative can lead to faster reaction and response time and lower costs, a more secure operating environment and a clearer understanding of what is happening in the company – all of which can boost the risk culture. Consider a simple example of a large multinational company that operates in many countries and carries a host of risks (operating, commodity, financial, operational) which are distributed throughout various business divisions. To keep things clear and simple, the firm's management can make sure that the decision-making process regarding risk is flat (e.g., delegated authorities), a single risk policy covering each risk type is devolved to every risk-taking center, uniform metrics are used throughout the organization and only a single committee considers large risk transactions. Simplicity of this kind – in an organization that has thousands of employees and dozens of offshore locations – can greatly enhance the understanding and management of risks.

Implementing the common sense, clarity and simplicity directive is, like implementation of the three Cs, somewhat complex, because it depends on the behaviors of each individual working in the firm. That said, executive management can set the tone by demanding that their senior managers approach business and risk management in a non-bureaucratic and transparent style, and by holding them to account during the management performance review process. Senior managers must take charge of the process by demanding the same of their managers, and so on. Furthermore, executive managers should do everything in their collective power to push for the flattest possible organization in the governance structure so that multiple layers of complexity and bureaucracy are reduced, avoided or eliminated.

Imperative 13: building credibility

We have discussed at various points the desirability of creating a partnership approach to the management of risks so that decisions, reactions and behaviors are automatic rather than forced, and employees view each other as having the same goals rather than divergent ones. This is a constructive approach to dealing with daily business matters, and is almost certain to yield better results than a confrontational approach. After all, confrontation can lead to conflict and a deterioration in the fundamental behaviors that a company needs in order to have a strong risk culture (e.g., communication, accountability, exchange of information, ethical behavior).

Not surprisingly, a partnership approach built on credibility is not always easy to achieve. Consider that for risk managers to be regarded as valued partners in helping the firm achieve its financial goals, they must be viewed, in the first instance, as being credible with regard to experience, actions and decisions. In practice, this can be accomplished only by demonstrating, and using, certain skills and behaviors:

- Undoubted technical expertise
- Sound business knowledge
- Willingness to proffer constructive views and opinions
- Creativity in seeking solutions
- Willingness to make tough decisions and assume responsibility
- Clarity in communications
- Efficiency and responsiveness in decision-making
- Consistency in decision-making
- Willingness to allow more risk to be taken when it makes sense to do so

When risk professionals follow this approach to business matters they accomplish several goals: they show themselves to be willing partners and consultants rather than traffic cops (while still maintaining independence and prudent judgment), and they make it clear that they recognize the broader corporate goals that must be achieved: value maximization while remaining within the defined risk philosophy and risk appetite set by the directors on behalf of the shareholders. The credibility they gain in this process will then lead to a self-reinforcing cycle: risk professionals will be sought out by business colleagues for prudent advice, this advice will be proffered and followed, the desired results will be achieved – and so on, in a repetitive cycle.

The same must apply to business leaders. They must be equally willing and able to build credibility with their risk partners so that risk managers take them seriously with regard to both business matters and risk matters. Again, this will come from practicing certain behaviors, some of which are simply an inverse of what we have described immediately above:

- Undoubted technical expertise
- Sound risk management knowledge, always on display as the front-line defense
- Willingness to work toward a restructured risk management solution
- Willingness to walk away from a risky deal when it is not the right thing for the firm or the client
- Willingness to provide risk partners with lead time to think about a potential risk exposure
- Consistency in decision-making

These are all behaviors which will let risk managers know that their business partners are serious about risk management.

Implementing the credibility imperative is the work of each and every individual in a firm. No single implementation plan can be created and pushed down from the top, although progress in terms of the behaviors above can be charted during the annual review process and through 360-degree evaluations.

Imperative 14: promoting mutual respect

Another key to creating the business/risk partnership is to ensure that there is mutual respect between the two groups. Like credibility, respect cannot be forced into being; it must develop gradually, over time, as the two parties learn to work together in a professional, constructive and collegial fashion, and as they demonstrate sensitivity to one another's viewpoints and positions. In the end, if business and risk professionals have mutual respect for one another, this supports the risk culture.

As we have stated, business and risk managers need to work together constructively, while retaining a healthy tension between business generation and the management of exposure. Having mutual respect and striving for goals that benefit the company as a whole does not mean sacrificing principles and integrity, or abandoning the core mission for which each set of professionals is responsible. Mutual respect develops as employees act in a mature and professional manner, continuously try to build a better understanding of other fields, emerge as solution seekers rather than naysayers and communicate clearly and concisely. Fundamentally, both groups must be respectful of the company's overarching business strategy, risk philosophy and profit and risk targets, and must adhere to these imperatives at all times.

Mutual respect between parties can emerge only over a period of time, which may mean several years. We cannot reasonably expect professionals to have an instant respect for others simply because such behavior is desirable. This cannot be forced. Thus, for example, if the head of a business line and the head of the corresponding risk management function work together for a period of months or years, gain experience of each other's capabilities, cooperate and maintain an open line of communication for both support and critique, then a feeling of mutual respect will likely develop. This respect will strengthen the operating environment around them. Naturally, if respect is heartfelt and mutual, it will carry forward when one or both move into new roles. We can well imagine how if this behavior is repeated by all employees, the culture will indeed be strengthened.

As with credibility, implementing the concept of mutual respect cannot be forced or demanded of professionals; it must develop over time through the actions and experiences of employees. Again, it can be reinforced through performance evaluations, but it cannot be implemented through a specific plan or on a specific timeline.

Imperative 15: developing a risk memory

A company is a living organism that evolves through changes in experience, strategy, environment and competition. The combination of these dynamic forces means that the company itself must learn, change and adapt – or else lose ground to others. This is a natural process, meant to make the company relevant at the current time. We can certainly imagine that if the GEs, Daimlers, IBMs and JP Morgans of the world had remained static rather than dynamic, had chosen to preserve the status quo rather than evolve, they would have been overtaken by others. The issue at hand is how a company learns from its experiences – what works, what does not, how things can be improved, how a new marketplace or economy will affect operations and so forth. The topic is complex and involved, and has been the subject of a great deal of academic study over the years.

To narrow the scope somewhat for our own discussion, we can look at how the same issues apply to risk matters. A company that seeks to improve its risk management capabilities must be in a position to learn from its mistakes and successes. It needs to know what forces, factors or processes helped minimize or avoid losses, which ones contributed to negative surprises, which ones improved or hampered the efficiency of risk management, which ones added to or subtracted from risk awareness, which situations or events proved untenable or unmanageable, and so on. Ignoring all of these experiences leads, of course, to repeating the sometimes painful lessons of history – again and again, potentially at a great cost to shareholders and other stakeholders.

Accordingly, those seeking to strengthen risk culture should build and use a framework that captures the institutional memory of risk. A company's leaders should create the mechanisms and forums for a periodic revisiting of historical events. Naturally, these mechanisms and forums have to be lasting, have to continue operating and contributing even when responsible professionals move into new roles, are promoted or leave to pursue other interests. The memories must remain for future professionals to reference. In practical terms, this means considering the following framework:

- Archiving very positive and very negative risk events in a database that adequately recounts the experience – background, risk factors, results, decisions, conclusions, corrective actions. The events to be included in such a database can be set at any relevant threshold (eg., a certain dollar or euro amount).
- Detailing, through internal audit reports or other post mortem documents, the results of large losses, and making these results available for review to senior business and risk leaders.
- Developing a habit of regularly including "senior statesmen" in risk committees and relevant crisis meetings so that they can share, firsthand, their own experiences of a particularly difficult risk situation.
- Requiring the board of directors to record their own thoughts on special risk situations in which they were involved. These are likely to have been significant because they involved directors in the discussion and decision-making.
- Ensuring that risk crises at other firms are discussed, in general terms, within relevant risk meetings to determine whether there are any lessons to be learned from competitors which can be put to use internally.

These are all simple steps that can be taken so that business and risk leaders do not forget what others at the firm have been through with regard to risk issues. Developing this memory is a relatively straightforward, and useful, way of strengthening culture.

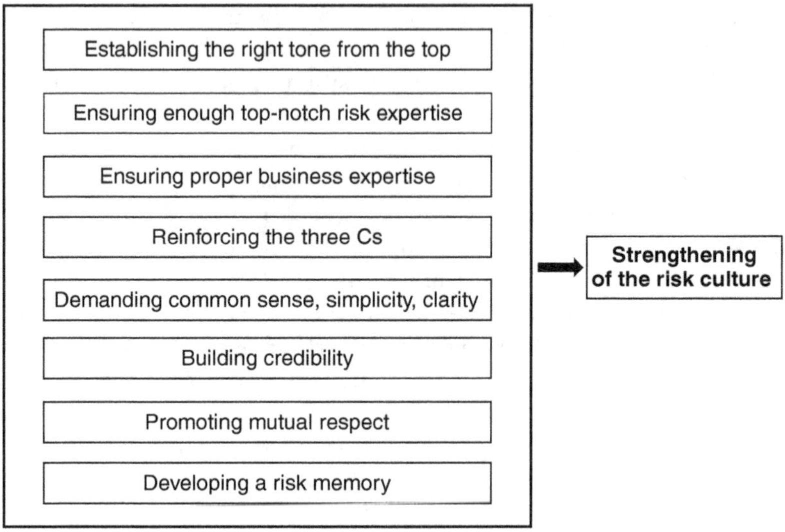

Figure 7.2 Knowledge and behavior imperatives

Implementing the risk memory imperative begins with executive management, which must initially provide the support and resources for the project. Thereafter, the chief risk officer should drive the process, using the knowledge and experience of the risk function to collect all relevant past information on the firm's risk experiences and coordinating with the technology department to create the right kind of database and platform. On an ongoing basis, the risk department should pursue two different tasks: first, continuing to contribute to the database and other forums and mechanisms any experiences which might provide useful knowledge in the future; second, engaging with business colleagues in the review of past events as applied to a current issue or problem to come up with alternative solutions. Naturally, business managers should be encouraged to contribute as much as possible to the database and to make ongoing use of information.

Ultimately, implementing the behavioral imperatives above is essential if an institution is to progress in building its risk culture. It is worth emphasizing, once again, that unlike the structural and governance changes we described in the previous chapter, the behavioral changes and are nebulous, which means they need extra attention and a leadership spotlight in order to be effective.

More broadly, in the these two chapters we have put forward a series of imperatives (summarized in Figure 7.2) which we believe can help a company build or strengthen its risk culture. Some of these are relatively straightforward to implement and follow, while others are much more difficult and time-consuming. In order to help a firm jump-start the process, we shall consider, in Chapter 9, several simple steps based on the imperatives that each of four groups of interested parties – directors, executives, business leaders and risk managers – can take. The intention behind the jump-start program is to help a company build momentum behind the entire effort. It can then proceed with an orderly implementation of the remainder of the imperatives, assigning responsibility as outlined for each of the points.

8 Gauging Progress and Success

In the previous two chapters we described some of the structural and behavioral changes a firm can implement in order to build or strengthen its risk culture. The next issue we need to consider relates to progress and success – specifically, how a firm knows it is moving in the right direction in achieving its goal of creating a risk culture that spreads throughout the organization. Accordingly, in this chapter we shall consider how a company can gauge its progress and success, focusing on time frame, short- versus medium-term actions and metrics of success. We shall also introduce a link between the imperatives of Chapters 6 and 7 and the diagnostic test from Chapter 2: as a company begins to implement the imperatives, it can retest itself via the diagnostic framework to determine its progress.

Time frame

The first point to consider in our evaluation of success relates to timing and time frame. In the corporate and financial world, where the pressure to perform and succeed is enormous, and where the patience of stakeholders is sometimes rather limited – particularly in jurisdictions that emphasize short-term share price movements – it is obviously desirable that a risk culture be implemented or enhanced quickly. Thus, after going through some diagnostic process, identifying weak points, creating a plan to bridge the gaps and implementing that plan, a company's leadership may hope that the roots of a risk culture will take hold and begin the transformational process. The company may even believe it can be transformed in a few months or quarters.

While that may be a desired goal, the fact is that the time frame is typically much, much longer: the development of a proper risk culture can take several – sometimes many – years to achieve. That might seem like a long time, but we know that building and deepening a risk culture involves changing the practices, behaviors and character of a firm – something which obviously does not happen in the span of weeks or months. It is important to remember that we are considering the creation of a risk culture, not the development of a risk process or a risk model. A process or a model represents a finite series of steps leading to a defined and measurable goal, such as the creation of a risk management decision-making framework, a set of risk policies that dictate the parameters of dealing in a risky business or a portfolio model to assess the risk and exposure of an entire portfolio of risk-sensitive business. Once these elements have been defined, they can be developed and then implemented; the end result will be clear. And the time frame will typically be rather short, certainly when considered in the context of the corporate lifespan. Thus, a process or a policy could be developed and enacted within a matter of weeks or months; a risk model, with appropriate coding and back testing, might take a few months up to a year, or perhaps two.

The same is not true for the development of a risk culture, where we are talking about changing the character of the institution to make it more risk-aware. Since corporate culture is something which develops over time, through leadership tone, management style, interactive behaviors, business strategy and other imperatives we have discussed above, it is not realistic to think that it can be changed in weeks or months, or even a few years. To be sure, a very small organization can complete the task more rapidly than a very large one, as changing the attitudes and behaviors of a few dozen or hundred employees (e.g., a hedge fund) is quicker than doing so for tens of thousands (e.g., a bank). But the process is time-consuming in either case. A nautical analogy is helpful here: implementing a risk process or model can be likened to maneuvering a speedboat – quick, flexible, with an immediate ability to alter course; building the risk culture is similar to navigating a battleship – slow, methodical, and with a course that becomes apparent over the medium term. Plenty of leeway and advance planning are required to steer the battleship in a different direction. Of course, changing direction starts with a few small steps, such as plotting a new course and then making adjustments to speed and rudder position. But the end goal, a new destination, will only be reached over a longer period.

Short-term versus medium-term actions

Although changing a risk culture required a potentially lengthy time frame, a company's leaders should not be disheartened, as the process can start quickly: a firm can parse its risk culture implementation plan into short- and medium-term increments, assigning success metrics to each phase in order to demonstrate progress and to build the momentum necessary to create the deepest, broadest and most effective risk culture.

To put this topic into context, let us gather the structural and behavioral enhancements covered in Chapters 6 and 7 and consider how these might be segregated into an action plan covering the short and medium terms. We shall extend the example in the next section by assigning to each factor a metric of success to illustrate how a company could reasonably gauge its progress.

- *Imperative 1*: defining a common risk philosophy. This step can be seen as a short-term action. While definition of the philosophy requires some thought and the philosophy must be synchronized with business strategy, it is a proactive step that can be taken in a matter of weeks. By the time it has gone through various iterations and has been considered by the board of directors, and other governance bodies, some months may have passed, but it is still a short-term activity.
- *Imperative 2*: formalizing the risk appetite. Risk appetite, like risk philosophy, can be defined and structured in a relatively short time frame of several weeks to several months. Although a proper analysis of financial resources, stress tests, leverage and liquidity constraints, and target credit ratings can be a time-consuming exercise (particularly in a large organization with many dimensions of risk), the task is easily accomplished in the short term when the correct focus is assigned.
- *Imperative 3*: assigning accountability. Accountability is part of the risk governance model, granting particular business and risk professionals and overarching committees authorities for decision-making. The design of the governance framework and the dissemination of authorities can occur relatively quickly as part of the overall risk process design. It can again happen in a matter of weeks or months, and thus qualifies as a short-term action.
- *Imperative 4*: developing the correct incentives. The creation of a proper incentive structure which motivates business and risk experts to align their professional efforts in a particular direction (one which leads to the creation of high-quality, properly risk-adjusted business) is again an activity that a company, through its directors, executive managers and human resource professionals, can design and implement in relatively short order. There is nothing particularly time-consuming about the effort and, once implemented, it can be maintained with ease.
- *Imperative 5*: building operational sophistication. Recall from Chapter 6 that building operational sophistication is a multi-part initiative that involves creating the right risk structure, organization and governance, defining the mandates for individual businesses and control functions, investing in a minimum level of technological infrastructure and building a backbone of relevant and reliable data. Not surprisingly, this effort is rather more involved, and is likely to take more time to implement, than the imperatives immediately above. While the creation of an appropriate structure and governance and the definition of operating mandates can be accomplished in a period of months, the implementation of the technology infrastructure

and the creation of meaningful data streams that can be used to guide the firm must generally be regarded as a multi-year process. Progress in these areas, particularly in support of strengthening or building the risk culture, must be synchronized accordingly; no shortcuts can be taken.

- *Imperative 6*: rotating personnel. Shifting professionals between business and control functions as a way of disseminating professional skills, technical expertise and risk knowledge can, in theory, be planned quickly within the human resource function. In practice, the execution process is rather more involved, as it relies on the identification and monitoring of particular individuals, the synchronization of compensation levels across disciplines, the management of career paths over time, the physical movement of professionals to different parts of the company or the world, and so on. Thereafter, time must be allowed to gauge the actual contributions of professionals in their new roles: even for the most senior employees, this is a process that will take at least several quarters. In light of these factors, we must view this essential initiative as medium-term.
- *Imperative 7*: injecting new blood from outside the firm. The practice of regularly bringing in new professional talent from outside the firm must be seen as ongoing, repeated year in and year out. As such we should not view this as a short-term deliverable, but as a continuous one that plays out over the medium term. In addition, it is generally true that identifying and recruiting experts from other firms takes many months, particularly for more senior executives, who may have contractual restrictions that bar them from joining another competitor until after a 3- or 6-month "gardening leave." Therefore, the new blood imperative is a medium-term step.
- *Imperative 8*: establishing the right tone from the top. Ensuring that top managers and board directors have an appreciation for risk, take the topic seriously, and lead by example when it comes to risk strategies, appetite and exposures is an essential behavioral element that is part of a continuing process within a firm. While directors and executives may display the right behaviors from the moment they join and participate in a company's strategic and tactical management, their efficacy in establishing the right tone will likely not be known for some time – until they have a proven track record of doing the right thing on risk matters and have had a demonstrable impact on the actions of lower-level managers and employees. The tone from the top directive must therefore be considered a medium-term initiative; while it may begin immediately, it takes time to become apparent.
- *Imperative 9*: ensuring enough top-notch risk expertise. We have noted the importance of having top risk talent in place throughout the organization, in all lines of defense: from directors and executives to business managers, to risk managers, to controllers and auditors. Even though the level of expertise will vary by seniority and function, it is clear that the presence of

such risk talent is fundamental to proper business and risk management and furtherance of the risk culture. From an action standpoint, this is a process that can begin immediately, by hiring or identifying professionals with the right risk expertise or by sending professionals at various levels to appropriate internal or external training or on rotations where they can deepen their skills. That said, we must view the process as one that takes months or years to achieve. That the right degree of risk expertise exists becomes evident over time, as a real program takes hold.

- *Imperative 10*: ensuring proper business expertise. The professional expertise that is essential in properly managing business segments is a combination of academic study, general job experience (in the industry, for example) and specific job experience (within the company). This kind of expertise is gained over a period of time. Whether the expertise is gained organically by nurturing professionals (on the job and in light of the specific characteristics and imperatives of the company) or recruited externally (through the new blood imperative), the main point is that this imperative is medium-term, rather than short-term, in nature.
- *Imperative 11*: reinforcing the three Cs. The three Cs of risk culture – communication, coordination and cooperation – evolve through a continuous, medium-term process built on the foundation of personal relationships and a cooperative spirit. In short, these fundamental elements of corporate culture are not short-term fixes that can be put in place and left to work their magic; they take time to develop and flow through the organization and, as noted, their success relies heavily on the dedicated efforts and interactions of individuals. It would be unrealistic to suppose that a robust regimen of communication, coordination and cooperation could be instituted in weeks or months. To be sure, enabling actions can begin immediately and will hopefully spread and build quickly, but the actual learned behaviors will take years to be fully integrated into the firm.
- *Imperative 12*: demanding common sense, simplicity and clarity. Common sense, simplicity and clarity are characteristics of an organization and its practices that can be reinforced through short-term implementation of a governance model that reduces bureaucracy, flattens the organization, assigns authorities and mandates clear reporting. However, the practical implementation of, and continuous adherence to, these mandates take time to do properly and effectively, and should be seen as part of a medium-term change in the mindset of responsible professionals. Just because something is mandated from above does not mean it will be successfully implemented or properly followed. This becomes evident only with time and experience.
- *Imperative 13*: building credibility. Credibility of professionals on both sides of the fence is an essential element of a strong risk culture and, as we might expect, develops over time as business and control professionals get to

know one another and become familiar with each other's skills, experiences and perspectives. Credibility comes from repeatedly doing the right thing, making the right decisions, treating people and processes with respect and demonstrating a high degree of professionalism and cooperation. Clearly, these elements cannot be inculcated or proven overnight: they require time to develop on their own, so we must consider this fix to have a medium-term horizon.

- *Imperative 14*: promoting mutual respect. As in the point immediately above, promoting mutual respect between all of the lines of defense that are meant to protect a firm's interests while maximizing shareholder value is a slow, time-consuming effort which cannot be rushed. A professional (regardless of responsibility) cannot demand that a colleague respect what he or she does. That respect can only be earned through positive actions, over time. This must be seen as another medium-term enhancement to the risk culture.
- *Imperative 15*: developing a risk memory. Creating the institutional memory that allows a firm to rewind through its history to examine how past crises were treated or how a risk challenge was successfully handled or overcome is, by its very nature, a medium- to long-term process. The issue is not really about creating mechanisms (e.g., databases, forums) for reviewing the lessons of history (which can be done quickly from a mechanistic standpoint) but about accumulating a wealth of past experiences which can be applied to a current or anticipated situation. Such a risk memory builds slowly, over time, and there is nothing that can be done to hasten the process.

Thus, we have segregated the key structural and governance, knowledge and behavioral steps that can help a firm build or strengthen a risk culture into short- and medium-term actions. The main point, illustrated in Figure 8.1, is that a company can actively take steps today to begin the process (indeed, all of the steps outlined above can arguably begin at once). However, the company must also be willing to exercise appropriate patience and discipline; not everything can be accomplished this quarter or even this year. In fact, discipline is particularly important, because those responsible within the firm must make sure the proper focus is maintained at all times.

Metrics of success

With some sense of the timeline for implementing imperatives which can boost a firm's risk culture, we shall now consider how a company can measure the success of its implementation process. To do so we identify metrics which a company can use to gauge progress, and then synchronize those metrics to provide a sense of success (or failure).

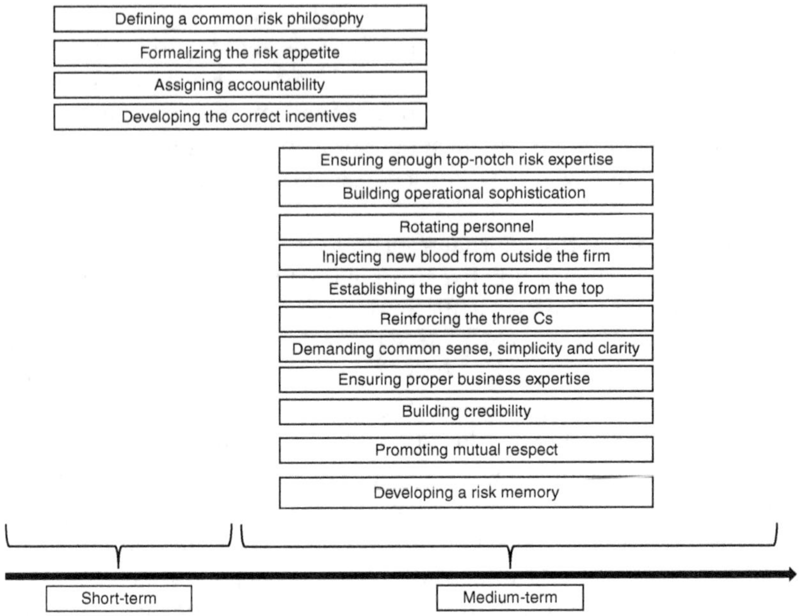

Figure 8.1 Timeline of action steps

We noted earlier in the book that one of the most challenging aspects of the topic of risk culture is that it can be nebulous, qualitative and subjective in its character. This necessarily means that measuring success, both in the aggregate and for individual imperatives, is challenging. Nevertheless, some attempt, however imperfect, must be made. Let us therefore consider various sample metrics, along with their associated ease of measurement (i.e., simple, medium, difficult or, in some cases, not objectively measurable).

- *Imperative 1*: defining a common risk philosophy. In terms of metrics, this is one of the easiest imperatives for a firm (and its stakeholders) to gauge. The metric is simply the completion of a statement that describes the firm's risk philosophy (and which has been promulgated through internal and external channels so that it is clear to everyone). The process and the end result need not be complex. Ease of measurement: simple.
- *Imperative 2*: formalizing the risk appetite. Like definition of the philosophy, formalization of the risk appetite is easy to gauge. After the intensive process of determining the appropriate risk appetite (in line with total risk capacity, credit ratings, leverage, liquidity and the other variables commonly used to shape the appetite) the result is easily evidenced: a declaration of the

amount the firm is willing to put at risk, in total and in granular or operative form. Ease of measurement: simple.

- *Imperative 3*: assigning accountability. In most companies, accountability (or responsibility) for business-related tasks as well as risk-related duties is generally defined formally. Initial definition can be via board-approved governance and organizational structures which assign duties (accountabilities) to specific professional positions. The ongoing performance of the individuals in these professional positions is typically assessed through periodic (quarterly, semi-annual, annual) performance reviews, which indicate whether an individual is adhering to those duties and powers for which he or she is accountable. In both cases the process lends itself to easy measurement. Ease of measurement: simple.
- *Imperative 4*: developing the correct incentives. As we have seen, a comprehensive program to provide the correct financial incentives for those taking or creating risk and those managing risk is essential to proper behavior and proper risk culture. Fortunately, a compensation policy, typically created by human resource professionals, in conjunction with executive management, and approved by the board of directors, is easy to create and verify. The comprehensive policy will contain details of how, and in what form, individuals will be compensated, with proper ties between revenues and risks. While the specifics of the policy will remain an internal matter (for employees at relevant levels), its actual existence is easy to track and verify. Ease of measurement: simple.
- *Imperative 5*: building operational sophistication. The operational sophistication imperative brings us into slightly more challenging territory. To be sure, some parts of this initiative are reasonably easy to gauge. For instance, development of the proper structure, organization and governance can be evidenced through board directives that approve them. Their existence can easily be confirmed (at least internally). Individual mandates which indicate what businesses and risks a given business unit can deal in and what delegated authorities risk managers enjoy can also be measured easily: they either exist or they do not. More complex are those elements which involve technology and data. As we have seen, some minimum infrastructural standards are vital in an era when business is based on complex, cross-border dealings; a firm cannot operate efficiently and securely without a robust technology platform that automates many aspects of its business, or without data which accurately tracks revenues, risks, capital usage and other dimensions of operational and financial control. The main question is whether the technology and data are up to the task and are effective in reinforcing the proper risk culture. Potential metrics that can be considered include the amount of investment in technology; the efficiency and accuracy of

financial reporting, risk reporting and operational processing; the speed at which monthly financial closeouts and reconciliations occur; and the number of operational errors. The technology- and data-related metrics can be customized to the specific business model of the firm, and can be tracked and reviewed by management and auditors regularly. While not simple, the process is quantifiable. Ease of measurement: simple to medium.

- *Imperative 6*: rotating personnel. The rotation of professionals between business and control functions, and within different segments of the control function, is guided, in the first instance, by a specific policy created by human resources which institutionalizes the process. The measurement of this task is quite easily done: either the policy exists or it does not. Once the process is in place (and it should be an institutional, rather than periodic, ad hoc, process), tracking rotations – a good proxy for measuring this imperative – is again relatively straightforward: a database which indicates movement in and out of particular departments can keep the task organized and reveal the amount of cross-departmental contact. Of course, one of the key reasons for personnel rotation is to ensure adequate sharing of expertise and a better appreciation for the viewpoints of other groups. These, unfortunately, cannot be readily measured or tracked; they must simply be allowed to take hold and flourish over time. The rotation process is merely a way to facilitate the goal of knowledge and behavior dissemination. Ease of measurement, rotation: simple; subsequent strengthening: not objectively measurable.
- *Imperative 7*: injecting new blood from outside the firm. Bringing in new professionals from outside the firm carries the idea of incorporating new perspectives, skills and knowledge which can benefit a company and its culture. Measurement of this imperative is straightforward: the human resource function can manage a database which identifies the number of professionals entering into business or control functions from outside the firm over the quarter or year. However, and in line with the point immediately above, the main reason for hiring external talent is to strengthen the fabric of the risk culture by bringing in a fresh set of eyes and different, but complementary, experiences. This strengthening, unfortunately, cannot be measured quickly or objectively – it must simply develop over time. Ease of measurement, external recruitment: simple; subsequent strengthening: not objectively measurable.
- *Imperative 8*: establishing the right tone from the top. As we move now to consider some of the knowledge and behavior imperatives, it is clear that gauging the tone from the top is a subjective exercise – one that does not lend itself to clear and concise metrics. To be sure, it is possible to consider how often directors and executives speak about risk management matters, or attend risk committees or lead discussion and debate on risk

philosophy and risk appetite. A count can be tallied, and we might argue that a company could insist that its directors and executives be present at a minimum number of sessions or that they co-author a certain number of strategic risk documents every year. That is all well and good and very easy to measure. However, it misses the real point of the imperative, which revolves around natural, and not forced, behavior regarding the right tone. The tone regarding risk matters (and other dimensions of control) is something which appears (or does not appear) organically, over time, and cannot really be measured objectively. Ease of measurement: attendance at meetings, public declarations and communiqués on risk matters: simple; setting the right behaviors: not objectively measurable.

- *Imperative 9*: ensuring enough top-notch risk expertise. The adequacy of the risk expertise that exists within a firm is measurable, at least in a general sense. Gauging how many risk experts are working in each of the main lines of defense is impractical in a company with tens of thousands of employees, but gauging the expertise that exists within the board, the executive team and the top management of business lines, risk management and control functions is a much more practical task: in this case we might be referring to several hundred or several thousand professionals, at most. Their risk skills can be gauged in several ways: human resource professionals can screen backgrounds, looking for specific job experience that relates to risk; the performance of individuals in a risk-related setting (e.g., risk committees) can be verified by superiors or colleagues through a 360-degree assessment; and risk-related tests can be administered to executives to examine their specific knowledge of risk fundamentals and advanced concepts, as relevant. Naturally, if executives in key positions are found to be lacking in some area, they can go through additional training or rotations to fill out their experience, as noted in the last chapter. Ease of measurement: simple.
- *Imperative 10*: ensuring proper business expertise. Determining the depth of business expertise in the ranks of directors, executives, business leaders and risk managers follows along the same lines noted immediately above. The same concepts that apply to risk expertise are readily applicable to business expertise, and the mechanisms used to measure depth of knowledge can be replicated for business skills. Thus, all identified managerial professionals should be evaluated with regard to their knowledge of the company's specific business, with additional exposure, rotation or training implemented as needed. Ease of measurement: simple.
- *Imperative 11*: reinforcing the three Cs. Our three Cs – communication, coordination and cooperation – act as the glue between business and control professionals, allowing them to work in a transparent and synchronized manner on issues, opportunities or problems of mutual interest. The formal communication that occurs between different parties, such as meetings,

committees, tele-conference calls and e-mail exchanges, can of course be measured. However, this is a red herring, as the success of communication depends not on quantity, but on quality. This aspect, which is what helps strengthen the culture, cannot be gauged in terms of any specific success metrics; neither, for that matter, can coordination and cooperation. In fact, the evidence of progress in all three Cs comes over time, in a more subtle form (e.g., no surprises, efficient processing, clear decisions based on common information). Ease of measurement: not objectively measurable.

- *Imperative 12*: demanding common sense, simplicity and clarity. Objectively measuring common sense, simplicity and clarity in employees in a meaningful way is, again, very difficult (if not impossible). These are characteristics whose presence creates an efficient and well-synchronized risk process in which risk decisions are made clearly, consistently and rapidly, without an excess of unnecessary work or time. The successful result of these desired behaviors is a strong and efficient approach to risk which is measurable (e.g., speed of decision-making, accuracy of risk decisions); however, the actual measurement of common sense, or simplicity, or clarity is not. Ease of measurement: not objectively measurable.
- *Imperative 13*: building credibility. Credibility is another important aspect of the business/risk relationship and is, unfortunately, difficult to measure objectively through standard metrics. To be sure, the level of credibility displayed by risk professionals to their business peers, and vice versa, can be evidenced informally and anecdotally (especially over an extended period) by examining interpersonal relationships, considering the tone of dialog, verifying adherence to constructive engagements and performing a 360-degree evaluation. These, however, cannot be considered clear, objective metrics; in all cases they lend themselves to a degree of subjectivity and opinion, suggesting that it is difficult to know just how successfully credibility has penetrated the organization. Ease of measurement: not objectively measureable.
- *Imperative 14*: promoting mutual respect. Mutual respect, like credibility, is earned over time on the basis of professionalism, skills, communication and partnership mentality. Not surprisingly, this makes this imperative, too, somewhat difficult to gauge objectively – so the same anecdotal and subjective tools noted immediately above must be brought to bear. Ease of measurement: not objectively measureable.
- *Imperative 15*: developing a risk memory. Memory of past success and failures and its application to the current state of affairs can actually be measured with some degree of objectivity. Once the database and other vehicles for storing and communicating a firm's lessons from history have been created (which is quite measurable), the practice of reviewing these events on a periodic or ad hoc basis can easily be measured: a firm simply needs to have a tracking mechanism in

place to show how often past material is reviewed and discussed – and, hopefully, used to good effect. Ease of measurement: simple.

As we can see from this brief overview of success metrics, some imperatives can be tracked concisely and objectively; others cannot, as they depend much more on subjective views. This is hardly surprising when we consider that some imperatives are based on mercurial human behaviors. That said, a firm at least has some tools that it can put to work in monitoring progress on individual imperatives.

This brings us to our next important point: the clear distinction between the metrics noted above and the idea of measuring the successful implementation of a risk culture. Being able to track the components that go into creating or improving a risk culture is important, but it does not guarantee successful embedding of that culture. As we have noted repeatedly, this is not a box-checking exercise. Accordingly, it is advisable to use the sample metrics (along with others specific to a company or an industry) to measure progress in implementing *the minimum standards that will help foster the risk culture.* The broader measurement of the success (or lack thereof) of a firm's entire risk culture must fall back on some of the overarching themes we introduced earlier in the book, such as wise and prudent risk decisions that benefit both the firm and its clients; no surprise unexpected losses; a good understanding of what risks the firm takes, why and in what quantity; the diffusion of skills and understanding between business and control professionals; and a general atmosphere in which all employees are risk-aware and doing the right thing. This is the ultimate way of measuring success.

Let us now revisit a version of the diagnostic test diagram from Chapter 2 (shown as Figure 8.2). While each theme can be assessed subjectively, we can use the metrics above to make the process more objective and precise, essentially completing the circle: we can link each of the structural and behavioral steps noted above to specific portions of our diagnostic spectrum.

A company may choose to retest itself using the diagnostic framework every year or two to see how it is faring. To be sure, this is a subjective test and one that requires honesty, but it can prove to be a valuable iterative process of self-assessment.

Failure and lack of progress

While we prefer to talk about metrics of success and the eventual implementation of a robust culture, we would be remiss if we completely ignored instances of failure. Not every firm that wants to create a risk culture will be able to do so, and failure may come for one of many reasons, including those we have discussed previously: lackluster management support, insufficient risk resources

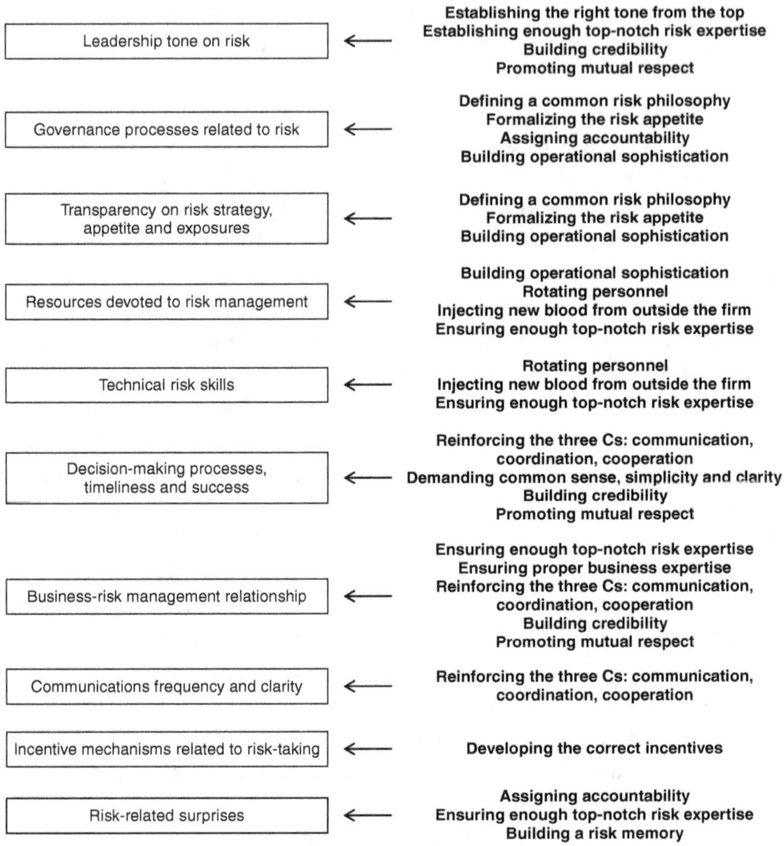

Figure 8.2 Matching imperatives with diagnostic issues

and expertise, unwillingness on the part of business managers to engage constructively in the process, breakdown in communications and so on.

In addition, it is entirely possible that a firm will be only partially successful in its quest: it may be able to implement some of the imperatives we have discussed, thereby taking some steps toward building a culture, but it may face difficulties in getting the full program in place. This means that a risk culture will exist, but it will not be as strong as desired and will not provide internal or external stakeholders with all of the expected benefits.

Failure (or lack of progress) can be detected through the same metrics we have outlined above. Let us briefly consider these.

- *Imperative 1*: defining a common risk philosophy. Either the firm might fail to define a risk philosophy at all or it might define a nebulous and convoluted philosophy, leaving too much to the interpretation of different parties.

- *Imperative 2*: formalizing the risk appetite. The firm might not create a risk appetite at all, it might create one that it changes frequently (e.g., several times per year) or it might define the appetite in a way that is not understood by those affected – any or all of which breed confusion.
- *Imperative 3*: assigning accountability. The firm's governance processes might not clearly delegate authority and assign accountability (instead keeping such authority with a committee or a few senior managers), meaning it will have failed to create an environment where skilled professionals are allowed to play a role in the company's fate.
- *Imperative 4*: developing the correct incentives. The firm might fail to create a compensation scheme that encourages risk takers to behave in a rational manner, allowing them instead simply to take risk that leads to a high current-period payout (regardless of the longer-term consequences). The firm might also fail to ensure that compensation for control professionals, including risk managers, is not directly tied to the success of the units they are meant to oversee.
- *Imperative 5*: building operational sophistication. The firm might not do what is necessary to build its operational platform: it might fail to create the right governance processes, diminish the role of the risk function, not define clearly the business mandates for managers, not invest sufficiently in technology or fail to create a meaningful data warehouse populated with useful information. Any combination of these shortcomings can prove problematic.
- *Imperative 6*: rotating personnel. The firm might choose not to rotate control and business professionals, meaning that they will not broaden their experience, come away with a better understanding of or perspective on the work of their colleagues or share their own knowledge and experiences. If this happens, the firm will have failed to take advantage of a simple mechanism that builds knowledge and partnerships.
- *Imperative 7*: injecting new blood from outside the firm. A firm might choose not to hire professionals from outside, preferring instead to recirculate the existing professionals into different positions. This will limit severely the chance of gaining new perspectives, thoughts and experiences and will make the entire corporate culture rather insular.
- *Imperative 8*: establishing the right tone from the top. The firm's directors and executives might prefer not to spend much time on risk issues or to bring risk management to the forefront by establishing essentials such as philosophy, appetite and profile. Naturally, the rest of the company might manifest a similar lack of interest as a result.
- *Imperative 9*: ensuring enough top-notch risk expertise. The company might not resource the risk function with the best possible talent, and might

simply prefer to make do with whatever personnel it has. It might also fail to push business leaders to demonstrate a minimum level of risk expertise, meaning that a key line of defense will be weak.

- *Imperative 10*: ensuring proper business expertise. Similar to the previous point, the company might not require that its risk and control managers demonstrate a good understanding of the firm's business, how it creates revenues or the link between risk and revenues. This suggests the control side of the firm be limited in its ability to add value.
- *Imperative 11*: reinforcing the three Cs. The firm might not actively promote, support or require formal or informal mechanisms for continuous communication and coordination between groups, preferring that everyone do what he or she feels is best. This may generate confusion, misinformation or a silo mentality.
- *Imperative 12*: demanding common sense, simplicity and clarity. As above, the company might choose not to implement the simplest and leanest organization and the most efficient decision-making process, allowing more bureaucratic and opaque mechanisms to persist.
- *Imperative 13*: building credibility. The firm's leadership might not particularly care whether business and risk managers demonstrate, in a bilateral sense, a minimum level of credibility when dealing with risk-related issues; furthermore, they might not demand any change in behavior to make improvements. These failures will almost certainly affect the partnership approach.
- *Imperative 14*: promoting mutual respect. As above, the company's leaders might not worry about whether mutual respect is shown between the different groups, tolerating disrespect and conflict as a matter of course and not worrying about altering behaviors with the same consequences.
- *Imperative 15*: developing a risk memory. The firm's leaders might not implement a database to collect the history of risk-related decisions, conflicts and outcomes, and they might not actively encourage or promote forums where these lessons of history can be analyzed, debated and discussed. An opportunity to capitalize on past mistakes and successes will have been squandered.

Again, a company and its leadership may intend to pursue a risk culture but may fail to implement some or most of the imperatives we have discussed, as evidenced by the failures we have just noted. Whether these failures are the result of ignorance, insufficient resources, lack of attention or some other reason will obviously depend on the beliefs and priorities of each company and its management team.

As we have noted, a company's relative success or failure in implementing or strengthening its risk culture will be evident from its risk management results, its financial results and its overall corporate performance. A company that has worked on some or all of the imperatives and set up a method for gauging progress should then take a step back and examine how it is conducting risk-related business and how that impacts its internal operations and financial results. This is, after all, the ultimate gauge of a company's success in this area.

So, a firm that avoids surprises and makes good risk decisions that at once help protect the shareholder and maximize the value of the enterprise – all in a constructive, partnership manner – will have achieved the goal of creating the successful risk culture. Equally, the firm that remains susceptible to surprise and makes bad risk decisions that threaten shareholders and enterprise value, and which operates in a contentious manner, will not have succeeded in creating the right culture.

9
Concluding Thoughts

We are reaching the end of our journey into risk culture. It remains in this chapter to summarize some of the key takeaways from the book in order to reinforce the main concepts. We shall also explore, through some speculative analysis, what might have happened to the companies described in the case studies in Chapter 5 had they focused earlier in their corporate lives on creating a robust risk culture; this analysis will help us reinforce some of the benefits of a strong risk culture. We shall then consider a simple jump-start program, based on the imperatives from Chapters 6 and 7, which lets four key groups of professionals take some easy steps to get the risk culture process started. We shall conclude with some ideas on what might happen next in the field of risk culture.

The key takeaways on risk culture

We have considered several issues relating to risk culture, including definitions, characteristics of strong and weak cultures, real examples of deficient risk cultures, mechanisms to build and strengthen cultures and metrics to measure progress along the way. This section provides a brief reminder of the main takeaways from each topic.

- *Risk culture reflects an awareness of risk throughout the organization*: every employee, regardless of function, should be risk-aware, and should behave in a way that reflects an understanding of the positive and negative results which risk can bring.
- *The tone at the top sets the stage for risk matters*: if a firm's leaders believe in being risk-aware and give risk issues the time, effort and resources they deserve, then others in the company will follow their lead. If leaders do not care, no one else will.

- *Risk culture is a qualitative dimension of the risk management process*: it is sometimes nebulous, and can take years to fully inculcate in a firm. This makes it challenging to implement properly.
- *Risk culture is ongoing*: it never stops, and must be continuously nurtured if it is to be effective. Since a company's business and the environment in which the company operates change over time, it is important that a similar evolution occur within the culture.
- *Creating or strengthening a risk culture is based on a series of imperatives*: some of these are structural and organizational in nature, while others center on knowledge and behavior. Both sets are required to properly embed the culture.
- *Measuring success is a tricky task*: some imperatives can be measured relatively easily, while others do not lend themselves to any obvious metrics. Measuring risk culture as a holistic concept depends for the most part on tracking a company's performance with regard to risk issues over a period of time.
- *External stakeholders can help push a firm in the direction of building or strengthening a risk culture*: but there are definite limits to what they can do. Ultimately, a firm and its leaders must want to create a proper risk culture; if the passion and dedication are not there, no amount of external pressure will ever make a company create the culture it requires.
- *Each firm will have its own unique culture*: this will reflect the firm's specific characteristics and idiosyncrasies of its history, national background, business and operations. Accordingly, we should not expect there to be a common way of measuring risk culture across firms, and we should not assume that one way is better or worse than another. Provided the essential elements of a risk culture are present and in force, allowances can, and should, be made for the unique elements of each company's approach.

These are some of the major themes we have introduced in this book, and which form the backbone of the topic of risk culture. They should, of course, be well understood by those seeking to implement or improve their own culture.

A brief "what if?" analysis

In Chapter 5 we discussed the problems that some prominent companies have experienced as a result of ignoring the basic tenets of a strong risk culture. We also noted, quite importantly, that the examples selected were just the tip of the iceberg: the number of companies and public institutions that have experienced similar issues (with varying degrees of severity) is in the hundreds, if not thousands.

In light of the building and strengthening imperatives discussed in previous chapters and the key takeaways summarized in the section above, let us consider how some of our case study companies might have avoided, or at least minimized, the financial and reputational damage they suffered had they thought to develop a risk culture at an earlier time. To be sure, this involves some 20/20 hindsight and some speculation, as we cannot know whether a strong risk culture would absolutely have altered the outcome. However, we must learn from past disasters if we are to protect against the next one, so this slightly speculative exercise is worthwhile.

Barings

The Barings incident in the mid-1990s helped focus many financial firms on the need to shore up their risk controls and ensure proper segregation of front and back office functions and systems; it also made clear the need to thoroughly question how revenues are generated. All of that came too late for Barings, of course; the question that remains is what might have happened had the firm been characterized by a strong risk culture at that point in time:

- Barings directors would have set a risk appetite commensurate with its relatively moderate trading activities and limited capital base.
- Executive managers would have required a robust P&L explain process in the bank's financial control function and comprehensive daily risk reporting, particularly from its overseas locations and offshore subsidiaries. They also would have ensured proper funding and support for the internal risk management function, taking care that overseas locations were properly staffed.
- Business managers operating relatively low-risk businesses (e.g., arbitrage) would have questioned thoroughly any continued outsized profitability.
- Barings' risk managers would have been able to challenge the business units and question their strategies; importantly, they would have had a functioning P&L explain process which would have enabled them to spot discrepancies between revenues and risks.
- The firm's financial control function would have developed and maintained a P&L explain process and would have established an escalation chain for large margin funding requirements.
- Auditors would have ensured proper security checks of the front-end IT platform.

Enron

Until Lehman's failure in 2008, Texas-based energy giant Enron had the distinction of being the largest corporate failure in US history. Again, we can speculate on what might have happened had the company had a strong risk culture:

- Enron's directors would have been knowledgeable about the company's energy and commodity trading portfolio and would have established an appropriate risk appetite and questioned the company's strategy of entering into so many risky markets simultaneously. Directors would also have had sufficient expertise to understand the firm's growing risk profile and leverage, preventing them from becoming too large.
- Executive leadership would have established a greater balance between the company's goals of generating revenues and protecting the capital and liquidity base – reinforcing the concept of balance and partnership. It would also have disallowed any internal incentive scheme where employees in a control function could profit from revenue-based activities they were directly or indirectly responsible for overseeing.
- The company's business managers would have properly evaluated the risk and return on each new business venture and avoided significant cross-subsidies.
- Enron's risk management function would have been well resourced and supported in its attempts to bring the company's diverse risk-taking operations under control. It would have had the power and authorities to make risk decisions and would have served as a partner rather than traffic cop.
- The CFO and audit functions would have served as real lines of defense rather than aiding and abetting, or ignoring, instances of financial misreporting and fraud. Special purpose entities would have been kept under close control and scrutiny.

Parmalat

One of the most stunning corporate fraud and bankruptcy cases in European history, Parmalat exemplifies the problems that occur when a charismatic and well-ensconced executive team can control operations and hide dealings. Had the company featured a strong risk culture:

- Parmalat's directors would have insisted on clarity regarding the company's large and growing business empire, and would have demanded transparency regarding the global acquisition strategy.
- The firm's executive team would have ensured line managers were being forthright about their operations, including business strategies, financial performance and acquisition plans.
- Parmalat's CFO would have had full and unquestioned access to all of the company's financial records and financial information.

- The company's risk managers would have been fully aware of Parmalat's offshore special vehicles, and would have thoroughly analyzed and monitored their use and performance.
- Financial controllers would have had an excellent handle on the books and records of each subsidiary and the consolidated group, and would have ensured strong controls were in place for both financial and managerial accounting processes.

Lehman Brothers

Lehman holds the distinction of being the largest-ever US bankruptcy, seemingly brought to its end by a truly weak risk culture. Let us consider some of the specific safeguards that would have existed with a strong risk culture:

- Lehman's board of directors would have been sufficiently risk savvy to challenge the CEO's desire to continue amassing risk positions, and would have been steadfast in defining and maintaining a prudent risk appetite. It would have created a compensation policy that discouraged aggressive risk takers from building up illiquid risks and excessive tail risks.
- The CEO and other executive leaders would have pressed for more internal awareness regarding risk, and would have married the business strategy with a risk appetite.
- Lehman's risk management function would have been empowered to challenge the businesses, and would have prevented investment in large, concentrated positions in illiquid real estate and complex mortgage securities. Risk managers would have been able to insist trading desks remain within the granted risk limits (as part of the appetite) instead of continuously exceeding them. The risk function would have illustrated the potential downside of excessive leverage and illiquid risk on the firm's revenues and balance sheet, and would have been free to discuss the findings with executives and directors.
- Other aspects of Lehman's control infrastructure, including financial control and accounting, would have provided important safety nets: the groups would have insisted on more accurate valuation and pricing earlier in the crisis, which might have allowed bad news to come out before things were so far advanced.

Fannie Mae

The case of Fannie Mae, and its counterpart Freddie Mac, illustrates the difficulties that can arise when a listed corporation with a public mission lacks a strong risk culture, is engaged in very risky business and is subject to political pressures; the ultimate burden in this case has fallen to US taxpayers. If Fannie

Mae had had a strong risk culture, the picture might have been appreciably different:

- Fannie Mae's directors would have defined a risk appetite that capped leverage at more modest levels and disallowed heavy concentrations in subprime assets. Directors would also have been able to critique and challenge the firm's exposures on a regular basis, particularly before they became so large.
- Fannie Mae's executive leaders would have played a strong role in keeping political pressures for lower underwriting standards at bay. They would have ensured a robust control environment with top risk management resources and clear financial and accounting controls. They would also have crafted a more precise business strategy synchronized with available returns, and disallowed a build-up of risky assets on such a slim base of capital. Indeed, the capital base would have been strengthened as part of the process.
- Business leaders responsible for the subprime portfolio would have had a strong grip on the downside scenario (a collapse in housing prices and a rise in delinquencies and defaults) and would have drawn up contingency plans together with the risk management team.
- Risk managers would have been empowered to raise a red flag before risky exposures grew out of control, and would have been diligent in enforcing risk limit allocations within the overall risk appetite. They would have worked closely with business leaders on understanding the potential disaster scenarios. Risk managers would also have stress tested the assumptions underpinning their mortgage valuation models and made appropriate recommendations regarding reserve levels.
- Financial controllers and auditors would have ensured a proper, robust environment for keeping books and records which produced reliable and accurate end-of-period financial and management information.

AIG

The example of AIG is remarkable for the size of the insurer's risk-related losses and the fact that, as a manager of risk, it ought to have been far more risk-aware. Had AIG been a risk-aware institution:

- The directors would have been far more aggressive in challenging the risk profile of the derivatives unit and would have insisted on more transparency around the entire operation; they would have ensured that regulators took a closer look at the operation. The directors would also have developed an appropriate risk strategy and appetite for the entire firm and created appropriate compensation policies to discourage booking of long-term tail risk.

- AIG's executive management would have had strong controls on the firm's non-insurance business lines and supported a robust risk management view of the operation. The leadership team would not have allowed the derivatives subsidiary to operate in such a flexible manner, outside the confines and norms of the rest of the organization.
- Risk management would have had a louder voice in the firm and flagged potential problems in the derivatives business. Risk limits would have been strictly enforced under an overarching risk appetite.
- Internal controllers would have analyzed the quality of controls and accounting deficiencies and pushed for corrective actions long before any financial accounting problems could occur.

BP

While the case of BP did not involve financial distress or bankruptcy, it did involve significant financial penalties (in the billions of dollars), significant reputational damage and, unfortunately, loss of life in two of the three events discussed. If BP had featured a strong risk culture:

- BP's executive leadership would have promoted a culture of challenge and communication, allowing those closest to the scene at pipeline sites and drilling rigs to speak openly about problems, or potential problems, without fear of reprisal. Management would have been responsive to these issues, acting as a matter of course to enact thoughtful solutions.
- The operational and safety risk management processes at the sites would have been sufficient to alert management before problems became disasters. In addition, management would have ensured adequate resourcing of all safety and risk management processes, investing the necessary amounts to prevent disasters.
- Business managers and risk managers would have had thorough, well-designed contingency plans to deal with stress scenarios or fat tail events, which tend to appear more often than expected.

Olympus

The flaws inherent in Olympus' risk culture allowed directors and executive leaders to hide losses and fabricate financial statements for more than 20 years, reflecting the iron grip that top managers and directors had over the entire operation. Had the firm featured a true risk culture:

- Olympus' directors would have limited speculative financial engineering transactions to a small proportion of the company's revenues through a defined risk appetite and a clear risk strategy.

- The company's executive leaders would have promoted free and open communications, allowing business managers to convey good and bad news and letting risk managers challenge both business strategies and risk positions.
- The company's financial control and audit functions would have been equipped to detect financial statement errors and misreporting and to institute controls sufficient to disallow any short- or medium-term discrepancies and verify the integrity of controls on an ongoing basis.

UBS

The Swiss banking giant has suffered from multiple instances of risk control failure in its major trading locations (the US, London, Zurich) and across various risk types and classes. Had the bank developed a strong risk culture over the years:

- Directors would have established an appropriate risk philosophy and appetite, along with proper incentive benchmarks for both risk takers and risk managers. They would have charged executive leadership with enforcing these imperatives, and would have challenged the wisdom of placing large proprietary bets on risky emerging market, credit and mortgage assets.
- The CEO and leadership team would have implemented a sound business and risk strategy and would have avoided unclear trading mandates within the firm (e.g., the proprietary activities of the bank and the proprietary activities of Dillon Read). The executives would have had access to meaningful risk reports revealing concentrated pockets of risk.
- Business managers would have had a strong risk/return discipline and followed a robust capital allocation process that would have reduced or eliminated major portions of the bank's proprietary risk-taking.
- The risk management function would have been empowered to cut back aggressively on risks and would have acted as a true management group rather than a limit controlling function.
- Internal auditors would have helped ensure the integrity of IT access into front office and back office trading systems.

MF Global

MF Global is simply another in a long line of financial failures. Interestingly, for the last two years of its existence the broker was led by Jon Corzine, who, as one-time CEO of Goldman Sachs, had led a bank that for many years prided itself on a strong risk culture. If the broker had had a strong risk culture:

- MF's directors would have established and reinforced a firm-wide risk appetite that limited both leverage and concentrated risk.

- MF's executive management would not have pursued an excessively risky strategy involving leveraged bets on concentrated risks in assets which were effectively a gamble on political outcomes. The risk profile would have been far more prudent.
- The chief risk officer would have been able to freely communicate concerns to the board of directors, and would have been protected in so doing. Communication between risk management and executives and directors would have been constructive, not confrontational.
- The company's infrastructural controls and monitoring capabilities would have been sufficient to track positions and client funds with ease and accuracy.

Again, these case summaries are speculative. We cannot know for sure what would have happened had Lehman, Parmalat, BP and others had a strong risk culture: they might have avoided problems completely, they might have been able to react swiftly when they encountered problems or they might have minimized some, but not all, of the damage. It seems unlikely, however, that they would have had to deal with the same extent of financial and reputational losses had they had at least some semblance of a risk culture in effect.

A jump-start program

Earlier in the book we presented the imperatives that we feel are necessary to bring a company's risk culture up to speed: ready and able to respond to the challenges and opportunities of the operating environment. And, as we have seen, implementing the imperatives is a combination of short- and medium-term actions, some easily measurable and others less so. We shall present in this section a simple jump-start program that can get a company up and running on the road to broader implementation of the imperatives. Under this scheme, each of four key groups of professionals within the typical corporate structure is charged with performing five simple tasks. Each task can be done quickly and inexpensively, helping a company build momentum on its risk culture journey.

Directors

1. Define the company's risk philosophy and risk appetite.
2. Establish the company's risk governance and structure simply and clearly, giving prominence to the risk management function.
3. Set the executive and employee incentive program.
4. Understand and openly discuss the company's key risk exposures.
5. Communicate frequently to all employees on the importance of risk issues.

Executives

1. Synchronize the company's business and risk strategies, ensuring they are consistent, relevant and realistic.
2. Chair and actively participate in the company's risk committees.
3. Properly resource the company's risk management efforts.
4. Understand and openly discuss the company's key risk exposures.
5. Communicate frequently to all employees on the importance of risk issues.

Business managers

1. Understand and openly discuss the risk exposures affecting each business line.
2. Challenge and critique the risk/return profile of each piece of new business or business initiative.
3. Communicate regularly and constructively with risk management partners.
4. Adhere diligently to the risk limits granted under the risk appetite.
5. Train employees on risk matters.

Risk managers

1. Set the risk limits for each business under the overall risk appetite and monitor them regularly.
2. Dissect the P&L of each business and relate it to risks taken.
3. Communicate regularly and constructively with business partners.
4. Analyze what could go wrong and discuss potential mitigating measures or protections with business managers and executives.
5. Train employees on business matters.

These are all simple, easy-to-implement steps that a company's leadership should enact as a matter of urgency. They must, of course, be tied into the broader, more time-consuming imperatives described earlier in the book. Their main purpose is to quickly create awareness about risk. Returning, again, to a previous work by this author and a colleague: "The best approach is to have as many people as possible feeling ownership of risk management."[1]

The future of risk culture

As we conclude this book we must consider the future of risk culture in an operating environment that has become riskier in recent years – and which shows no signs of becoming less risky. The entire concept of risk management has become something of a given in most industries: companies, and their leaders, recognize that risk has to be managed actively. Thus, what might have seemed opaque or mysterious one or two decades ago (certainly in any industry other than financial services) now seems almost commonplace. Companies and public institutions operating in all segments and spheres are at least generally aware of risk and risk management processes. To be sure, surveys indicate that these firms embrace the concept with differing degrees of intensity and resourcing, but the issues are by now well known to virtually all.

Given this, the idea of implementing a risk culture – now and in the future – cannot be as alien as it once might have appeared. If many firms have already begun or completed the process-oriented risk management tasks, they can now turn to the qualitative and behavioral issues we have touched on in this book. They can approach these more nebulous issues with a greater degree of comfort and awareness, much as they do other corporate initiatives that depend on people, experience, judgment and doing the right thing.

Whether this process will be uniformly successful across all industries and firms remains to be seen. We have seen that different stakeholders can apply direct or indirect pressure on a company's leadership to focus on the issue of risk culture. Naturally, this assumes that the stakeholders have a vested interest and feel as if they can make a difference by applying such pressure. However, we know that it is ultimately a company's leadership that must be willing to embrace and drive these changes. No one can force a company's directors and executives to adopt a risk culture. Outsiders can apply certain sanctions, such as withdrawing capital or funding, lowering credit ratings or taking business to a competitor, but while these sanctions might be unpleasant and even disruptive, they are unlikely to be destructive. The issue, therefore, rests largely in the hands of the leaders. They must determine whether the various benefits to be derived from a strong risk culture are sufficiently compelling. These benefits, as noted in Chapter 3, include:

- A governance mechanism that is well crafted, understood and followed
- A risk awareness that permeates the organization and permits a close link between business and risk strategies
- An expert population that is equally skilled in business and risk matters
- Mutual respect between revenue generators and control professionals
- Multiple lines of defense that consider and evaluate risk matters equitably
- Free flow of information and strong lines of communication between all parties
- A general attitude of doing the right thing when it comes to risk

These benefits help leaders become prudent guardians of the firm's financial resources, reputation and goodwill, allowing good business to be transacted and corporate value to be maximized.

But the issue is still a complex one. In the final analysis we must consider whether the creation of a robust and effective risk culture is possible in an era of anonymous public corporations and bureaucratic government entities. Do such institutions really have enough incentive, enough skin in the game, to make them diligently accountable for creating a risk-sensitive environment? Or is the only truly successful risk culture to be found in proprietorships, partnerships and other organizational structures where the owners or partners are at once the business generators and risk capital providers? Is the direct tie between capital at stake and risk awareness the only link that matters? Let us briefly consider the case of Goldman Sachs. During the 1980s and 1990s Goldman was regarded as an aggressive and savvy, but generally wise, risk taker: it understood its risks, it balanced risk and return, it gave risk management a prominent seat at the executive table, it rotated all risk takers through risk management, it had strong risk skills throughout the firm and it rarely posted surprises. It is conceivable that some of the success Goldman had in building the right kind of risk culture came from the fact that it was a partnership: the partners were risking their own capital, not that of some anonymous shareholders. That made all the partners risk-aware, and they were able to drive this vision and behavior throughout the firm. After Goldman went public in 1999 at least some key elements of its risk culture seem to have been lost: it began taking unwise bets, it did not give risk management the same attention, it did not do the right thing for its clients, it paid risk takers enormous amounts without tying the compensation explicitly to tail risks – and it eventually stumbled, both financially and reputationally. Its fierce risk culture became a thing of the past, and the firm became a lightning rod for criticism in the aftermath of the 2008–2009 financial crisis. Is it a coincidence that the risk culture weakened after the public offering, when the capital at risk belonged to others rather than the partners?

The same point can be made about various other partnerships that actively take risks, such as venture capital and private equity funds, buyout firms and hedge funds: the managing principals collectively have a lot at stake financially and tend to be very sensitive to risk issues. Further examples of successful risk cultures can be drawn from the ranks of the Swiss private banks, which appear to have steered a steady course over many years – managing their financial and risk resources and protecting their reputations and goodwill, all while successfully serving clients. It again comes as no surprise that most of these banks are organized in partnership form (with certain limited liability elements, to be sure).

Despite the fact that partnerships may be more likely to embrace the idea of risk culture – if only to selfishly protect the partners' capital – it is our view that all firms, regardless of construct, must strive to do the same. While it may be more difficult when the ownership equation is different, it is still possible for any firm to create the right risk culture. We believe that the trend toward such sensible action will continue.

Two other points bear consideration. First, the idea, practice and implementation of a risk culture must be seen as applicable across every industry that is exposed in some way to risk (including those in the public sector). There has long been a belief that risk management is the sole preserve and concern of the financial services industry. After all, the thought goes, firms in this industry – banking, insurance, securities, asset management – are in the business of risk. Risk is the commodity that they deal in, and so that is their issue and concern. This is, of course, all true. But it is wrong to think that risk concerns only financial services. As we have tried to illustrate throughout this book, through multiple examples and case studies, risk is a concern for every industry. Every company, in every industry, is exposed to some type of risk. Of course, many times these risks are non-financial: they can relate to reputation, operational variables, business conditions, property damage and so forth. But we should make no mistake: these are risks that need to be managed, and they can be managed much more effectively through a robust risk management process which is built atop an indisputable risk culture.

The second point to emphasize is that the issue is global, crossing national boundaries. We know that leaders in different countries have different approaches to the management of business. Some are very short-term oriented, while others are keyed into the medium term; some vest a great deal of authority in executives, while others prefer to rely on multiple boards; some prefer a very hierarchical structure and approach, while others like a flat process; some emphasize revenue growth, while others are more attuned to bottom line; and so forth. There is no "right" or "wrong" answer or approach: the point is that unique approaches exist. The same applies to the management of risk. In some countries risk management is very prominent and aggressive, while in others it is more passive; in some cases risk is managed more by committee, while in others it is managed through delegated authorities; in some cases the approach is strongly quantitative, while in others it tends toward the qualitative; and so forth. Despite these differences, there is a common thread: a strong risk culture benefits risk management, regardless of the form of that risk management. Thus, an automotive firm in Germany, a bank in the US, a steel company in Japan and a commodity trading firm in Brazil – all exposed to different kinds of risks and all managing their risks in different ways – can still deal with risk issues most effectively when they enjoy a strong risk culture. The practical manifestation of the strong risk culture applies regardless of national origin.

Given these two points, we might expect that, in the future, consideration and implementation of risk culture will be taken up by companies in all industries, across all national borders. If this is, in fact, the case, then internal and external stakeholders will be the ultimate beneficiaries. It is also quite possible that the systemic risks that periodically flow through the global economy will be better held in check, and will pose less of an existential threat. While we recognize, and have tried to demonstrate, that this is a medium-term exercise that takes years to accomplish, the benefits to be derived make it a worthwhile investment.

Notes

1 Successful Risk Management

1. For instance, see E. Banks, *Risk and Financial Catastrophe* (Basingstoke: Palgrave Macmillan, 2010) for a consideration of risks segregated into pure and speculative (i.e., whether a risk can cause only losses or whether the possibility for profits also exists), catastrophic and non-catastrophic (i.e., the degree to which a risk is infrequent but of high severity or frequent but of low severity), and financial and non-financial (i.e., whether the risk derives from financial indicators or operating variables). These classifications, which simply add another degree of dimensionality to the discussion, do not alter the general risk management framework laid out in this chapter.
2. Portions of this discussion draw on E. Banks, *Risk and Financial Catastrophe* and *Finance*, 2nd edn (London: Routledge, 2010).
3. This follows the inverse price/yield relationship, where a rising yield relates to a falling price and vice versa.

2 A First Look at Risk Culture

1. G. Morgan, *Images of Organization* (Thousand Oaks, CA: SAGE, 2006).
2. E. H. Schein, *Organizational Culture and Leadership*, 4th edn. (San Francisco: Jossey-Bass, 2004).
3. C. Levy, E. Lamarre, and J. Twining, "Taking Control of Organizational Risk Culture" (New York: McKinsey & Co., February 2010).
4. J. M. Fallon and A. Hoon, "What's Your Company's Risk Culture?" (Directorship.com, 2010).
5. KPMG, "Never Again? Risk Management in Banking beyond the Credit Crisis" (New York: KPMG, 2009).
6. Towers Perrin, "Assessing Your Company's Risk Culture" (New York: Towers Perrin, 2008).
7. "Point of View: S&P's Fresh Look at Risk," http://www.pwc.com/us/en/point-of-view/enterprise-risk-management-standard-poors.jhtml.
8. Ibid.
9. S. J. Dreyer, "Standard & Poor's Looks further into How Nonfinancial Companies Manage Risk" (New York: S&P, June 2010).
10. Institute of International Finance, "Reform in the Financial Services Industry: Strengthening Practices for a More Stable System" (Washington, DC: IIF, 2009).
11. Ibid., section AIII.I.
12. Committee of European Banking Supervisors, "High Level Principles for Risk Management" (London: European Banking Authority, 2010).
13. Risk Management Association, "Enterprise Risk Management: A Definition," *RMA Journal*, 88(6) (February 2006): 18–20.
14. See http://www.theirm.org/events/documents/Perspectivesonriskculture_James_Maxwell.pdf.

15. E. Banks, *The Simple Rules of Risk* (Chichester: John Wiley, 2002).
16. Ibid., p. 25.
17. Ibid., p. 28.
18. Ibid., p. 30.
19. Ibid., p. 33.
20. Ibid., p. 35.
21. Ibid., p. 39.
22. Ibid., p. 41.
23. Ibid., p. 45.
24. Ibid., p. 46.
25. Ibid., p. 52.
26. Ibid., p. 53.
27. Ibid., p. 54.
28. Ibid., p. 55.
29. Ibid., p. 56.
30. Ibid., p. 92.
31. Ibid., p. 101.
32. Ibid., p. 103.

3 Institutional and Regulatory Considerations

1. Risk Management Association, "RMA Announces Results of ERM Survey" (Philadelphia: RMA, 2006).
2. Many published works on the credit crisis and its origins and resolutions are available. I have written about the subject in various volumes, including *Risk and Financial Catastrophe* (Basingstoke: Palgrave Macmillan, 2010) and *See No Evil: Uncovering the Truth behind the Financial Crisis* (Basingstoke: Palgrave Macmillan, 2010).
3. KPMG, "Never Again? Risk Management in Banking beyond the Credit Crisis" (New York: KPMG, 2009). The study included a survey of 500 senior managers from large institutions involved in risk and risk management.
4. Deloitte, "Global Risk Management Survey," 6th edn. (New York: Deloitte, 2009). The survey is conducted every two years among financial institutions representing $19 trillion in assets.
5. See C. Levy, E. Lamarre, and J. Twining, "Taking Control of Organizational Risk Culture" (New York: McKinsey & Co., February 2010).
6. It is not uncommon, in some systems, for directors to be put up for nomination on a staggered basis, with only a portion up for confirmation or reconfirmation each year.
7. This assumes, of course, that an adequate amount of collateral is taken, and that its value is sufficient to repay the outstanding loans should liquidation be necessary.
8. Some exceptions occur in cases of severe financial distress, where directors may face a specific duty to protect the rights of creditors. However, this is reserved for dire cases.
9. This has, of course, occurred repeatedly in the financial markets over the years: banks have lost business permanently or temporarily when flawed sales practices have come to light – viz. Drexel, Bankers Trust, Merrill Lynch, UBS and so forth.
10. Moody's, "Moody's Risk Management Assessment Methodology" (New York: Moody's, July 2004).

11. Moody's, "Best Practices for a Board's Role in Risk Oversight" (New York: Moody's, August 2006).
12. Ibid., p. 3.
13. See, e.g., S. J. Dreyer and D. Ingram, "Standard & Poor's to Apply Enterprise Risk Analysis to Corporate Ratings" (New York: S&P, May 7, 2008).
14. S. J. Dreyer, "Standard & Poor's Looks further into How Nonfinancial Companies Manage Risk" (New York: S&P, June 2010).
15. Standard and Poor's, "Summary of Standard & Poor's Enterprise Risk Management Evaluation Process for Insurers" (New York: S&P, 2007).
16. In the interests of disclosure, I was part of the IIF working group that discussed and analyzed the entire range of issues, and which ultimately developed the "Final Report on Market Best Practices for Financial Institutions and Financial Products."
17. Institute of International Finance, "Final Report on Market Best Practices for Financial Institutions and Financial Products" (Washington, DC: IIF, 2008).
18. Institute of International Finance, "Risk Culture" (Washington, DC: IIF, 2009), AIII.3.
19. Committee of Sponsoring Organizations of the Treadway Commission, "Embracing Enterprise Risk Management" (Durham, NC: COSO, 2011), 1.
20. Basel II served as an update, enhancement and expansion of the original 1988 Basel Accord.
21. During the corporate scandals of the early 2000s, various accounting firms were found to have been conflicted in acting both as auditors and as consultants on revenue-generating activities. This was perhaps most apparent in the case of Andersen, Enron's auditor and business consultant. The conflicts between the two roles and the failure by Andersen to detect Enron's fraud (along with criminal charges filed by US regulators) led to the eventual collapse of Andersen.

4 Deficiencies and Problems I: Concepts

1. In 2003 Richard Dunn and I wrote that failures in risk management are a combination of "1. Poor senior management decision-making on risk, 2. Lack of risk governance, 3. Unclear risk appetite, 4. Inadequate liquidity management, 5. Insufficient checks and balances, 6. Avoidance of common sense, 7. Flawed risk infrastructure". E. Banks and R. Dunn, *Practical Risk Management: An Executive Guide to Avoiding Surprises and Losses* (Chichester: John Wiley, 2003), 12–14.
2. Moody's has put this situation into context very nicely: "In several major corporate governance failures of recent years, boards either did not understand the culture within the organization, including the attitude toward risk-taking, or ignored the culture and instead focused on short-term corporate performance." Moody's, "Best Practices for a Board's Role in Risk Oversight" (New York: Moody's, August, 2006), 3.

5 Deficiencies and Problems II: Cases

1. A straddle is an option strategy that consists of a put option and a call option at the same strike price and maturity.
2. The financial aggrandizement was significant, with the CFO collecting a reported $30 million and the treasurer another $10 million from these "internal investments."

3. G. Morgenson, "Behind Insurer's Crisis, Blind Eye to a Web of Risk," *New York Times*, September 28, 2008.
4. BP, "Fatal Accident Investigation Report, Isomerization Unit Explosion, Final Report" (Texas City: BP, December 9, 2005), 154.
5. Ibid.
6. B. Walsh, "Oil Spill: The National Academy of Engineers Spreads the Blame Around," *Time*, November 17, 2010.
7. Indeed, shortly after ascending to the chief executive position in November 2011, Sergio Ermotti indicated that one of his primary goals was to strengthen the bank's "weak risk culture."
8. D. Wakabayashi and P. Dvorak, "Panel Calls Olympus 'Rotten' at Core," *Wall Street Journal*, December 7, 2011.
9. Ibid.
10. Ibid.

6 Building and Strengthening I: Structure and Organization

1. Various bodies and regulators have put forward their own structural prescriptions for enhancing risk culture (and enterprise risk management). For instance, COSO (which we briefly discussed in Chapter 3), lists the following as imperatives:

   - Policies and action plans to embed ERM processes into the organization's functional units such as procurement, IT, or supply chain units
   - Development and communication of a risk management philosophy for the organization
   - Development of board and corporate policies and practices for ERM
   - Further discussion and articulation of a risk appetite for the organization and/or significant business units, including quantification
   - Establishment of clear linkage between strategic planning and risk management
   - Integration of risk management processes into an organization's annual planning and budgeting processes
   - Committee of Sponsoring Organizations of the Treadway Commission, "Embracing Enterprise Risk Management" (Durham, NC: COSO, 2011), 8.

2. Institute of International Finance, "Final Report of the IIF Committee on Market Best Practices: Principles of Conduct and Best Practice Recommendations. Financial Services Industry Response to the Market Turmoil of 2007–2008" (Washington DC: IIF, July 2008).
3. http://www.coso.org/documents/COSOBoardsERM4pager-FINALRELEASEVERSION82409_001.pdf.
4. http://www.theiia.org/guidance/standards-and-guidance/ippf/standards/full-standards/?search=risk appetite&C=3118&I=8317.
5. http://www.soa.org/files/pdf/news-erm-fact-sheet.pdf.
6. For instance, the IIF points out the following critical distinction: "The main point is to make it clear to all that risk appetite is not a statement of the maximum amount of risk the firm could take but instead a reasonable guide to prudent risk taking. It should be kept in mind that the buffer between appetite and capacity makes some allowance for modeling error as well as the danger of severely adverse and

perhaps unanticipated market conditions." Institute of International Finance, "Risk Appetite" (Washington, DC: IIF, 2009), AII.3.

7 Building and Strengthening II: Knowledge and Behavior

1. E. Banks and R. Dunn, *Practical Risk Management: An Executive Guide to Avoiding Surprises and Losses* (Chichester: John Wiley, 2003), 89.
2. It is worth recalling the results of the KPMG survey cited in Chapter 3, which indicated that board expertise in risk matters was thought to be lacking in nearly half of the companies surveyed.

9 Concluding Thoughts

1. E. Banks and R. Dunn, *Practical Risk Management: An Executive Guide to Avoiding Surprises and Losses* (Chichester: John Wiley, 2003), 90.

Selected References

Aon (2009, August). "Enterprise Risk Management: S&P Enhancement White Paper." New York: Aon.

Banks, E. (2002). *The Simple Rules of Risk*. Chichester: John Wiley.

Banks, E. (2010). *Finance*, 2nd edn. London: Routledge.

Banks, E. (2010). *Risk and Financial Catastrophe*. Basingstoke: Palgrave Macmillan.

Banks, E. (2010). *See No Evil: Uncovering the Truth behind the Financial Crisis*. Basingstoke: Palgrave Macmillan.

Banks, E. and Dunn, R. (2003). *Practical Risk Management: An Executive Guide to Avoiding Surprises and Losses*. Chichester: John Wiley.

Buehler, K., Freeman, A. and Hulme, R. (2008). "Owning the Right Risks." *Harvard Business Review* 86(9):102–110.

Committee of European Banking Supervisors (2010). "High Level Principles for Risk Management." London: European Banking Authority.

Committee of Sponsoring Organizations of the Treadway Commission (2010). "Current State of Enterprise Risk Oversight and Market Perceptions of COSO's ERM Framework." Durham, NC: COSO.

Committee of Sponsoring Organizations of the Treadway Commission (2011). "Embracing Enterprise Risk Management." Durham, NC: COSO.

Deloitte (2009). "Global Risk Management Survey," 6th edn. New York: Deloitte.

Dreyer, S. J. (2010, June). "Standard & Poor's Looks further into How Nonfinancial Companies Manage Risk." New York: S&P.

The Economist (2011, February). "The Gods Strike Back." London: Economist Publications.

Fallon, J. M. and Hoon, A. (2010). "What's Your Company's Risk Culture?" Directorship.com.

Financial Stability Board, Senior Supervisors Group (2009, October). "Risk Management Lessons from the Global Banking Crisis of 2008." Basel: Bank for International Settlements.

Institute of International Finance (2008, July). "Final Report of the IIF Committee on Market Best Practices: Principles of Conduct and Best Practice Recommendations. Financial Services Industry Response to the Market Turmoil of 2007–2008." Washington DC: IIF.

Institute of International Finance (2009). "Reform in the Financial Services Industry: Strengthening Practices for a More Stable System." Washington, DC: IIF.

Institute of International Finance (2009). "Risk Appetite." Washington, DC: IIF.

Institute of International Finance (2009). "Risk Culture." Washington, DC: IIF.

Institute of International Finance (2011). "Implementing Robust Risk Appetite Frameworks to Strengthen Financial Institutions." Washington, DC: IIF.

Kirkpatrick, G. (2009). "The Corporate Governance Lessons from the Financial Crisis." Paris: Organisation for Economic Co-operation and Development.

KPMG (2009). "Never Again? Risk Management in Banking beyond the Credit Crisis." New York: KPMG.

Levy, C., Lamarre, E. and Twining, J. (2010, February). "Taking Control of Organizational Risk Culture." New York: McKinsey & Co.

Moody's (2004, July). "Moody's Risk Management Assessment Methodology." New York: Moody's.
Moody's (2006, August). "Best Practices for a Board's Role in Risk Oversight." New York: Moody's.
Morgan, G. (2006). *Images of Organization.* Thousand Oaks, CA: SAGE.
Risk and Insurance Management Society (2011). "An Overview of Widely Used Risk Management Standards and Guidelines." Washington, DC: RIMS.
Schein, E. H. (2004). *Organizational Culture and Leadership*, 4th edn. San Francisco: Jossey-Bass.
Towers Watson (2011, March). "Measuring Risk Culture." New York: Towers Watson.

Index